יִידיש אויסגאַבעס און פֿאָרשונג

Jiddistik Edition & Forschung

Yiddish Editions & Research

Herausgegeben von Marion Aptroot, Efrat Gal-Ed,
Roland Gruschka und Simon Neuberg

Band 2

த

אַבֿרהם סוצקעווער Avrom Sutzkever

זינגט אַלץ נאָך מייַן וואָרט
Still My Word Sings

לידער   Poems

ייִדיש און ענגליש   Yiddish and English

אַרויסגעגעבן און איבערגעזעצט   Edited and translated
פֿון העדער וואָלענסיאַ   by Heather Valencia

d|u|p

Yidish: oysgabes un forshung
Jiddistik: Edition & Forschung
Yiddish: Editions & Research

Herausgegeben von Marion Aptroot, Efrat Gal-Ed,
Roland Gruschka und Simon Neuberg

Band 2

Avrom Sutzkever: *Zingt alts nokh mayn vort*
Avrom Sutzkever: Still My Word Sings. Poems. Yiddish and English.
Edited and translated by Heather Valencia

Library of Congress Control Number: 2021933382

Bibliografische Information der Deutschen Nationalbibliothek
Die Deutsche Nationalbibliothek verzeichnet diese Publikation in der Deutschen
Nationalbibliografie; detaillierte bibliografische Daten sind im Internet über
http ://dnb.d-nb.de abrufbar.

Typografie, Satz, Umschlag: Efrat Gal-Ed
Hauptschriften: Adobe Garamond, Hadassah EF
ISBN 978-3-11-074563-4
ISSN (Print) 2702-9425
ISSN (Online) 2702-9433

אלי עמיר
סופר ועיתונאי

אינהאַלט

Contents

Foreword

The aims of this book are threefold: to provide a broad and representative selection of Sutzkever's poetry in Yiddish for readers of the language; by means
of the parallel-text format to facilitate the journey into Sutzkever's poetry for
students or lovers of Yiddish for whom translations can provide useful help;
and to acquaint non-speakers of Yiddish with the work of one of the great
poets of the twentieth century.

Not only is this volume the first bilingual edition of Sutzkever's work to
present a generous selection of poetry from all periods of his creative life, but
it also comprises the widest selection of his poems in Yiddish to date. Almost
all the volumes of poetry are represented, and there are examples from every
decade. Of his longer epic poems, two appear here: *Siberia* and *Ode to the
Dove*, both of which are essential to an understanding of the poet's creative
development and *ars poetica*.

From such a huge oeuvre, produced over such a long period of time, the
task of making a selection is a formidable one. An effort has been made to
represent as many facets of his rich and varied poetic creation as possible, but
inevitably, personal responses to particular poems have played a role in the
selection.

A further deciding factor was the issue of translatability. While the immense and much-discussed question of whether poetry *can* be satisfactorily
translated from one language to another cannot be considered here, certain
aspects of translating Yiddish, and specifically Sutzkever's, poetry into English, must be mentioned.

Modern Yiddish poetry, to a greater extent than the poetry of other cultures, has kept rhyme and meter as a prominent feature, and Sutzkever is
extraordinarily accomplished and inventive in this respect. He exploits with
great virtuosity the symbolic potential of combining and contrasting in
rhyme the various components of the Yiddish language – Germanic, Slavic
and Hebrew – as is evident in the introductory poem of אין פֿײַער־וואָגן (*In
fayer-vogn*, In the Fiery Chariot), for example (p. 115), and he plays with the
semantic components and sounds of the language to create rhymes of sparkling originality. His poetry spans the registers with ease, from high lyrical
style to the informal conversational tone. He has enriched the Yiddish language by colorful, evocative neologisms, many of which are almost untranslatable, since they are very specific to the Yiddish language itself.

From these indications, it can be seen that translation into English poses many problems. The dissimilarity of English and Yiddish mean that the rhymes are not readily transferable and much of the word play that derives from the interaction of the different components of Yiddish is not easily conveyed. The tone of a poem in Yiddish can sometimes seem over-romantic or melodramatic in English. Thus some poems have been omitted which I would have liked to include, because I was unable to achieve an satisfactory translation. For example, rhyme and meter are, I believe, integral to the ballad form, and several ballads resisted my attempts to create an English version which did not descend into bathos. (The reader can judge how successful or otherwise the one ballad included here, "Grains of wheat," p. 101, has turned out to be.)

Overall, given the aims of the book, the strategy adopted was to create English versions which stood alone as poems in their own right, while keeping as close as possible to the language, imagery and intentions of Sutzkever's originals. I have not striven to achieve rhyme at all costs, but have used rhyme or assonance only when it suggested itself and could, in my view, be achieved without doing too much violence to the original. To compensate for the infrequency of rhyme, I have tried to achieve something of Sutzkever's rhythm and flow – not necessarily by using the same meter, but finding a meter which gave a similar movement to that of the original work.

Sutzkever laid great emphasis on the order of individual poems in his collections of poetry; overall he proceeds on a chronological principle, but within cycles and series of poems which are united under a title, he shapes them differently, with the opening and closing poems often having particular significance for the cycle or series. Throughout I have remained faithful to the order in which he has presented them in the two-volume *Poetic Works* of 1963, which comprises most of his creative work to that date. There is however one striking exception to the generally chronological system of the *Poetic Works*: Sutzkever places his long poem *Siberia* at the very beginning, even before the poems of his youth, as a signal of its seminal importance to him as a poet, and the present volume does the same. The publishing history of the poems written during the war period is particularly complex, but in the *Poetic Works*, Sutzkever has organized these poems in strict chronological order, according to the dates on which the poems were written, and this has been retained here.

For poetry published after 1963, the order of publication dates of Sutzkever's various books of poetry, and of individual poems within each volume has been followed. Throughout, I have placed dates and places under poems only when Sutzkever does so himself, with one exception: in the three volumes in which they appeared, the *Poems from my Diary* were grouped under the various years of their creation, but here I have placed the date under each poem, in order to make it easier for the reader to follow their chronological progression.

The selection of poems is preceded by Sutzkever's מײַן לעבן און מײַן מײַן ליד (My Life and My Poetry). This is the slightly abridged text of a talk given by Sutzkever at the Jewish Public Library in Montreal on 24 May, 1959. It gives the reader a flavor of Sutzkever's lively speaking style, and fascinating insights into his poetic credo and the evolution of his ideas.

After the selection of Sutzkever's poetry there is a section of notes, giving the publishing history of each poem and discussing any interesting or obscure cultural or linguistic points. The volume concludes with my essay on Sutzkever's life and work.

I am indebted to many people for their help during the preparation of this volume. First and foremost, I am very grateful to Sutzkever's daughters, Rina and Mira Sutzkever, for giving me permission to publish their father's work and my translations as well as photographic material; over the years I have had many fruitful and interesting conversations with Mira, who has always encouraged my work. I would also like to thank Tamar Guy for permitting the publication and translation of the final poem, which was discovered recently among the possessions of her late father, Shalom Rosenfeld.

Yitskhok Niborski of the Medem Centre, Paris, has always been unstinting in sharing his incomparable knowledge of Sutzkever's poetry and Yiddish literature in general, and has answered many linguistic and literary queries. Rabbi Mark Solomon and my friend Oron Joffe have helped me greatly on issues of Hebrew language and Jewish culture. Two friends, also poets, Irene Evans and Leah Zazulyer, read early versions of some of the poems and made very constructive comments, as did members of my Edinburgh Yiddish group, whose enthusiasm has spurred me on. I have also benefitted from many lively discussions with Peter Comans, the translator of Sutzkever into German.

For their help and encouragement over the years, I should like to thank two friends: Helen (Khayele) Beer of University College, London, who has given me so many insights into Yiddish language and culture, and my former colleague at Stirling University, Brian Murdoch, who in the early 1980s introduced me to Sutzkever's work and started me on my Yiddish journey.

This book would not have been possible without Marion Aptroot and Efrat Gal-Ed of Heinrich Heine University, Düsseldorf: I am most grateful to the former for supporting the project, and for her careful and sensitive editing of the manuscript, and to the latter for turning it into such a handsome volume. I am indebted to Daria Vakhrushova for her painstaking work in creating the typed version of Sutzkever's Montreal talk, and providing some helpful notes.

To all these people I express my sincere thanks. Any shortcomings and mistakes in the book are entirely my responsibility.

I dedicate this book to my husband, Mike Valencia.

Heather Valencia
Thornhill, Stirling
September 2017

Transcription of Yiddish

As is clear from the text of the original poems, Yiddish is written in the Hebrew alphabet, from right to left. In this volume the Yiddish is spelled according to the YIVO rules of modern Yiddish orthography. The German, Slavic and occasional other European components and modern internationalisms are written entirely phonetically, whereas the Hebrew-Aramaic components of Yiddish are written as they are in Hebrew – though their pronunciation in Yiddish is slightly different – that is to say, almost entirely in consonants. The transcription of all the components of Yiddish in this volume, however, is phonetic, according to the system which was devised for English speakers by scholars of YIVO, the Jewish Research Institute in New York.

Hebrew and Yiddish do not have capital letters. It has become the convention when transcribing Yiddish into Roman letters to capitalize the first word of a sentence and proper nouns (in hyphenated names, only the first part of the name is capitalized: e. g. *Nyu-york*). The first word only of a title is capitalized, unless it contains a proper noun within it.

The transcription of personal names is somewhat complicated. Where a name is used in a Yiddish text, strict YIVO transcription is used: thus, Mark Shagal, Perets, Sholem-aleykhem, Vilne. In an English text, where there is a different well-known spelling of the name, then that is used: Marc Chagall, Peretz, Sholem Aleichem, Vilna. Thus, in an article or title in Yiddish the spelling "Sutskever" is given, whereas when referring to the poet in an English context, the more common spelling "Sutzkever" is used. In different sources, Sutzkever's first name is given variously as Abraham, Avraham, and Avrom. Although Sutzkever used "Abraham" when writing his name in an English context, he is always referred to by the Yiddish pronunciation of his name: Avrom Sutzkever, and this more authentic version has been chosen for the present volume.

Pronunciation

The pronunciation of the YIVO transcription system is virtually self-evident for speakers of English, but a few aspects should be noted:

kh is always pronounced at the back of the throat, like the composer *Bach*, or the Scottish *loch*;

zh denotes a sound that is not very common in English: the sound represented by *si* in *vision*, or the final syllable of the borrowing from French: *massage*;

ay represents the diphthong in the English words *try* or *goodbye*, whereas *ey* represents the diphthong in the English words *they*, or *stay*;

in *ng*, the *g* is always pronounced – e. g., whereas in standard English the *g* is not pronounced separately in *singing*, it is in Yiddish *zingen*, to sing;

y denotes the sound (semivowel) at the beginning of *Yiddish*, even when it occurs in the middle of a word, e. g. *filosofye* (philosophy), it is never a vowel;

e at the end of words is always pronounced, e. g. *milkhome*, (war).

All vowels in Yiddish are short. Where two vowels occur together (other than the diphthongs *ay*, *ey* and *oy*), both are pronounced separately, e. g. *flien* (*fli-en*, to fly).

מײַן לעבן און מײַן ליד

[...] איבערגענומען בין איך הײַנט פֿון אָט דעם אָוונט, וואָס ער ווערט אײַנגעאָרדנט דורכן ייוואָ, און אַז איך זאָג דעם קלאַנג ייוואָ, זע איך פֿאַר זיך די גרעסטע דערהויבנקייט אין ירושלים־דליטע אין משך פֿון די לעצטע צוואַנציק יאָר ביזן חורבן. ערשט אין דער געטאָ־צײַט האָט זיך אַנטפּלעקט אין מיר דער גרויסער כּוח צום ייִדישן וואָרט, איך זאָל אים ראַטעווען פֿון אונטער די חורבֿות. איך זאָל אים ראַטעווען פֿון די דײַטשישע נעגל, וואָס האָבן זיך אײַנגעקלאַמערט אינעם הייליקן ייוואָ. און איך זע פֿאַר זיך אַ גרופּע פֿאַרמאַטערטע ייִדן, פֿאַרפּײַניקטע, וואָס קר מען אין ייוואָ בעת דער דײַטשישער אָקופּאַציע, אויף צוואַנגס־אַרבעט צו פֿאַקן די מאַטעריאַלן, די דײַטשן זאָלן זיי קענען אָפּשיקן אין דײַטשלאַנד אין זייער מו־ זעום „יודען־פֿאָרשונג אָנע יודען." און אָט זע איך פֿאַר זיך ווי איך נעם צונויף די כּתבֿ־ידן פֿון י. ל. פּרץ, וויקל זיי אַרום מיט אַ שטריק און לאָז זיי אַראָפּ אַנטקעגן דער געביידע פֿון דער עס־עס, פֿון דער צוווייטער זײַט גאַס, פֿון דער צווייטער זײַט גאַס, און עס קומט די ליטווינקע שימעיטע, שטעלט אײַן דעם לעבן און זי נעמט פֿון מיר אָפּ פּרצעס כּתבֿ־ידן און זי באַהאַלט זיי אין אוניווערסיטעט־ביבליאָטעק. און אַזוי ווי עס זײַנען געהאַנגען די כּתבֿ־ידן צווישן הימל און ערד, אַזוי זײַנען געהאַנגען דעמאָלט אונדזערע לעבנס. און ווען די שטאָט איז באַפֿרײַט געוואָרן, און איך בין געלאָפֿן צום ייוואָ, איז די געביידע געוווען פֿאַרברענט, נאָר צוויי אײַזנס האָבן זיך פֿון איר אַרויסגעשטרעקט, ווי צוויי אײַזערנע הענט, און האָבן געשריען צו די הימלען. און שטענדיק ווען איך הער דעם קלאַנג ייוואָ, זע איך און איך הער דעם געשריי פֿון די אײַזערנע ייוואָ־הענט אין ווילנע.

My Life and My Poetry

[…] Today I am deeply moved by this evening that has been organized by YIVO. Indeed when I say the word YIVO, and hear its sound, I see before me something of the greatest nobility in [Vilna], the Jerusalem of Lithuania, in the twenty years preceding the Holocaust. It was not until my time in the ghetto that the great power of the Yiddish word revealed itself within me, demanding that I should save it from being buried under the ruins. I was to save it from the Germans, who had got their claws into our sacred YIVO. And I see before me a group of exhausted, tormented Jews, forced laborers, who had come into the YIVO building during the German occupation to pack up the materials so that the Germans could send them to Germany for their museum dedicated to "Research on Jews without Jews."[1] And now I see myself gathering up manuscripts of I. L. Peretz[2], binding them together with string and lowering them to the ground, right opposite the SS building on the other side of the street; Shimayte,[3] a Lithuanian woman, takes Peretz's manuscripts from me and hides them in the University Library, risking her life in doing it. Just as these manuscripts dangled between heaven and earth, so did our lives at that time. When the city was liberated, I ran to the YIVO building, but it had been burnt down. All that remained were two iron rods sticking out from the ruins like two iron hands, screaming to the heavens. Whenever I hear the sound "YIVO", I see the iron YIVO hands in Vilna, and hear their screaming.

This is an abridged version of a talk given by Sutzkever at the Jewish Public Library in Montreal on May 24, 1959, as part of a farewell evening to honor the poet, who had been visiting the Yiddish-speaking community there (Sutzkever 1959, audiofile). Since this was an oral presentation, it was occasionally necessary to tighten up the syntax and eliminate some repetitions and impromptu remarks, in order that it should read more smoothly as a written text. The standard YIVO spelling system is used, eliminating dialect pronunciation, but influences of Sutzkever's Lithuanian dialect are still apparent where the neuter grammatical gender is absent and masculine and feminine forms are used where the standard Yiddish form is neuter. In both versions, omissions are indicated by three dots and square brackets.

1   See p. 243 f.
2   Yitskhok Leybush Peretz (I. L. Peretz, 1852–1915), one of the early modern Yiddish writers. Peretz had furthered the work of young writers and was deeply revered. See also p. 87 and 257.
3   Shimayte: Ona Simaite (1894–1970) helped many Jews in the Vilna ghetto, for example finding hiding places, delivering mail, providing false passports and bringing weapons and ammunition into the ghetto. She was sent to Dachau then to a concentration camp in occupied France, but was liberated by allied forces on September 10, 1944.

[...] איך דערמאָן זיך, ערבֿ דער צווייטער וועלט־מלחמה איז פֿאָרגעקומען
אין ווילנע דער צוזאַמענפֿאָר פֿון די רבנים. חיים גראַדע באַשרייבט עס אין זיַין
לעצטן בוך. איך געדענק אָבער אַ וואָרט פֿון דעם חפֿץ חיים פֿון ראַדין, אַז ווען מע
האָט אים געבעטן, ער זאָל עפֿענען די פֿאַרזאַמלונג, האָט ער ניט געוועלט. האָט
מען אים געזאָגט: סטייטש, איר זיַיט דאָך דער צדיק־הדור, טאָ פֿאַר וואָס רעדט
איר מיט אַ זינדיקער רייד? אַזוי האָט מען אָנגעהויבן אים אייַנצוריידן מיט כּל־מיני
עפּיטעטן און ער האָט אַלץ אַלע אָפּגעוואַרפֿן. שפּעטער האָט מען געזאָגט: איר זיַיט דאָך
דער עלטסטער פֿון אונדז. דאָ האָט ער ניט געקענט לייקענען, און געבויגענערהייט
איז ער אַרויף אויף דער בינע און האָט געזאָגט איין פּסוק, אַ געוואַלדיקן פּסוק. ער
האָט געזאָגט אַזוי: פֿאַראַן אין שמות איין פּסוק וואָס איז גילטיק געווען אַ מאָל בעת
ייִדן האָבן געמאַכט מזבחות. איז דעמאָלט בעת ס'וועט אַרויפֿגיין דער כּהן צי ווער,
פֿלעג ער קענטיק גיין אָנגעטאָן אין לייכטע קליידער, איז געווען פֿאַראַן אַן אָנזאָג:
ולא תעלה במעלת על מזבחי אשר לא תגלה ערותך עליו! טאָרסט ניט אַרויפֿגיין
אויף דער בינע, אויף דער מזבח, אין דער הויך, אויפֿן טרעפּ, צום מזבח, מע זאָל
ניט אַרויסזען דיַין נאַקעטקייט. האָט עס דער חפֿץ חיים פֿאַרטיַיטשט אַזוי: זאָלסט
ניט אַרויפֿגיין מיט דיַינע מעלות אויפֿן באַלעמער, מע זאָל ניט זען דיַין נאַקעטקייט.

ווייל איך ניט, מיַינע טיַיערע פֿריַינד, ריידן וועגן זיך, וועגן מעלות. דעריבער
וואָלט איך ניט געוואָלט גערעדט ביַים ים ריידן אויף דער טעמע וועגן לעבן און מיַין ליד
דערצײלן וועגן מיַינע פּאָעטישע מעלות. נאָר בלויז ווי ווייַט מעגלעך אָביעקטיוו
דערנענטערן אײַך צו דער לאַבאָראַטאָריע פֿון מיַין שאַפֿן און צו דער ביאָגראַפֿיע
פֿון מיַין דיכטונג, ווייַל די אמתע ביאָגראַפֿיע פֿון אַ דיכטערס לעבן – דאָס איז זיַין
שאַפֿונג, ווי די ביאָגראַפֿיע פֿון דעם נבֿיא איז זיַין נבֿואה.

אַ גאַנץ לעבן שטעלט זיך פֿאַר פֿאַעט אײביקייט־פֿאַקן, און
כאַטש ער שטעלט זיי, דאַכט זיך, ניט אויף זיַין לייב, נאָר אויף פּאַפּיר, איז אָבער
זיַין לייב און זיַין נשמה אינעם פּאַפּיר, און דאָס פּאַפּיר טוט אים אומענדלעכער ווי.
כדי דער פֿאַעט זאָל דערגרייכן זיַין ציל, מוזן די פּאַקן אָננעמען, מוזן זיי ווירקן אויפֿן
לייענער, און במילא באַקומט די קונסט אַן אימוניטעט קעגן פֿאַרגעסנקייט און קעגן
דעם דיכטערס אייגענעם פֿאַרגאַנג.

צוויי געשעענישן האָבן שטאַרק באַווירקט מיַין לעבן אין די פֿריִע יאָרן. די ערשטע
– מיַין קינדהייט אין סיביר. מיַינע ערשטע זיבן־אַכט יאָר אין וויַיטן צפֿון, ווו מיַין
מאַמע־לשון, כאַטש מע האָט געשריבן וועגן מיר, אַז איך בין אַ גוטער ייִדיש־קענער
מעג איך אָבער אויסזאָגן דעם סוד, אַז מיַין ערשט לשון, וואָס איך האָב גערעדט אין
מיַין קינדהייט, איז געווען קירגיזיש. ווייַל איך האָב זיך געפֿונען צווישן קירגיזן, מיט

[...] I remember that before the Second World War a conference of rabbis took place in Vilna – Chaim Grade describes it in his most recent book. I recall something that the Chofetz Chaim[4] of Radin said. When he was asked to open the meeting, he was unwilling to do so. So they said to him: "But you are the great holy man of this generation, so why are you transgressing like this?" They kept trying to persuade him by using all sorts of epithets, but he still refused. Finally they said: "You are the most senior of us all." This he could not deny, and with a bowed head he went up onto the stage and quoted one verse [of the Tanakh], but what a powerful one! He said: "In Exodus there is a verse which refers to the period when Jews made sacrifices on an altar. When the High Priest or someone else went up to the altar, he would apparently go dressed in a light garment, because it was said: 'And you shall not go up by steps to my altar, that your nakedness be not exposed on it.'[5] That is to say: you must not go up on the stage, in other words, [...] up on high, to the top of the steps, to the altar, so that people do not see your nakedness." This the Chofetz Chaim interpreted to mean: you should not go up to the reading desk with your virtues on display, so that people do not see your nakedness.

Therefore, my dear friends, I do not want to talk about myself and my virtues. And, speaking on the subject of my life and my poetry, I would not want to talk about my virtues as a poet, but rather – objectively, as far as possible – allow you to approach the laboratory of my creation and the biography of my poetry, because the true biography of a poet's life is his created work, just as the biography of a prophet is his prophesy.

His whole life long the poet, it seems to me, injects himself with what I would call "eternity pox." And though he does not inject them into his body, but onto paper, nevertheless his body and soul are in the paper, and that paper causes him never-ending pain. For the poet to achieve his goal, these pox must become active, and must infect the reader. In this way his art and the poet himself acquire immunity against oblivion.

Two events strongly influenced my early life. The first – my childhood in Siberia. Although people have written of me that I have a good knowledge of Yiddish, in fact during my first seven or eight years in the far north [...] my mother tongue, my first childhood language, was Kirghizian. I was living

4   Israel Meir Kagan (1839–1933), born near Grodno in the Russian Empire, was a very influential rabbi of the Musar movement, who became known by the title of his first book: Chofetz Chaim (the desirer of life), published in 1873. He settled in Radin where he founded a famous yeshiva.
5   Exod. 20: 26.

זיי זיך געשפּילט און זיך אויסגעלערנט דעם דאָרטיקן לשון. און די בילדער אין סיביר,
אין מײַן פֿריִער קינדהייט, אַ כּותער אין ווײַטן סטעפּ, הינטערן אירטיש, פֿאַרשנייט,
איבערן סטעפּ טראָגט זיך אַן אויסגעצויגענער געוווי פֿון אַ וואָלף. דער טאָטע אין
דער האַלב־טונקלקייט פֿון כּותער שפּילט אויף זײַן רויטער פֿידעלע אַ ייִדישן ניגון,
און איך נעם אויף מיט אַלע חושים די קלאַנגען פֿון דער פֿידל וואָס מישן זיך מיטן
געוווי פֿון דעם וואָלף, און ס׳דאַכט זיך מיר, אַז איך הער אויפֿן בײַדעמל, ווי די
טײַבעלעך פּיקן זיך אויס פֿון די אייער. און פֿאַר טאָג גייט די זון אויף פֿון שניי אַרויס
ווי אָנגעטאָן אין אַ פֿײַערדיקן פּעלץ, איך, אַ זעקס־יעריקער, קום אַרויס באַגעגענען
דעם טאָג, און איך זע אינעם שניי די שפּורן פֿון אַ חיה. און פֿון ווײַטן זע איך, ווי
די חיה לויפֿט, און איר אָטעם קרײַזלט זיך אַרויף אינעם פֿראָסט, אין די הויכן, און
נאָך אַן אָטעם גייט אויף, אַן אָטעם פֿון אַ קימען, אַ רויך. און מײַן אייגענער קליינער
אָטעם קלעטערט, קלעטערט, און פֿון די דרײַ אָטעמס ווערט אויסגעצווײַגן איבערן
סטעפּ אַ געצעלט. אָדער בײַ נאַכט ווען די לבֿנה ליגט אַ פֿאַרפֿראָרענע מיטן נאָז אין
שניי, און דער שניימענטש וואָס איך האָב אָקאָרשט אויסגעקנאָטן, איז וואָס מער
איך קוק אויף אים, דוכט זיך מיר אויס אַז ער טאַנצט אַנטקעגן די שטערן.

די דאָזיקע בילדער־דימענטן וואָס זײַנען אַרײַן אין די ערשטע יאָרן אין מײַן
נשמה, פֿינקלען פֿאַר מיר און אין מיר דורך אַלע פֿינצטערנישן. זיי האָבן מיר
געטרייסט און באַאָלדיקט און באַהאַלדיקט אויך אין גאָטאָ. זייער זינגענדיקע ליכטיקייט פֿאַרשאַפֿט
מיר תּמיד הנאה. און ווען איך בין אַלט געווען אַ יאָר צען שוין אין ווילנע, האָבן
יענע סיבירער קלאַנגען און פֿאַרבן גענומען מאָנען אין מיר אַ תּיקון, איך זאָל זיי
געבן ווערטער. איך זאָל זיי געבן צום עסן ווערטער. און געוויס, מער אינטויִטיוו
ווי באַוווּסטזיניק האָב איך דעמאָלט דערשפּירט דעם אָנזאָג פֿון רב נחמן בראַצ־
לאַוער, אַז ווער עס האָט וואָס צו שרײַבן, און ער שרײַבט ניט, איז געגליכן צו
איינעם וואָס דערהרגעט די אייגענע קינדער. און אַזוי איז געבוירן מײַן ערשטע
פּאָעמע ,,סיביר", וואָס אירע אָפּשטראַלן קאָן מען געפֿינען אין כּמעט מײַנע אַלע
שפּעטערדיקע שאַפֿונגען ביז הײַנט צו טאָג. אַפֿילו אין ,,געהיימשטאָט" פֿינקלט
אַרײַן, וואָרקעט אַרײַן מײַן קינדהייט.

אויסער מײַן קינדהייט האָט געמאַכט אויף מיר אַ שטאַרקן רושם אין די פֿריִע
יאָרן אַ מעשׂה. אַ מעשׂה וואָס מײַן מאַמע, ע״ה, האָט מיר דערציילט וועגן איר
טאַטן, דעם מיכאַלישאָקער רבֿ, רב שבתי פֿײַנבערג, מײַן זיידע. מײַן זיידע איז גע־
ווען אַ גרויסע פֿערזענלעכקייט, האָט געשריבן אין משך פֿון דרײַסיק יאָר אַ פּירוש

among the Kirghiz, and playing with them, so I learned their language. And the images of the Siberia of my early childhood were a snow-covered hut in the distant steppes, beyond the Irtish River, and the long drawn-out howl of a wolf resounding over the steppe. In the semi darkness of the hut Father plays a Jewish melody on his red fiddle and with all my senses I absorb the sounds of the fiddle that blend with the wolf's howling, and it seems to me that I can hear the little baby doves in the attic pecking their way out of their eggs. At dawn the sun rises out of the snow, looking as if it was clothed in a fiery fur. And when I, a six year-old child, come out to greet the day, I see in the snow the tracks of an animal. From afar I see the animal running, and its breath spirals upwards in the frost, up towards the sky, and another vapor rises, the smoke from a chimney. My own little breath clambers, clambers up to meet them, and the three breaths join to form a tent across the steppe. Or at night I see the moon lying frozen, with her nose in the snow, and there is the snowman which I have just finished carving; the more I look at him, the more it seems to me that he is dancing towards the stars.

These precious images which entered my soul in my earliest childhood are like diamonds which still sparkle before me and within me through every kind of darkness. They comforted me and gilded my life even in the ghetto. Their singing brightness always fills me with delight. And when I was about ten years old and already living in Vilna, those Siberian sounds and colors began to demand of me that I should do them justice and give them words. Words to nourish them. And then, more instinctively than consciously, I heard within me the saying of Reb Nakhmen Bratslaver[6], that whoever has something to write, but does not write it, is like someone murdering his own children. And thus my first long poem "Siberia"[7] was born; its resonance can be found in almost all my later poetic works right up to the present day. My childhood even sparkles and coos its way into "Secret City."[8]

Apart from my childhood, one other thing which made a strong impression on me in my early years was a story my mother o"h, told me about her father, my grandfather, the Rabbi of Michalishok,[9] Reb Shabse Feinberg. He was an eminent personality who in the course of thirty years wrote a com-

---

6   Nakhmen Bratslaver (Nahman of Bratzlav, 1772–1810), the great-grandson of the Baal Shem Tov, the founder of Hasidism. He was a famous Hasidic rabbi, the founder of the Bratslav Hasidim, and a writer of mystical tales.
7   See p. 56.
8   Sutzkever 1963 (I): 443–537. "Geheymshtot" (Secret City) is a moving narrative poem about a group of Jews hiding in the sewers of Vilna during the Nazi terror.
9   Michalishok is the Yiddish name for the town which is called Mikhalishki in Russian, Michaliszki in Polish. It lies to the north east of Vilna, and is now in Belarus.

אויפֿן מגן־אבֿרהם. ער האָט זיך אויך איבערגעשריבן מיט ניט קיין אַנדערן ווי לעוו
טאָלסטוי, און בײַ מײַן מומען איז ביזן יאָר נײַן און דרײַסיק נאָך געווען אויפֿגעהיט
פֿיר בריוו טאָלסטויס צו מײַן זיידן, וועגן רעליגיעזע ענינים.

דערצײַלט מיר מײַן מאַמע, אַז נאָך דעם ווי איר עלטסטער ברודער, מײַן פֿע־
טער לייזער, איז אַנטלאָפֿן אין מיטן נאַכט קיין אַמעריקע, ווײַל אים האָט זיך אויס־
געדאַכט, אַז טאַטע־מאַמע האָבן ליב די קלענערע, ייִנגערע קינדער מער פֿון אים,
האָט דער זיידע זיך איבערגענומען פֿון דער זאָרג און ער איז קראַנק געוואָרן. [...]
און אין דער דאָקטער פֿון שטעטל האָט געהייסן, ער זאָל פֿאָרן קיין ווילנע. דער
שמש האָט אײַנגעשפֿאַנט דעם פֿערד אין אַ שליטן, אויסגעשפֿרייט מיט שטרוי, און
דער קראַנקער זיידע אין אַ ווינטערדיקער נאַכט האָט זיך אַרײַנגעזעצט אין שליטן,
און מײַן מאַמע איז מיט אים מיטגעפֿאָרן. און דער זיידע האָט געהייסן מײַן מאַמען,
זי זאָל מיטנעמען זײַן כתבֿ־יד אין אַ רענצל. און אײַדער זיי האָבן זיך אַרויסגעלאָזט
אויפֿן וועג, האָט ער נאָך געבעטן, מע זאָל אַרויספֿאָרן אויפֿן בית־עולם וווּ דעמאָלט
איז שוין געלעגן זײַן ווײַב, עטל, ווײַל טאַמער שטאַרבט ער אין ווילנע, זאָל ער זיך
געזעגענען פֿריִער מיט איר. די מצבֿות זײַנען געווען פֿאַרשנייט, דער בית־עולם
פֿאַרוויִט, נאָר דער זיידע האָט אויסגעפֿונען די מצבֿה פֿון זײַן פֿרוי, ווי זי וואָלט
עפּעס אַרויס לעבעדיק פֿון דער ערד אַ פֿאַרשנייטע, און ער האָט זיך מיט איר
געזעגנט.

דער וועג איז געווען אַ פֿאַנטאַסטישער. וועלף מיט גזלנים מיט אַ שענק,
אַנצושרײַבן אַ גאַנצן בוך, און אין אַ פֿאַר טעג אַרום, פֿאַר טאָג, זײַנען זיי געקומען
אין ווילנע. געקומען אין ווילנע און אַרײַנגעפֿאָרן צו מײַנע קרובֿים אויף סטע־
פֿאַן־גאַס. נאָר ווי דערשטוינט איז געוואָרן מײַן מאַמע, ווען אַרײַנטראָגנדיק די זאַכן
אין שטוב, האָט זי באַמערקט, אַז דער רענצל, מיטן כתבֿ־יד וואָס דער זיידע האָט
געשריבן דרײַסיק יאָר איז נעלם געוואָרן! זי האָט געוווּסט, אַז קוים דערוויסט זיך
דערפֿון דער זיידע, וועט פּלאַצן זײַן האַרץ. איז זי געוואָרן זייער טרויעריק און זי איז
אַוועקגעלאָפֿן צו רב חיים־עוזר גראָדזשינסקי, פֿרעגן אַן עצה וואָס מע טוט.

האָט ר' חיים־עוזר אויפֿגערופֿן די ווילנער רבֿנים און האָט געטראַכט, וואָס
מע קען טאָן כּדי צו ראַטעווען דעם זיידן. און
נאָך אַ לאַנגע שמועסן, האָבן די רבֿנים באַשלאָסן אויפֿצוהענגען איבער די איבער
הונדערט ווילנער קלייזלער און בתי־מדרשים אַ קול־קורא צו די ווילנער גנבֿים, צו
די חשובֿע ווילנער גנבֿים. אַז אויב אין משך פֿון דרײַ טעג וועט ניט אָפּגעטראָגן ווע־
רן צום רבין דער געגנבֿעטער רענצל מיט דעם וואָס איז דאָ אינעווייניק, וועלן אַלע
ווילנער גנבֿים אַרײַנגעלייגט ווערן אין אַזאַ פֿינצטערן חרם, אַז זייער אוראייניקלער
וועלן ניט אַרויסקריכן...

און מײַן מאַמע, אַ פֿאַרטרויערטע, מיט אַ תּפֿילה אויף די ליפּן, איז געזעסן אין
פֿאַדערצימער און געוואַרט וואָס וועט זײַן. דער זיידע האָט עפּעס דערשפּירט, אַז

mentary on the book *Magen Avraham*[10]. He also corresponded with no less a personage than Leo Tolstoy, and until 1939 my aunt had in her possession four letters from Tolstoy to my grandfather, on religious issues.

My mother told me that after her eldest brother, my Uncle Leyzer, had run away to America in the middle of the night because he imagined that his parents loved the younger children more than him, my grandfather was so distressed that he became ill. [...] The doctor of the shtetl prescribed that he should go to Vilna. One winter night the *shames*[11] harnessed the horse to the sledge padded with straw, and my sick grandfather settled down in it, my mother traveling with him. Grandfather told my mother to take his manuscript with her in a satchel. Before they started on their journey, he asked to be driven to the cemetery where his wife Etl lay, in order to say farewell to her, in case he should die in Vilna. The cemetery was desolate and the gravestones were covered with snow, but my grandfather found his wife's gravestone, looking as if she herself had risen, alive, from the snow, and he said his farewells to her.

The journey was like a fantasy: wolves, robbers, an inn – one could write a whole book about it – and after a few days, before daybreak, they arrived in Vilna and went to my relatives on Stefan Street. But how astounded my mother was when she realized, as she was bringing their things into the house, that the satchel with the manuscript which my grandfather had spent thirty years writing, had disappeared! She knew that if my grandfather found out, his heart would break. So she was extremely distressed and rushed off to see Rabbi Chaim Ozer Grodzinski,[12] to ask his advice.

Reb Chaim Ozer called the Vilna rabbis together to consider what could be done to save my grandfather. The manuscript would have to be found. And after long discussions, the rabbis decided to put up a proclamation in every one of the over a hundred small synagogues and prayer houses, appealing to the honorable Vilna thieves. It declared that if the stolen satchel and its contents were not handed in to the rabbi within three days, then all the thieves in Vilna would be placed under such a severe edict of excommunication, that even their great-grandchildren would not be able to escape it...

My mother meanwhile, deeply grieving, with a prayer on her lips, sat in the front room waiting to see what would happen. Grandfather sensed that

10   The מגן אברהם (*Magen Avraham*, Shield of Abraham) is an important 17th century commentary on the שולחן ערוך (*Shulkhan Arukh*, The Prepared Table), the major compilation of Jewish laws.

11   Shames: the beadle of a synagogue.

12   Chaim Ozer Grodzinski (1863–1940) was an eminent Halakhic authority and Talmudic scholar in Vilna who answered halakhic questions from all over the world.

ס׳איז ניט גלאַטיק, ווען ער האָט געבעטן, קראַנקערהייט, מע זאָל אים געבן דעם
כתב־יד, האָט די מאַמע אַלץ געזאָגט תירוצים און תירוצים, אַז די דאָקטוירים דער־
לויבן ניט אַזוי און אַזוי ווייַטער, אָבער ביז וואַנען קען מען ציִען? און אָט זיצט אַ פֿאַר־
טערטע די מאַמע, און עס גייט שוין באַלד אַריבער דער דריטער טאָג... זי איז שוין
פֿאַרריאָוסט.

און מיט אַ מאָל דערהערט זיך אַ קלאַפּ אין טיר. און עס גייט אַרײַן אַ ייִד, באַצירט
מיט אַ גלאַנציקן קאָזיריק – ווי סע הייסט אין ווילנע – ברילילק, און מיט שטאַרקע,
ברענענדיקע שוואַרצע אויגן, און אין האַנט ציטערט אים דער באַקאַנטער רענצל.
און דער גנב זאָגט צו דער מאַמען: „איך וויל איבערגעבן נאָר דעם רבין אַליין, נאָר
דעם רב אַליין". לויפֿט די מאַמע גלייך אַרײַן צו איר טאַטן, דערציילט אים די גאַנצע
געשיכטע, און פֿאַרלױפֿט, אַז שוין געפֿונען, געפֿונען, שרעק זיך ניט, און עס גייט
אַרײַן דער גנב, שטעלט אַוועק דעם רענצל אויף אַ בענקל, לאָזט אַרונטער דעם
קאָפּ, און די אויגן פֿאַרלױפֿן אים מיט ציטערדיקע טרערן, און ער גיט אַ זאָג צו מײַן
קראַנקן זיידן. „זיידע, זאָגט ער, בענטשט מיך!" האָט דער קראַנקער זיידע אויפֿ־
געהויבן דעם קאָפּ, באַקוקט דעם גנב, און ער האָט אים געענטפֿערט: „קינד מײַנס,
וואָס קען איך דיך בענטשן? איך בענטש דיך, דו זאָלסט נישט זײַן קיין גנב."

די דאָזיקע מעשׂה, אַז עס קען פֿלאַצן דאָס האַרץ צוליב אַ כתב־יד, צוליב דעם
וואָס די האַנט האָט געשריבן עפּעס מיט אַ בלייַער צי מיט טינט, האָט אויף מיר,
אויף מײַן פֿאַנטאַזיע געמאַכט אַ געוואַלדיקן רושם. איך האָב אָנגעהויבן צו גלייבן,
אַז דער עצם שרײַבן איז אַ הייליקע זאַך. און ס׳איז טשיקאַווע פֿאַר מיר אַליין, אַז
ווען מײַן מײַן האַנט, עפּעס ווי די האַנט וואָלט געוואָן אַ מענטש פֿאַר זיך אַליין, האָט
אָנגעהויבן צו פֿירן מיט אַ בלייַער איבער שורות פּאַפּיר און אויסצווווועבן מײַנע
ערשטע סיבירער לידער, האָב איך קיין אַנונג ניט געהאַט, אַז ס׳איז פֿאַראַן שוין
אַ גרויסע ייִדישע דיכטונג, אַז מיר פֿאַרמאָגן אַ לייוויק, אַ יהואש, אַ קולבאַק. וויִל
גראַד איך, וואָס איך שטאַם פֿון רבנים, גראַד איך – אַזוי האָט זיך גענמאַכט – האָב
געלערנט אין ווילנע און אין אַ פּוילישער גימנאַזיע [...]. ס׳וועט אויך זייַן ניט קיין
באַרימערייַ, ווען איך וועל זאָגן, אַז בייַם שרייַבן מײַנע ערשטע לידער האָב איך ניט
געהאַט קיין שום ידיעות וועגן דער פּאָעטישער קונסט, וועגן די געזעצן פֿון פּאָעזיע,
וועגן ריטעם, בילד און מישונג פֿון קלאַנגגען, נאָר געפֿילט האָב איך יאָ, שוין דע־
מאָלט, אַז ניט נאָר פֿייגל־געזאַנג, נאָר אויך שטומע שטיינער האָבן זייער מוזיק. און
אַז ייִדיש איז אַ מעכטיקער ים, וואָס זייַן יעדע כוואַליע האָט איר באַזונדערן ניגון.

די גרויסע אַנטפּלעקונג איז פֿאַר מיר פֿאָר געקומען דעמאָלט, ווען כ׳האָב זיך באַקענט
נענטער מיט דער ייִדישער פּאָעזיע. אָבער דעם אמת מוז איך זאָגן, אַז איך בין אַ
ביסל דערשראָקן געוואָרן. פֿאַר וואָס? ס׳איז מיר אויסגעקומען מאָדנע, וואָס וויכ־

something was up; when, ill as he was, he asked her to give him the manuscript, she made excuse after excuse, saying that the doctors would not permit
it, and so forth, but how long was she going to be able to keep this up? So
there she sat, in tears, and the third day was drawing to a close... she was in
despair.

Suddenly they heard a knock at the door, and in came a man wearing a
cap adorned with a shiny kazirik, as the visor of a cap is called in Vilna; a man
with piercing, burning black eyes – and in his hand trembled the familiar
satchel. The thief said to my mother: "I want to hand this over to the rebbe
himself, to no one else but the rabbi." So my mother went straight to her
father and told him the whole story, finishing by assuring him that he needn't
be alarmed, it was already found. The thief came in, put the satchel on a
chair, hung his head, and, his eyes filling with trembling tears, he addressed
my sick grandfather: "Grandfather," he said, "bless me!" My sick grandfather
raised his head, looked at the thief, and answered: "My child, what blessing
should I give you? My blessing is that you shall no longer be a thief."

This story, which shows that one's heart can break for the sake of a manuscript, for the sake of something which the hand has written with pencil
or ink, made a powerful impression on me, on my imagination. I began to
believe that the act of writing itself was holy. I myself find it curious that at
the time when my hand, – as if the hand itself were an independent human
being – began making lines on paper with a pencil, weaving my first Siberian
poems, I had no idea that there existed a great body of Yiddish poetry, that we
had a Leyvik, a Yehoash, a Kulbak.[13] For it so happened that I of all people, a
descendent of rabbis, was educated in Vilna in a Polish high school [...]. I am
not boasting when I say that when I wrote my first poems I had no knowledge
of the art of poetry, of poetic rules, rhythm, image, the mingling of sounds –
but nevertheless even then I felt that not only birdsong, but also dumb stones
have their own music. And that Yiddish is a mighty sea, whose every wave has
its own special melody.

For me the great revelation came when I became better acquainted with Yiddish poetry. But to tell the truth, I was rather taken aback. Why? Because it

13   H. Leyvik (pseudonym of Leyvik Halpern, 1888–1962): Yiddish poet and dramatist, famous
for his play דער גולם (*Der goylem*, The golem). Yehoash (pseudonym of Solomon Bloomgarden,
1870–1927), poet and translator of the *Tanakh* into Yiddish. Moyshe Kulbak, poet, dramatist and
prose writer (1896–1937), born in Sutzkever's birthplace, Smorgon.

טיקע ייִדישע פּאָעטן, וואָס האָבן געלעבט מיט אַ פֿערציק-פֿופֿציק יאָר צוריק און
געוווּען שטאַרק באַרימט, איז איצט, ווען איך האָב זיי געלייענט, האָבן זיי מיר אויס־
געזען שפּראַכלעך און פֿאָרמעל פֿאַרעלטערט.

פֿאַר וואָס, האָב איך געטראַכט דעמאָלט, זײַנען די דאָזיקע וויכטיקע פּאָעטן
אין משך פֿון פֿערציק-פֿופֿציק יאָר אַזוי פֿאַרעלטערט געוואָרן? איך האָב געוווּסט,
אַז אַלטער ווײַן איז גוט, אָבער פֿאַרעלטערטער ווײַן טויג ניט. מיר האָט זיך אויך
אויסגעדוכט, אַז מע ווערט עפּעס בײַ אונדז געבוירן שוין פֿאַרעלטערט. און נאָך
מער האָט עס מיך פֿאַרוווּנדערט, ווען איך האָב געלייענט פּוילישע פּאָעטן, למשל
מיצקעוויטשן. שאַפֿונגען געשריבן מיט הונדערטער יאָרן צוריק, און ווי מעכטיק
עס פֿליעסקען די שטראָפֿן. [...] איך האָב אויך דערפֿילט, אַז מײַנע חושים זײַנען
זײַער שפּירעוודיק, און יעדער פֿעלער אין אַ ליד שטערט מיר די הנאה, וואָס פֿאָ־
זיע מוז פֿאַרשאַפֿן. און איך האָב אַזוי לאַנג שטודירט ייִדיש ביז איך האָב זיך אַפֿילו
אויסגעלערנט אַלט-ייִדיש און אָפּגעגעבן צוויי יאָר איבערצוזעצן אויף מאָדערנעם
ייִדיש אליהו בחורס „באָווע-בוך". איך האָב אויך אָנגעהויבן צו שרײַבן לידער
אין אַלט-ייִדיש, גלײַכצײַטיק האָב איך אָנגעהויבן באַנוצן אַ סך נעאָלאָגיזמען,
ווערט-שאַפֿונגען, אַלץ פֿאַר דער מורא איך זאָל ניט פֿאַרעלטערט ווערן.

ווען ס׳איז דערשינען מײַן ערשט בוך – ריכטיקער, מײַן צווייט בוך, „וואָלדיקס"
– אין 1940, וואָס איז מסתּמא געווען דער לעצטער ייִדישער בוך אין אייראָפּאַ, ווײַל
שפּעטער איז געקומען דער גרויסער חורבן, – האָט וועגן דעם בוך געזאָגט מײַן
חבֿר פֿון „יונג ווילנע", טאַלאַנטפֿולער פּאָעט, אַ זײַער טאַלאַנטפֿולער פּאָעט, שמ־
שון כהן, – האָט ער געזאָגט וועגן אָט דעם בוך מײַנעם „וואָלדיקס", אַז איך האָב
אָנגעשריבן „די לידן פֿון יונגע ווערטער". [...]

אַ פּאָעט איז דער גרעסטער עקספּלואַטאָר. די גאַנצע וועלט צווינגט ער צו אַר־
בעטן פֿאַר זײַנע לידער. דאָס געוויין פֿון אַן ערשט געבוירן קינד און די גסיסה פֿון
אַ זקן, די שטערן גיבן ליכט זײַנע ווערטער, און סײַ די שטילקייט, און סײַ דער שטו־
רעם גיבן אים זײַער געהיימען ריטעם. אַ גליווואַרעם איז פֿאַר אים אַזוי וויכטיק ווי
די זון און אַ רעגנטראָפֿן אויפֿן שויב ווי די ניאַגאַראַ, וועלכע איך האָב איצט געזען
צום ערשטן מאָל אין מײַן לעבן.

seemed strange to me that these important Yiddish poets, who had lived forty or fifty years before[14] and were very famous, now seemed to me, when I read them for the first time, to be both linguistically and stylistically out-of-date.

Why, I wondered then, have these famous poets become so old-fashioned in the course of forty or fifty years? I knew that old wine is good, but that wine which is out-of-date is not. I formed the opinion that perhaps we [Yiddish poets] are born already out-of-date. My amazement intensified when I read Polish poets, for example Mickiewicz.[15] Their works were created hundreds of years earlier, and yet how powerfully their verses resound [...] I also perceived that my feelings are very sensitive, and every weakness in a poem disturbs for me the pleasure which poetry must give. So I studied Yiddish until I had even learned Old Yiddish and spent two years translating Elye Bokher's *Bovo-bukh*[16] into modern Yiddish. I also started writing poems in Old Yiddish,[17] but at the same time I started using many neologisms, word creations, all because I was afraid of becoming old-fashioned.

My first book – or, more accurately, my second book – *From the Forest*[18] appeared in 1940, and was probably the last Yiddish book to be published in Europe because soon after that came the great *khurbm*.[19] Shimshon Kahan, my friend from *Yung Vilne*,[20] a very talented poet, said about it that I had written "The sorrows of young *verter*."[21] [...]

The poet is the greatest exploiter of all. He forces the whole world to work for his poems. The crying of a newborn child and the death agony of an old man. The stars give light for his words, and both silence and storms give him their secret rhythms. A glowworm is as important for him as the sun, and a raindrop on a windowpane means as much to him as the Niagara Falls, which I have just seen for the first time in my life.

14   This is a slight exaggeration. Most of the most famous Yiddish poets he would have encountered at that time (apart from Yehoash) were only about fifteen or twenty years his seniors, and many were still alive when he started reading Yiddish poetry in the 1930s (See p. 237).
15   Adam Mickiewicz (1798–1855), famous Polish Romantic poet, dramatist, essayist and translator. His most famous work is the epic poem *Pan Tadeusz*.
16   The sixteenth-century בבא־בוך *Bovo-bukh*, written by Elye Bokher (pseudonym of Elia Levita, 1469–1549), is based on the Italian romance Bovo d'Antona, which is in turn based on the Anglo-Norman romance *Bevis of Hampton*.
17   Sutzkever 1963 (I): 201–204.
18   Sutzkever's first book לידער (*Lider* Poems) appeared in 1937. See p. 240.
19   חורבן (*khurbm*): destruction, devastation, disaster. The term is used in Yiddish for three great catastrophes in Jewish history: the destruction of the first and second Temples, and the Holocaust of 1939–1945.
20   Yung Vilne (יונג ווילנע, Young Vilna), a group of poets active in Vilna before the Second World War. See p. 239 for more detailed information on Sutzkever's relationship with them.
21   Shimshon Kahan is making a play on the Yiddish "*verter*" (words) and their homophone "Werther", the name of Goethe's tragic hero in the novella *Die Leiden des jungen Werther* (The Sorrows of Young Werther, 1774).

דער פּאָעט שאַפֿט שטענדיק, אויך אין חלום. ריכטיקער געזאָגט – אויך זײַן
חלום שאַפֿט פֿאַר אים. ניט צו דערקלערן די סודות פֿון דער יצירה. מען קען צער-
גלידערן אַלע עלעמענטן פֿון וועלכע עס באַשטייט זײַן ליד, אָבער די פּראָטאָפּלאַז-
מע פֿונעם ליד, דער סוד וואָס מאַכט לעבעדיק אַלע עלעמענטן און פֿאַראייניקט זיי
אין אַ האַרמאָניש לעבן איז אומדערקלערלעך. סלאָוואַצקי האָט זיך אויסגעדריקט,
אַז ער שרײַבט נאָר דאָס, וואָס מלאָכים זאָגן אים אונטער. און דאָס וואָס מען רופֿט
דיכטערישע משוגעתן, האָבן אויך צו מאָל אַ טיפֿן זינען. דער בלינדער מילטאָן
פֿלעגט ליגן אויף אַ קאַנאַפּע, דער קאָפּ אַראָפּגעלאָזן אויף דער ערד, און דעמאָלט,
ווען זײַן בלוט איז אַרײַן אין קאָפּ, ווען ער פֿלעגט פֿון אײַנגענעם בלוט פֿאַרשיכּורט
ווערן, פֿלעגט ער אימפּראָוויזירן זײַן „פֿאַרלוירענעם גן־עדן". טורגעניעוו שרײַבט
אין אַ בריוו צו זײַנעם אַ פֿרײַנד: „אין דער צײַט פֿון אַן אָפּעראַציע האָב איך געזוכט
די ווערטער מיט וועלכע איך וואָלט קענען גענוי איבערגעבן דעם אײַנדרוק וואָס
עס מאַכט דאָס מעסער, ווען ער שנײַדט זיך אַרײַן אין לײַב."

און איך אַליין, ס׳איז שווידערלעך דאָס צו דערציילן, נאָר איך געדענק דאָס
זייער גוט: דאָס איז געווען אין 1941, אין דער צײַט פֿון אַ שחיטה אין געטאָ, ווען
איך בין געלעגן אויף אַ בוידעם באַהאַלטן, און בלויז אַ נאָדלליכט איז אַרײַן פֿון
אויבן צווישן די דאַכלעקס, האָב איך געזען ווי [...] לעבן מיר, ליגט אַ טויטער ייִד.
ס׳איז געווען הייס, איז געווען נאַקעט זײַן לײַב. האָב איך גאָר פֿאַרגעסן, אַז דאָ ליגט
אַ טויטער, און כ׳האָב גאָר פֿאַרגעסן ווי איך געפֿין זיך אַליין, און אָנטאַפּנדיק מיט
די פֿינגער אַ שטיקעלע קויל האָב איך גענומען שרײַבן ווי אויך פֿאַרפיר אַ ליד אויפֿן
לײַב פֿונעם טויטן.

אַ דיכטער, אמת געזאָגט, קומט ניט קיין דאַנק פֿאַר זײַן פֿאַר זײַן ווערק, ווי עס קומט ניט קיין
דאַנק דעם קערנדל וואָס צעוואָקסט זיך שפּעטער אין אַ בוים פֿול מיט פֿירות. ער
גיט בלויז אָפּ דאָס, וואָס אים איז געגעבן געוואָרן. זײַן שׂכר באַקומט ער וועדליק
דעם טעם און דער פֿאָרעם פֿון זײַנע פֿירות, וואָס זײַן ווערק ברענגט אַרויס. ער
שרײַבט אַ גאַנץ לעבן, דער פּאָעט, ער שרײַבט אָן אַ שיעור. ס׳איז אָבער זייער זעלטן
ווען ער שרײַבט אָן אַ שיר.

אָבער וואָס איז אַ שיר, אַ ליד? דאָס איז דאָס, וואָס דער נבֿיא ישעיהו זאָגט: בורא
ניבֿ שׂפֿתים – איך שאַף דעם ליפֿן־פֿרוכט. ווי עס ענדיקן זיך אַלע מעגלעכקייטן,
דאָרטן הייבט זיך אָן די קונסט. מען האָט געפֿרעגט רב ישׂראל פֿון רוזשין ווען עס

The poet never stops creating, even when he is dreaming. Or rather – even his dream creates for him, not to mention all the secrets of Creation. It is possible to analyze all the elements which make up his poem, but the "protoplasm" of the poem, the secret which breathes life into all these elements and unites them in harmony, is indescribable. Slowacki[22] declared that he only wrote what angels whispered to him. Even what is often described as the madness of poets sometimes has a deep meaning. The blind Milton[23] used to lie on a couch with his head hanging down to the ground, and it was then, when his blood flowed into his head, and intoxicated him, that he would improvise his "Paradise Lost". Turgenev[24] wrote in a letter to one of his friends: "During an operation I tried to find the words with which I would be able to convey exactly the impression the knife makes, as it cut into the body."

And I myself had an experience which is terrible to relate, but which I remember very clearly: in 1941, during a massacre in the ghetto, when I was hiding in an attic with only a tiny point of light coming in through the roof-tiles, I noticed, lying [...] beside me, a dead Jew. It was hot, and the corpse was naked. I completely forgot that it was a dead man lying there, I forgot entirely where I was, and groping around with my fingers I found a little piece of coal and started writing a poem on the body of the dead man, as if it were paper.

To tell the truth, a poet does not deserve any thanks for his work, any more than a tiny seed which grows into a tree laden with fruit deserves thanks. The poet simply gives back what he has been given, and he receives a recompense according to the taste and form of the fruits which his work produces. He writes his whole life long, the poet, he writes without limit – but seldom without a poem.[25]

But what is a poem? It is what the prophet Isaiah describes when he says "I create the fruit of the lips."[26] Where all possibilities end, there art begins. When Rabbi Israel of Ruzhin[27] was asked when the Messiah would come,

22 Juliusz Slowacki (1809–1849), Polish Romantic poet and dramatist.
23 John Milton (1608–1674), English poet whose epic poem *Paradise Lost* was published in 1667. Milton was completely blind by 1654, and dictated his later works to amanuenses. Sutzkever's poem דער בלינדער מילטאָן (*Der blinder Milton*, Blind Milton; Sutzkever 1963 (II):374) was inspired by this anecdote.
24 Ivan Sergeyevich Turgenev (1818–1883), Russian novelist, short-story writer and playwright.
25 This is a word play on the two (almost) homonyms דער שיעור (*der shier*), meaning "limit, measure" and דער שיר (*der shir*), "the poem".
26 Isaiah 57: 19.
27 Israel Friedman of Ruzhin (1796–1850) was a Hasidic rebbe who established an influential court in Sadigura, Bukovina and later in Austria. Later dynasties of Hasidim were influenced by the traditions of his court.

וועט קומען משיח, האָט ער גענטפֿערט: די וואָס ווייסן זײַנען דאָס ניט מגלה, די
וואָס זײַנען מגלה, ווייסן ניט. אַזוי איז אויך מיט פּאָעזיע. דאָס איז דער ענטפֿער.
אָבער לאָמיר זיך פֿאָרט פּרוּוון צוהערן צו אָט דער געטלעכער קול. מיצקעוויטש
האָט עס פֿאָרמולירט אַזוי: ווען ליבשאַפֿט אַזוי ווי דער זײַדוואָרעם וועבט מיטן
אינגעוועייד זײַן פֿאָדעם. אַנשטאַט ליבשאַפֿט וואָלט איך אפֿשר געזאָגט שיינקייט.
ווען שיינקייט.

וואָס איז פּאָעזיע? דאָס אַלץ וואָס דער גרויער מענטש ווייסט ניט, אַז ס׳איז
פּאָעזיע. און אפֿשר איז גערעכט די גרויסע דיכטערין עלזע לאַסקער־שילער וואָס
איז געשטאָרבן אין ירושלים אין אַ פֿאַרוואָגלטע, "טרוים פּלוס לאָגיק," האָט זי געזאָגט,
"דאָס איז פּאָעזיע"!

איך וועל זיך דערלויבן צו ברענגען עטלעכע אייגענע געדאַנקען און אַפֿאָריזמען
וועגן דיכטונג. דיכטונג באַפֿרײַט דעם מענטשן פֿון אינערלעכער פֿאַרשקלאַפֿונג.
דערפֿאַר איז לײַכטער צו גיין צום טויט מיט אַ ליד. פּאָעזיע הייסט: באַפֿרײַען זיך פֿון
די עמאָציעס און אַפֿילו באַפֿרײַען זיך פֿון דער פֿערזענלעכקייט. אָבער באַפֿרײַען זיך
דורך דיכטונג פֿון דער פֿערזענלעכקייט קאָן נאָר אַ דיכטערישע פֿערזענלעכקייט.

די מוזע באַפֿאַלט ווי אַ גזלן. בלויז מיט אַ גוטע לידער קען מען זיך אויסלײַזן
דאָס לעבן. וואָס מער דער פּאָעט איז רעאַליסטיש, אַלץ ווײַטער איז ער פֿון דער
רעאַליטעט, און וואָס מער דער פּאָעט איז פֿאַנטאַסטיש, אַלץ נעענטער איז ער צו
דער רעאַליטעט. לידער מוזן פֿאַרמאָגן אינהאַלטן. ניטאָ קיין אינהאַלטן קען מען
ניט אויסהאַלטן.

בלויז יענע יונגע פֿרוי געפֿעלט מיר, ווען איך קען זיך ניט פֿאָרשטעלן אַז יאָרן
וועלן באַזיגן איר שיינקייט. בלויז יענע דיכטונג געפֿעלט מיר, ווען איך קען זיך ניט
פֿאָרשטעלן אַז יאָרן וועלן באַזיגן איר שיינקייט.

אַ נאַקעטער מענטש קאָן זיך כמעט ניט פֿאַרטיידיקן, מעג ער האָבן אין האַנט
אַ מעסער. אַזוי אויך אַ נאַקעט ליד. נאַקעט אין פֿאָרעם קען עס זיך ניט פֿאַרטיידיקן
קעגן די אָנפֿאַלן פֿון דער צײַט און עס מוז באַזיגט ווערן. [...]

איך אַליין האָב געפּרוּווט דעפֿינירן דעם סוד פֿון פּאָעזיע אין אַ גאַנצער רײַ לידער.
[...] דאָס ערשטע ליד, "דיכטונג", האָט אַ שטיקל געשיכטע. זײַענדיק אין ירוש־
לים אין צום ערשטן מאָל אין אַ רעגנטאָג... און ווער עס האָט געזען ירושלים אין אַ
רעגנטאָג, וועט ניט פֿאַרגעסן סײַ ירושלים און סײַ דעם רעגן, ווייל דער רעגן גייט
עפּעס נידעריק און איר ווייסט ניט, ווו איז אַ שטוב און ווו איז אַ וואָלקן, און אַלץ
טראָגט זיך אין אַזאַ מיסטישן גערײַ, און איך האָב זיך געצוואַגן אין דעם רעגן און
געטראַכט, ניט פֿאַר אײַך געדאַכט, וועגן פּאָעזיע. אָבער איך האָב נאָך ניט אַנט־
פּלעקט דעם סוד. שפּעטער, ווען דער רעגן איז אַריבער און די זון האָט אָנגעהויבן
באַגלעטן און אויסצוטריקענען די בערג און די וואַסערן פֿונעם רעגן זײַנען אַרײַן
אונטן אין די אונטערערדישע קוואַלן, און ווען איך האָב פֿאַרנומען דעם גערויש

he answered: "Those who know do not reveal it, and those who reveal it, do not know." It is the same with poetry. That is the [correct] answer, but nevertheless, let me try to listen to that divine voice. Mickiewicz formulated it in this way: "to spin love just like the silkworm spins its thread from its own entrails."[28] Instead of "love", I would perhaps have said "beauty": the poet spins beauty.

What is poetry? Everything that the grey human being does not recognise as poetry. Perhaps the great poet Else Lasker-Schüler[29] who died, homeless, in Jerusalem was correct: "Dream plus logic", she said, "that is poetry!"

Let me take the liberty of presenting some of my own thoughts and aphorisms about poetry. Poetry frees the human being from inner slavery. For that reason going to one's death is easier with a poem in one's heart. Poetry means: freeing oneself from one's emotions and even from one's own personality. But to free oneself from one's own personality – only a poetic personality can achieve this.

The muse attacks like a bandit, and only with a good poem can one ransom one's life. The more realistic the poet is, the more distant he is from reality, and the more fantastic he is, the nearer to reality. Poems must have content, because one cannot be content without content.

I am only attracted to a young woman if I cannot imagine that the years will destroy her beauty. And I am only attracted to poetry if I cannot imagine that the years will destroy its beauty.

A naked human being can hardly defend himself, even if he has a knife in his hand. Nor can a naked poem. A poem which is not clothed in form cannot defend itself against the onslaught of time, and must be defeated. [...]

I have tried to define the secret of poetry in a number of poems. [...] The first of these, "Poetry," has a history attached to it. For the first time I was in Jerusalem on a rainy day... and whoever has experienced Jerusalem on a rainy day, will forget neither Jerusalem nor the rain, for the rainclouds are so low that you don't know where the buildings end and the clouds begin, and everything spins round in a mystical circle. I was letting myself be soaked by the rain and thinking (like the poetic fool I am!) about poetry. But I couldn't at that point manage to discover its secret. Later, when the rain had stopped and the sun had begun to caress and dry out the mountains, and the rain-

28   Mickiewicz: see footnote 15.
29   Else Lasker-Schüler (1869–1945), Jewish-German poet and dramatist whose work has affinities with that of the Expressionist movement. She lived in Berlin until 1937, then settled in Palestine. She described her feelings of isolation, which Sutzkever alludes to, in her late poems. Sutzkever wrote a poem about her (p. 147).

פֿון די קוואַלן אונטער דער ערד נאָכן רעגן, האָב איך בײַ זיך געטראַכט, אַז דאָס איז אייגנטלעך פּאָעזיע. ניט וואָס איך זע איצטער, נאָר דאָס וואָס איך האָב געזען, ס'איז באַהאַלטן געוואָרן, און [...] איך אַן בלויז, איך דער הער בלויז די מיסטישע ווידער־ קלאַנגען פֿון דעם וואָס איז געווען פֿריִער. האָב איך אָנגעשריבן, פֿאַרשטייט זיך, וועגן דעם דעמאָלט אַ ליד, דאָס איז געווען אין 1950.

דיכטונג

כ'לעבן, ס'איז געווען אַ העזה
צו קומען אויפֿן ציון־באַרג אין רעגן,
וווּ ס'קיניגט אין אַ פֿעסטונג פֿון חלומות
דער בעל־תהילים,
און טראַכטן וועגן –
כ'שעם זיך צו דערציילן – וועגן
דיכטונג.

און ס'איז געווען דאָס טראַכטן, ווי אַ האַנט
וואָלט אויסגעוואַקסן דעמאָלט פֿון מײַן מילגרוימיקן שאַרבן,
אַ האַנט מיט פֿינף צעבליצטע אויגן אויף די שפּיצן פֿינגער.
און ס'האָט די האַנט אַלזעעריש
געשוועבט אַרום דעם רעגן
ווי אַרום אַ יונגפֿרוילייַב,
און שיכּור פֿונעם פֿרעגן:
– וואָס איז דיכטונג?

צוריקוועגס, האָט אַ פֿײַגנבוים פֿאַרשטעלט
די נאַקעטקייט פֿון מײַן געדאַנק.
און אומגעשטילט, באַליידיקט,
בין איך אַראָפּ אין טאָל,
וווּ ס'האָט אַ בלישטשענדיקע יאַשטשערקע
אָפּגעקלעקט איר נאַסקייט אָן אַ שפּיץ פֿון רעגנבויגן.

ווען ס'איז ניט געבליבן שוין קיין סימן
פֿונעם גאַנצן רעגן, האָב איך מיט אַ מאָל דערהערט
ניגונים, שטימען – – –
פֿלייַצעניש פֿון וויִנענדיקע פֿידלען אונטער דר'ערד.

water had flowed down into the underground springs, I heard the sound of these springs under the earth after the rain, and thought to myself that this, really, was poetry. Not what I see now, but what I have seen, that is now hidden, and I simply sense, I just hear the mystical echoes of what has been before. I had this experience in 1950, and naturally I wrote a poem about it:

Poetry[30]

Indeed, it was audacious
to come up to Mount Zion in the rain,
where the writer of the Psalms
rules in a fortress made of dreams,
and think about –
I am ashamed to tell it –
think about poetry.

And as I thought, it was as if a hand
had grown out of my pomegranate skull,
a hand with five flashing eyes
upon its fingertips.
Then, like a visionary, the hand
floated over the rain
as if it were the body of a virgin,
It was intoxicated by my question:
What is poetry?

On the way back, a fig tree covered
the nakedness of my thought.
So, unsatisfied, offended
I descended to the valley,
where a gleaming lizard
dried off its wetness on the corner of a rainbow.

When no sign of the rain remained,
all at once I heard
melodies, voices – – –
a surging flood of weeping fiddles underneath the earth.

30 Sutzkever 1952: 96 f; 1963 (II): 87 f.

יענע אונטערערדישע אומזעעוודיקע שטראָמען,

יענע, וואָס צום טאַטע־רעגן זוכן זיי אַ ריכטונג –

ווי זאָל איך זיי אָנרופֿן בײַם נאָמען?

– דאָס איז דיכטונג!

און נאָך אַ קורץ ליד, וועגן זעלבן ענין:

אײַננעמען שטחים פֿון צײַט מיטן וואָרט,

זאַלבן אויף זיי דײַנע זויבערע זילבן;

וויקלען אין קלאַנגען־רצועות די מוסקלען,

אָנטאָן אַ שטילקייט אין ערדישע הויטן,

שפּאַלטן אַ גראַם ווי אַ מילגרוים און טרינקען,

לאָזן די גלידער פֿאַרשווימען אין לידער

ביז דײַנע לידער אויף ס׳נײַ ווערן גלידער –

אָט צוליב דעם ביסטו, ייִנגל, באַשאַפֿן.

און נאָך עפּעס וועגן פּאָעזיע וואָס איך האָב געשריבן:

פּאָעזיע

אַ טונקל־פֿיאָלעטע פֿלוים

די לעצטע אויפֿן בוים,

דין־הײַטלדיק און צאַרט ווי אַ שוואַרצאַפּל,

וואָס האָט בײַ נאַכט אין טוי געלאָשן

ליבע, זעונג, צאַפּל,

און מיטן מאָרגן־שטערן איז דער טוי

געוואָרן גרינגער –

דאָס איז פּאָעזיע. ריר זי אָן אַזוי

מען זאָל ניט זען קיין סימן פֿון די פֿינגער.

אָדער אפֿשר איז גאָר פּאָעזיע – דערהייבן די וואָכעדיקייט צו כּולו שבת ווי דאָס

האָט געוואָלט אונדזער פּרץ אין זײַן „גאָלדענע קייט"? דיכטונג – דאָס איז די האַר־

מאָניע פֿון אַלע סתּירות, דער שלום צווישן טויט און לעבן, די פֿאַרקנסונג פֿון פֿאָ־

רעם און אינהאַלט, פֿון עטיק און עסטעטיק. זאָל דאָס ניט פֿאַרשטאַנען ווערן אַז

Those unseen subterranean streams
seeking a way to reach the rain, their father –
What name should I give them?

– *That is poetry!*

And here is another short poem on the same theme[31]:

To conquer domains of time with the word,
anointing your spotless pure syllables with them;
to bind all your muscles in *tefillin*[32] of music,
and clothe your earthly skin in silence,
to split open a rhyme like a pomegranate, drink it,
and let all your limbs melt away into poems
until all your poems become limbs once again –
It was for this, lad, that you were created.

And another poem I wrote about poetry:

Poetry[33]

A ripe, dark purple plum
the last one on the tree,
thin-skinned and tender as the pupil of an eye,
which has by night extinguished in the dew
love, vision, trembling,
and with the morning star, the dew grew lighter, did not linger –
that is poetry. Touch it so gently
that not a trace remains there of your finger.

Or perhaps poetry consists of elevating the humdrum into a pure Sabbath, as our Peretz tried to do in his *Goldene keyt*?[34] Poetry is – all contradictions brought into harmony, peace between death and life, the fusing of form and content, of ethics and aesthetics. This does not mean that I want to preach a

31   Sutzkever 1957: 76; 1963 (II): 331.
32   תפֿילין, *tefillin*: phylacteries.
33   Cf. p. 151.
34   I. L. Peretz, *Di goldene keyt* (The golden chain), 1909. In the play a Hasidic rabbi attempts to hasten the coming of Redemption by prolonging the Sabbath, and refusing to allow the week to start.

איך גיי פֿרײַדיקן עסטעטיזירטע קונסט, חלילה. כ'האָב געהאַט אַ מאָל אַ חבֿר אין
„יונג ווילנע״, לייזער וואָלף האָט ער געהייסן. האָט ער מיר אַ מאָל אָפּגעהאַלטן
אויפֿן גאַס און מיר אַ פֿרעג געטאָן:

– זאָג מיר, האָט ער געפֿרעגט, וואָס איז עטיק און וואָס איז עסטעטיק? איך
בין געבליבן צעטומלט אין דער זומערדיקער היץ. און איידער כ'האָב באַוויזן צו
ענטפֿערן, האָט שוין לייזער וואָלף פֿאַר מיר געענטפֿערט אַליין. און ער האָט אַזוי
געענטפֿערט:

– עטיק איז עטיק, און עסטעטיק – עסטעטיק.

איך מיין ניט, חלילה, צו פֿרײדיקן די עטיק וואָס עס עסט עטיק, איך מיין יע אַז אַ
ייִדישער דיכטער דאַרף ברענגען אין זײַן געזאַנג יענע היילנדיקע שיינקייט וואָס גיט
כּוח צו לעבן. אַ שיינקייט וואָס איז גלייכצייטיק אַ ליבשאַפֿט צו אַל דאָס אמתע און
דערהויבענע וואָס צוזאַמען מיט שפּינאָזעס אינטעלעקטועלער ליבע צו גאָט איז
זי, טאַקע זי, די אינטעלעקטועלע ליבע צום מענטש, צום ייִד און צום ייִדישן פֿאָלק.

ווען איך רייד וועגן עסטעטיק, מיין איך אָט וואָס אָט וואָס פֿאַר אַן עסטעטיק: ווען די
לעצטע ווילנער ייִדן האָבן זיך געפֿונען באַהאַלטענע אין די קאַנאַליזאַציע־רערן
[...], און איך בין אין דאָרט געווען, האָב דאָרט געוואָגלט, און דער שטאַרקסטער
אײַנדרוק פֿון די שטאַרקסטע אײַנדרוקן איז בײַ מיר געבליבן אַ צימערל אונטער
דער ערד, אין די קאַנאַליזאַציע־רערן, אָן די ייִדן וואָס האָבן דאָרטן געוווינט...
(אַגבֿ דער וואָס האָט עס אויסגעאַרבעט געפֿינט זיך איצט אין טאַראָנטאָ, כ'האָב אים
באַגעגנט, גרשון אבראמאָוויטש, וואָס ער איז איינער פֿון די העלדן פֿון מײַן פֿאַעמע
„געהיימשטאָט״). וואָס האָט אויף מיר געמאַכט אַ געוואַלדיקן רושם איז אין אָט
יענעם צימערל וואָס לשם אײַנגענעמקייט האָט מען אויסגעקאַלכט די ווענט, און
דאָס וואָלט געווען גענוג אַז ייִדן האָבן נאָך געהאַט דעם חוש, ליגנדיק אין דער
ערד, אויסצוקאַלכן נאָך די ווענט. אָבער דאָס איז ווייניק. פֿאַרוווּנדערט האָט מיך
דאָרטן דער בלויער שלעקעלע אויבן וואָס איז געמאַכט געוואָרן. דאָס מיין איך
ווען איך רייד וועגן עסטעטיק. אַזאַ שיינקייט, אַ געפֿיל פֿון שיינקייט וואָס שטאַרקט
דעם מענטשן, וואָס גיט אים כּוח איבערצולעבן שיינקייט, וואָס גיט אים כּוח זיך
צו פֿרייען מיטן לעבן.

אָבער איבער אַלץ, ווי מיר דאַכט, איז דיכטונג פֿערזענלעבכקייט. וואָס גרעסער
די דיכטערישע פֿערזענלעבכקייט, אַלץ אוניווערסאַלער איר דיכטונג. עס גילט פֿאַרן

kind of aesthetisized art, God forbid! I once had a friend in *Yung Vilne* called Leyzer Volf.[35] He once stopped me in the street and asked me a question:

"Tell me," he said, "what is ethics and what is aesthetics?" I stood there, feeling rather stupefied in the summer heat. Before I could answer, Leyzer Volf answered the question himself:

"Ethics is ethics, and aesthetics – eats ethics."[36]

I certainly do not mean to preach the kind of aesthetics which "eats ethics", but I do believe that a Yiddish poet must bring into his song that healing beauty which gives us the strength to live: beauty that at the same time means love for all that is true and sublime. Combined with Spinoza's[37] intellectual love of God, this indeed constitutes intellectual love for the human being, the Jew and the Jewish people.

When I speak of aesthetics, this is the kind of aesthetics I mean: when the last Jews of Vilna were hiding in the sewage system [...], I was there, I wandered about there, and the greatest of all the powerful impressions this experience made on me remains that of a little chamber under the earth, among the sewage pipes, where the Jews lived. (By the way, the man who hollowed it out, Gershon Abramovitsh, now lives in Toronto. I met him. He was one of the heroes of my *poeme* "Secret City")[38]. The thing that made a huge impression on me was that in order to make it pleasanter, they had whitewashed the walls of that tiny room. That fact alone, that Jews crouching underground had retained such a strong sense of beauty that they whitewashed the walls, would have been enough. But there was more. I was astonished to see the blue canopy that had been installed there[39]. This is what I mean by aesthetics: this concept of beauty, a feeling for beauty that empowers the human being and gives him the strength to experience beauty [even in such a situation] and to rejoice in his life.

But more than anything, it seems to me, poetry is personality. The greater the poetic personality, the more universal his poetry. Ibsen's[40] dictum: "Be

35   Leyzer Volf (1910–1943), one of the founding members of the group *Yung Vilne* (see footnote 19), was a prolific poet now best known for his satirical and parodic verse.
36   In Yiddish: עטיק איז עטיק, און עסטעטיק – עסט עטיק (*etik iz etik, un estetik – est etik.*) Leyzer Volf's answer is a pun, as the verb "esn" (third person singular: "est") means "to eat."
37   Baruch Spinoza (1632–1677), Dutch-Jewish philosopher of Sephardic-Portuguese origin, seen as one of the great Rationalists.
38   Cf. fn. 8.
39   Cf. Sutzkever 1947: 140.
40   Henrik Ibsen (1828–1906), Norwegian playwright, poet and theatre director.

פּאָעט דער איבסעענישער פֿאָרזאָג: זײַ ווער דו ווילסט, נאָר זײַ ביזן סוף. ס׳איז אָבער
אַ גרויסע קונסט זיך צו דערקענען אויף אַ דיכטער. ווי זאָגט ערגעץ משה נאָדיר:
ניט אַלץ וואָס גלאַנצט ניט איז גאָלד.

נאָך פּלאַסטישער וועגן דעם באַטײַט פֿון פּערזענלעכקייט האָב איך געלייענט
אין קאָראַן: אײר ווייסט דאָר, איך בין אין ארץ-ישׂראלדיקער בירגער, [...] קומענדיק
אין לאַנד גענומען לייענמען דעם קאָראַן. [...] איך האָב געפֿונען דאָרטן אייניקע פּסוּ־
קים, וואָס האָבן מיך דורכגעצויטערט, דורכגעצירט בין איך געוואָרן לייענדיק
זיי. אין איין טייל רעדט זיך וועגן דער פּערזענלעכקייט. דאָרט ווערט עס גערעדט אין
צוזאַמענהאַנג מיט די רשעים. וואָס ווען מען טאָן מיט די רשעים ווען זיי וועלן קר־
מען אויף יענער וועלט? זאָגט דאָרטן דער בעל-הקאָראַן אַזוי: מע וועט אויסשטעלן
די רשעים אין אַ רייַ, און עס וועט צוקומען אַ שליח אַדער אַ מלאך און מיט ברע־
נענדיקן ליים וועט ער פֿאַרשמירן אַלעמענס פּנימער, איין פּנים זאָל זײַן פּונקט ווי
דער צווייטער. די גרעסטע קללה – אַנטפֿערזענלעכן! צונעמען די פּערזענלעכקייט.
דאָס איז, לײַדער, די קללה ניט פֿון יענער וועלט, נאָר פֿון אונדזער צײַט. ווען דער
מענטש פֿאַרלירט זײַן פּערזענלעכקייט אויף דער וועלט.

איך וויל אײַך דערצייַלן וועגן אַ פּאָעט וואָס האָט געשריבן וועגן דעם זעלבן עניין
אויף אַ מערקווירדיקן אופֿן. און דער פּאָעט איז פֿון אַ יידישן אָפּשטאַם. זײַן נאָמען איז
לעשמיאַן, באָלעסלאַוו לעשמיאַן. געבוירן אין זאַמאָשטש, אין דער זעלבער שטאָט
וואָס פּרץ. ער איז שוין, דאַכט זיך, געבוירן ניט קיין ייִד, אָבער פֿון ייִדישע עלטערן.
ער איז איינער פֿון די גרעסטע פּוילישע פּאָעטן. איך האָב אים געקענט, האָב אים
געזען אין וואַרשע אין זעקס און דרײַסיקסטן יאָר. אַ נידעריקער, געוואָן אַ פֿאַרוואָזאָר
אין אַן אַפּטייק. האָט ווער אים אָנגעקוקט האָט קיינער זיך ניט געקענט פֿאָרשטעלן,
אַז ער איז איינער פֿון די גרעסטע פּאָעטן אין פּוילן און אפֿשר איינער פֿון די גרעסטע
אין דער וועלט, לויט מײַן געפֿיל, לויט מײַן געשמאַק. אַ פּאָעט וואָס האָט באַשאַפֿן
אַן אייגענע שפּראַך און אַן אייגענע מיטאָלאָגיע, דורכגעברענט מיט אַ פֿאַנטאַסטיק
וואָס קען זיך פֿאַרגלײַכן נאָר מיט אַ באָדלער צי עדגאַר פּאָ. איז אָט דער באָלעסלאַוו
לעשמיאַן האָט ערב דער צווייטער וועלט-מלחמה, אין 1937, אָנגעשריבן אַ טראַק־
טאַט וועגן פּאָעזיע. ס׳הייסט טאַקע אויף פּוילש אַזוי – Traktat o poezji. ער האָט
דאָס געזאָלט פֿאָרלייענען אין דער אַקאַדעמיע אין קראָקע, אָבער אַ טאָג צי עטלעכע
טעג פֿאַר דעם איז ער געשטאָרבן, און דער כּתב-יד איז געבליבן ליגן. ער איז טאַקע
געווען שוין ניט קיין ייִד, אָבער די דײַטשע האָבן דעם מיט זיך ניט גערעכנט, און
זײַן טאָכטער און זײַן פֿרוי זײַנען פֿאַרשפּאַרט געוואָרן אין וואַרשעווער געטאָ, און
צוזאַמען מיט זיי דער כּתב-יד. די טאָכטער איז, דאַכט זיך, אויף אַ געוויסע צײַט
געווען אין ארץ-ישׂראל, מע האָט זי גערעטעוועט, און אין ענגלאַנד, אין יאָרן אַרום,
אין לאַנדאָן איז דערשינען דער דאָזיקער טראַקטאַט. דאָס איז אַ מערקווירדיקע
שאַפֿונג און עטלעכע אויסצוגן וויל איך פֿאַר אײַך איבערדערצייַלן, איבערלייענען,
ווייַל עס קלינגט ווי אַ נבֿואה.

who you want to be, but [carry it through] right to the end," applies to the poet. There is, however, a great art in recognizing oneself as a poet. As Moyshe Nadir[41] said somewhere: "Not all that does not glisten is gold."

In the Qur'an I read something even more vivid about personality: you know that I am an Israeli citizen, [...] and when I first came to the country, I started reading the Qur'an. [...] I found there some verses which made me tremble when I read them. There is one part where it speaks of personality, in the context of evildoers. What will happen to the wicked when they arrive in the world to come? The writer of the Qur'an says: they will be made to stand in a row, and a messenger or angel will come with burning lime, with which he will smear their faces, so that they all look the same. The greatest curse – to depersonalize! Removing the personality is, unfortunately the curse, not of the world to come, but of our time, when the human being is losing his personality in this world.

I want to tell you about a poet who wrote about the same issue in an extraordinary way. This poet is of Jewish origin. His name is Bolesław Leśmian.[42] He was born in Zamość, the same town as Peretz. I believe he was not born as a Jew, although he had Jewish parents.[43] He is one of the greatest Polish poets. I knew him, I saw him in Warsaw in 1936. He was a small man who worked as a pharmacist. If you looked at him you would never have imagined that he was one of the greatest poets in Poland or perhaps in the world – that is, according to my opinion and taste. He was a poet who created his own language and mythology that burned with a fantasy reminiscent of Baudelaire or Edgar Allan Poe. Before the Second World War, in 1937, Bolesław Leśmian wrote a tractate about poetry – it is called in Polish *Traktat o poezji*. He was to do a reading in the Academy in Krakow, but the day before, or a few days before, he died, and the manuscript was abandoned. Though he was not [officially] Jewish, the Germans ignored this and his wife and daughter were imprisoned in the Warsaw ghetto. They had the manuscript with them. The daughter was saved and, I believe, spent some time in Israel, and years later Leśmian's tractate appeared in London. It is an extraordinary work, and I would like to tell you about some extracts, to read them to you, because they sound like a prophecy.[44]

---

41   Moyshe Nadir, (pseudonym of Yitskhok Rayz 1885–1943), born in Eastern Galicia, emigrated to New York in 1898. Became famous as a Yiddish humorist and satirist.
42   Bolesław Leśmian (1877–1937), one of the most influential poets of the early 20th century in Poland.
43   It is clear that Sutzkever means that he was not registered or brought up as a Jew.
44   In fact Sutzkever only reads this one short statement from Leśmian's tractate!

אַזוי זאָגט דאָרט לעשמיאַן אין דעם טראַקטאַט וועגן פּאָעזיע: „ניצשע זאָגט אַרויס אין אַ אײנעם פֿון זײַנע ווערק אַזאַ אַפֿאָריזם: וואָס מען זאָל ניט זאָגן וועגן דער פֿרוי, איז אמת. מיר קענען איבעראַנדערשן און איבערקערן דעם זאַץ: וואָס מע זאָל זאָגן וועגן פּאָעזיע, וועט זײַן ניט אמת.“ פּאָעזיע מײַדט אויס יעדע באַצײַכענונג. אַ באַצײַכענונג איז פֿאַר דער פּאָעזיע אַ מין גלעזערנע טרונע וועלכע טויט מיט איר דורכזיכטיקײט.

איך האָב געזען אין אַ זאָאָלאָגישן גאָרטן בוטשאַנען וואָס האָבן זיך געדרײט אויף דער פֿרײַ און ניט געוויזן קײן חשק אַוועקצופֿליִען. ס׳האָט זיך געקענט דאַכטן, אַז אין דעם רוים פֿון גאָרטן האָט זיך געהאַלטן די אינסטינקטיווע צוגעבונדנקײט צום שטיקל ערד און צום עסן. איך האָב אָבער געהאָט אַ טעות. דער היטער פֿון באַ־ טאַנישן גאָרטן האָט מיר דערקלערט אַז כדי זײ צוצושמידן צום אָרט, האָקט מען אונטער מיט אַ שער אַ געוויסן טייל פֿון זײיערע פֿליגל. און דעריבער קענען ניט די פֿייגל באַנצן זײיערע פֿליגל. אַ מאָל דערמאָנען זיי זיך וועגן זײיער אײַנגעבוירענער באַפֿליגלטקײט און מיט פּלוצעמדיקן גלוין פּרוון זיי זיך אַ הייב טאָן – אָבער אומזיסט. זיי פֿאָכען נאָר אויפֿן אָרט מיט די פֿליגל, אָבער פֿליִען קענען זיי שוין ניט. מע האָט זיי אײַנגעשפּאַרט אין גאָרטן מיט אויסנאויסֿיקער באַפֿליגלטקײט און מיט כלומרשטער פֿרײַהײט, אַזוי אַז ס׳איז שווער מיטן ערשטן בליק צו באַנעמען דעם ווייטיקדיקן סוד פֿון זײיער ערדישן זײַן, פֿון זײיער רירעוודיקן אָבער תּפֿיסהדיקן דרייען זיך אין פֿאַרכישופֿטן קרייז פֿון זאָאָלאָגישן גאָרטן.

אָדער מען איז אַ פֿויגל, אָדער מען איז ניט. קײן האַלבע פֿויגל זײַנען ניט פֿאַראַן. ניט קײן פֿולקומענע פֿליגל פֿליִען אויף הערן אויף צו זײַן פֿליגל. אָדער דאָס וואָרט באַפֿרײַט זיך פֿון די געדאַנקען־צוימען [אָדער] ס׳נעמט אויף זיך מיטן אייגענעם ווילן די קייטן.

ס׳באַווײַזט זיך באַלד ווי וואָס האַלט אַ שול אַז מען דאַרף שרײַבן מיט ניט־באַפֿרײַטע ווערטער, מיט אידעיש־צוזאַמענגעשאַפּֿענע זאַצן, אַזוי, אַז דער געדאַנקען־אין־ האַלט זאָל אין הערשן אין זאַץ איבער דעם ניט־עמאַנסיפּירטן וואָרט. [...] דער מין פּאָעזיע שטרעבט אונדז צו פֿאַרכישופֿן ניט מיט דעם צויבער פֿון ווערטער נאָר מיט דעם אינהאַלט פֿון זאַצן. די ווערטער און לידער פֿון אַזעלכע פּאָעטן פֿאַרלירן זײיער אמתדיקע זעלבסטשטענדיקײט, זײיער געפֿילמעסיקע אומאָפּהענגיקײט, די לידער באַפֿרײַען זיך פֿון די שעפֿערישע קאַפּריזן, פֿון די ניסים און וווּנדערס אין דער איבערצײַגונג אַז פֿאַרכלינעוועט מיט אַלגעמיינע אידעיש־באַצייכנטע זאַצן וועלן זיי באַקומען ערנסטקײט, געזעלשאַפֿטלעכע וויכטיקײט און וועלן זיך פֿאַרלײַכטערן דעם וועג צו די נשמות פֿון דער ברייטער געזעלשאַפֿט.

אַזאַ פּאָעט באַמיט זיך ניט אויסצוטײלן, נאָר צו זײַן ענלעך צו דער סביבה. אָנשטאָט צו שטרעבן צום נײַעם, וואָס אין קונסט מיינט עס ניט איבערגעחזרטע אינדיוויוידואַליטעט, שטרעבט דער פּאָעט צו דעם קעגנזאַץ. וועגן קונסט ווייסן נאָר די פּאָעטן וועלכע קוקן מיט [...] חוצפּהדיקײט אין וועלט דורך אַ מאָדערנער ניט־אויסגעפֿונענער לאַרנעטע אין דער איבערצײַגונג אַז זיי דערנענטערן זיך צו דער פֿאַרפֿולקומטער צוקונפֿט.

Thus Leśmian says in his tractate about poetry: "Nietzsche writes this aphorism in one of his works: 'Whatever one says about woman, is true.' We can alter this sentence and turn it round: 'Whatever one says about poetry, will not be true.'" Poetry resists any definition. A definition is for poetry a kind of glass coffin, which kills with its transparency.

In a zoological garden I once saw storks that were roaming freely and showed no desire to fly away. I had the impression that in the garden they had an instinctive feeling of connection to that little piece of earth and to their food. But I was wrong. The storks' keeper explained to me that in order to chain them to that place, they cut off part of their wings with scissors, so that they cannot use them. Sometimes the birds remember their innate winged state, and, inspired by a sudden faith, they try to fly – but in vain. All they can do is stand and flap their wings, but fly they cannot. They have been imprisoned in the garden, apparently free to fly, so that at first glance it is is difficult to perceive the painful secret of their earthbound state, and the touching significance of their, captive, restless roaming around in the enchanted circle of the zoological garden.

Either one is a bird, or one is not. There are no such things as "half-birds". Incomplete wings are not wings any more. Either the word liberates itself from the confines of thought or it accepts the chains of its own free will.[45]

There is a school of thought which believes that one should write with unfree words, with sentences whose ideas hang together logically, so that in the sentence the thought content has precedence over the unemancipated word. [...] That kind of poetry tries to enchant us not with the magic of words but with the content of sentences. The words and poems of such poets lose their true self-sufficiency, their emotional independence, the poems liberate themselves from creative caprices, from miracles and wonders, because of the [poet's] conviction that when choked up with sentences of a general ideological nature they will take on seriousness and social importance, which will ease their path to the souls of the wider society.

A poet like this does not try to be distinctive, but to fit in with his environment. Instead of striving towards the new, which in art means unrehearsed individualism, that poet aspires to the opposite of this. The only poets who know anything about art are those who look [...] daringly at the world through a modern, still uninvented lorgnette, convinced that they are drawing closer to the perfect future.

45   Sutzkever actually says here "Either...and", but he clearly means to make the contrast between the the "confined" word and the "emancipated" word.

דער אומגלויבן אין יחיד אין זײַן אייגנאַרטיקייט און דער גלויבן אין קאָלעקטיוו אין אָפֿטע גרויע זיך איבערחזרנדיקע דערשײַנונגען מוז סוף־כל־סוף דערשטיקן די אומאָפּהענגניקע פֿרײַע מאַכט פֿון דער מענטשלעכער נשמה. די כוחות וואָס זײַנען ביז איצט געוועזן אַ באַצייכענונג פֿון אויספֿעלן אין יעטצטיקן טאַלאַנט ווערן אַ טאַלאַנט פֿון נײַע פּאָעטן, און זייער אַרימטע אייגנשאַפֿט איז רעכט צום טאַלאַנט. (דאָס זײַנען נבֿאיִישע ווערטער.)

דער כּוח און ווונדער פֿון דיכטונג און פֿון ייִדיש־דעלעקט לשון האָט זיך אַנטפּלעקט פֿאַר מיר דער עיקר אין אַ ווילנער געטאָ. דאָרט האָב איך באַאמת געקענט זאָגן: „החיים והמוות בידך ייִדיש לשון". די שפּראַר, מײַן ייִדיש, איז געוועזן דער כישוף־פֿאַנצער אָן וועלכן ס'האָבן זיך אָפּגעשלאָגן די פֿײַלן פֿון טויט. מיטן ליד בין איך אַפֿילו אין געטאָ געוועזן אַ פֿרײַער מענטש. פֿרײַ ביז דער אומענדלעכקייט.

איך דערמאָן זיך אין סעפּטעמבער 1941, ווען מיטן לעצט געבליבענעם ווילנער רבֿ, רבֿ גוסטמאַן (איצט אַ ראָש־ישיבֿה אין ניו־יאָרק), ווען אונדז בײַדע האָט מען געפֿירט שיסן צו די שעסקינער בערג. ס'איז געוועזן פֿאַר טאָג, גאָלדענער פֿרי, און מע האָט אונדז געפֿירט צווישן פֿאַרלאָזענע גערטנער. ייִדן זײַנען שוין ניט געוועזן, די גע־ רטענער זײַנען ווילד פֿאַרוואַקסן געוואָרן, און איך... גייענדיק צום טויט, האָב איך מיט אַ מאָל פֿאַרקוקט אויף די גרויסע טויען, אויף די גרינע קרויטבלעטער. כ'האָב דעמאָלט בײַ זיך זיך געטראַכט: קוק זיך אײַן, דו נאַר, וואָס האָט געלעבט באָלד דרײַסיק יאָר און האָסט קיין מאָל ניט באַמערקט, אַז אויף קרויטבלעטער זײַנען די טויען אַזעל־ כע גרויסע, גרעסער פֿון אומעטום. דאָס האָב איך דעמאָלט געטראַכט.

און ווען מען האָט אונדז בײַדן אַרויסגעפֿירט אין די בערג, אויף שעסקינער בערג און מען האָט אונדז געהייסן גראָבן פֿאַר זיך אַ גרוב, און ווען איך האָב געגראָבן די גרוב, און דערזען אַ ווערעמל און צעשניטן דעם ווערעמל, גראָבנדיק, האָב איך געטראַכט בײַ זיך: קוק זיך אײַן, אַ קליין ווערעמל, דו צעשנײַדסט אים, הערט ער ניט אויף צו לעבן, פֿאַרקערט, ס'ווערן צוויי ווערעמלעך, און ווײַטער אַ שניט – ווערן דרײַ. און דעמאָלט האָב איך טאַקע אָנגעשריבן אָט דאָס ליד „עקזעקוציע". אָנגעשריבן אין קאָפּ, און שפּעטער, ווען איך בין געבליבן לעבן, ווי איר זעט, ווײַל מע האָט געשאָסן איבער אונדזערע קעפּ, מע האָט זיך געוואָלט אַזוי צו זאָגן אַ ביסל אָנשפּילן מיט אונדז, נאָך דעם האָט מען אונדז דעם זעלבן טאָג אין געטאָ, – האָב איך פֿאַרצייכנט אָט יענע איבערלעבונג.

Lack of faith in the individual and his originality and the [contrary] belief in the collective, in its often grey, repetitive manifestations, must in the end stifle the free independent power of the human soul. The powerful features which until now have been used to denote a lack of contemporary talent will be considered a positive aspect in new poets, and their well-known characteristics will be accepted as talent. (These are prophetic words.)

The power and the wonder of poetry and of the Yiddish language revealed themselves to me above all in the Vilna ghetto. There I was able to say truly: "Life and death are in your hands, Yiddish language."[46] The language, my Yiddish was the magic armor which repelled the arrows of death. With my poetry I was a free man, even in the ghetto. Free for all eternity.

I remember how in September 1941 I was taken, together with Rabbi Gutsman, the last rabbi in Vilna, (who is now the head of a yeshiva in New York), to be shot in the Šeškinė hills. It was dawn, a golden morning, and we were led along between deserted gardens. There were no Jews left there, the gardens were very overgrown, and I – on the way to my death – suddenly began to stare at the large amount of dew on the green cabbage leaves. At that moment I thought to myself: "Have a good look at it, you fool, who have been alive for almost thirty years and haven't ever noticed that on cabbage leaves there is more dew than anywhere else." That is what I was thinking at that moment.

And when they led us both into the hills and told us to dig a trench for ourselves, and I was digging the trench, I spied a little worm which, as I dug, I cut in two, and I thought to myself: "Look at this little worm, when you cut him in two, he doesn't stop living, in fact the opposite: he becomes two worms, and with another cut, there are three." And in my head I wrote my poem "Execution".[47] I did survive, as you see, because in fact they shot over our heads – they just wanted to have a little game with us, so to speak, and led us back to the ghetto the same day – and later I wrote down this experience:

46 ‏החיים והמוות בידך ייִדיש לשון‎ (hakhayim vehamoves beyadekh, yidish loshn) This is a variation of a common Hebrew saying: ‏החיים והמוות ביד הלשון‎ (Hakhayim vehamoves beyad haloshn, Life and death are in the hands of language), denoting the power and importance of words. This Hebrew saying is in turn a slight misquotation of Proverbs 18: 21: ‏מות וחיים ביד־לשון ואהביה יאכל פריה‎ (Moves vekhayim beyad-loshon veohaveyho yokhal piryoh, Death and life are in the power of the tongue: and they that love it shall eat the fruit thereof.)

47 First published in Sutzkever 1945: 48, then as second section of ‏אַ טאָג בײַ די שטורמיסטן‎ (A tog bay di shturmistn, A day with the storm troopers) in Sutzkever 1948b: 29; Sutzkever 1953b: 116; Sutzkever 1963 (I): 254; Sutzkever 1968a: 22f.

גראָב איך אַ גרוב ווי מען דאַרף, ווי מען הייסט,

זוך איך בעת־מעשׂה אין דר׳ערד אויך אַ טרייסט.

אַ גראָב און אַ שניט, און אַ ווערעמל קליין

עס צאַפלט פֿון אונטן – דאָס האַרץ קען צעגיין.

צעשנײַדעט אים מײַן רידל און – ווּונדער דערבײַ –

צעשניטענערהייט ווערן צוויי, ווערן דרײַ.

און ווייַטער אַ שניט און ווערן דרײַ, ווערן פֿיר,

און אַלע די לעבנס באַשאַפֿן דורך מיר?

קומט ווידער די זון אין מײַן טונקל געמיט,

און אַ גלויבן נעמט שטאַרקן מײַן אָרעם:

אויב אַ ווערעמל גיט זיך ניט אונטער דעם שניט,

ביסטו ווינציקער דען פֿון אַ וואָרעם?

די גרעסטע אָנערקענונג וואָס איך האָב באַקומען פֿאַר פּאָעזיע איז געווען די פּרע־
מיע וואָס כ׳האָב באַקומען אין ווילנער געטאָ פֿאַר מײַן פּאָעמע „דאָס קבֿר־קינד‟.
די פּרעמיע איז באַשטאַנען אין אַ שריפֿט אויף פֿאַרמעט אָנגעשריבן, אונטערגע־
שריבן פֿון אַלע די דעמאָלט לעבעדיקע ייִדישע און העברעיִשע שרייַבער און אַ
גאָלדענע צען־רובלדיקע.

ווי שטאַרק עס איז דער כּוח פֿון ליד, דער כּוח פֿון ריטעם, האָב איך זיך איבערצײַגט
אין 1944, מערץ, ווען איך האָב אַ געדאַרפֿט, זייַענדיק אין די פּאַרטיזאַנישע וועלדער,
אַריבערגיין אַ מינענפֿעלד, אַ פֿעלד פֿאַרזייט מיט מינעס. און ווּ עס ליגן די מינעס,
האָט קיינער ניט געווּסט. האָב איך אויך געזען צעריסענע מענטשן, קעניטיק אַ פֿויגל
וואָס האָט ניט קיין קיין שׂכל, האָט זיך גראָד געוואָלט אַוועקעטאָן אויף אַ מינע און צע־
ריסן געוואָרען. ווי אַזוי, אין אַ וועלכער ריכטונג זאָל איך גיין? ווּ שטעלן דעם פֿוס?
איין ריר איז טויט, נישט שטעלן איז לעבן, האָב איך אַרייַנגענומען אין זיך אַ ניגון,
און אָט אין ריטעם פֿון יענעם ניגון בין איך געגאַנגען אַ קילאָמעטער לאַנג איבערן
מינענפֿעלד און איך בין אַריבער. נאָר אפֿשר קענט איר איצט דערמאָנען וואָס
פֿאַר אַ ניגון דאָס איז געווען? איך געדענק אים ניט.
די ביאָגראַפֿיע פֿון אַ ליד איז אַ סך לענגער ווי די דאַטע וואָס איז אונטערגע־
שריבן אונטערן ליד. איין ליד ווערט אַ מאָל אויסגעטראָגן דורך לאַנגע יאָרן, דורך
אַ גאַנץ לעבן. און אפֿשר קומט עס גאָר ווי אַן אָפּקלאַנג, אַ בענקשאַפֿט, אַ ירושה פֿון
טאַטן, פֿון זיידן צי פֿון אָדם הראשון, ווער ווייס? אָבער כּדי דאָס ליד זאָל געבוירן,
מוז עס באַפֿרוכפּערט ווערן מיט אַ סודותדיקער טרער, וואָלט איך געזאָגט. די

I'm digging a trench as I must, by command,
and I search in the earth: is there comfort at hand?

A dig and a spade cut, and up from below
a tiny worm wriggles – it touches me so.

My spade slices through him, but, amazing to see,
the cut-up little worm becomes two, becomes three.

Another spade cut, there are four, not just three,
have all these new lives been created by me?

And the sunshine returns to my dark gloomy mood,
and faith starts to strengthen my arm:

If a wee little worm won't submit to the cut,
what of you? Are you less than a worm?

The greatest mark of recognition I ever received for poetry was the prize I won in the Vilna ghetto for my *poeme* "The Grave Child". The prize consisted of a certificate written on parchment, signed by all the Yiddish and Hebrew writers who were alive then, as well as a gold ten-rouble coin.

It was in March 1944 that I realized how strong the power of the poem, the power of rhythm is. While living in the forests with the partisans, I had to cross a field scattered with live mines. No one knew exactly where the mines were sited. I saw human beings torn to pieces, and a bird that obviously had no sense, decided to sit on a mine and was blown to bits. I wondered how, and in what direction I should go. Where to put my foot down? One false move meant death, not putting my foot down was life, so I managed to get a melody into my head, and to the rhythm of that melody I walked for a kilometer across that minefield and got safely across. Perhaps you can remind me what the melody was? I can't remember.

The biography of a poem goes back a great deal further than the date written at the bottom. Sometimes a poem is carried within you for long years, sometimes throughout your whole life. And perhaps it comes like an echo, a yearning, an inheritance from your father, your grandfather or Adam himself, who knows? But in order for the poem to be born, I would say that it has to be fertilized by a mysterious tear. The tear, the sudden impulse, the

טרער, דער צאַפל, דער פֿינקל קען זײַן די באַוועגונג פֿון אַ צוווייג, אַ שמייכל, אַפֿילו
אַ לוויה. אָבער אָן דעם לעצטן אויפֿצאַפל וואָס פֿאַרוואַנדלט ווערטער אין געזאַנג,
אָן אָט דער קלייניקייט, וואָס איר נשמהדיקע פֿונקציע איז אומדערקלערלערלעך ווי
דער סוד פֿון לעבן, קאָן דאָס ליד ניט געבוירן ווערן. און עס טרעפֿט, אַז בלויז בײַם
אָטעם פֿון טויט בלאָזט אַרײַן דער פֿאַעט אין זײַן ליד לעבן.

די שטימונג, דאָס בילד און דער אויסדרוק פֿון מײַנע פּאָעמע, למשל, „ערבֿ
מײַן פֿאַרברענונג", האָבן ווי קוילן אין מיר געטלִיעט און געמאַנט אַ תּיקון פֿונעם
יאָר 1941, האַרבסט, ווען איך בין געצוווּנגען געוואָרן צו טאַנצן אַ נאַקעטער מיטן
אַלטן אַכציק־יעריקן רבֿ פֿון מײַן גאַס, הרבֿ קאַסל, אַרום ברענעדיקע ספֿר־תּורות.
בײַם האַרבסט פֿונעם יאָר 1949 אין ארץ־ישׂראל איז מיר נאָכגעגאַנגען אָט יענער
גרוילביבילד. די פּאָעמע האָט פֿאַר די אַלע יאָרן זיך געריסן צו דער פֿרײַ, ווי אַ געבונ־
דענער פֿויגל. אָבער ערשט דעמאָלט ווען איך האָב דערזען די וואָלקן איבערן כרמל
וואָס האָט אויסגעזען ווי דער אין פֿײַער פֿאַרכאַפֿטער רבֿ דעמאָלט בײַם שײַטער
מיט יאָרן צורוק, ערשט דעמאָלט, קענטיק, איז געשען אָט יענע באַפֿרוכפערונג, אָט
יענע טרער האָט אַ פֿינקל געטאָן און דעמאָלט האָט זיך די פּאָעמע געבוירן.

די טרער וואָס האָט באַשאַפֿן מײַן לידער־ציקל „אַ בריוו צו די גראָזן" איז גע־
ווען – איר וועט לאַכן – אַ לעצט געבליבענע פֿלוים וואָס איך האָב צופֿעליק, ניט
צופֿעליק באַמערקט אויף אַ סאָד ערגעץ אין גליל. די פֿלוים איז געווען אָפּגעפֿיקט פֿון
אַ הונגעריקן ראָב, און ס׳האָט זיך אַרויס אַנטפּלעקט איר בליטשטשענדיקער יאָדער.
גלײַך ווי איך האָב עס דערזען, זײַנען אָנגעלאָפֿן אין מיר קלאַנגען, אַסאָציאַציעס,
און אָט די וויערדיקע פֿיר שורות, וואָס האָבן אָנגעלאָפֿן אָנגעשטעקט דעם גאַנצן
לידער־ציקל אין אַ סכום סובלימירטע איבערלעבונגען פֿון דער סאַמע קינדהייט
ביז דעמאָלט.

> די געלע פֿלוים דערמאָנט אָן מיר אַליין,
> עס קלאַפֿט צעוויישן בײַדן אַ צוזאַמענדיקער אָדער:
> וויפֿל ס׳זאַל דער פֿעלדזנראָב ניט פֿיקן מײַן געבײַן,
> וועט ער ניט קאָנען אויפֿזיגלען מײַן בליטשענדיקן יאָדער.

אָבער גאָר צום סוף אַז איך האָב פֿיל אַזוי פֿיל גערעדט, ווילט זיך פֿאָרט פֿרעגן: וואָס
איז פֿאַרט פֿאַעזיע? וויל איך ענדיקן מיט אַ קורצער מעשׂהלע. עס קען קלינגען ווי
סימבאָליש, אָבער דאָס איז אַ מעשׂה פֿון מײַן איבערלעבונג, איינע פֿון מײַנע טיפֿע

spark can be the movement of a branch, a smile, even a funeral. But without the final impetus, which transforms words into song, without this tiny
thing whose spiritual function is as indescribable as the secret of life itself,
the poem cannot be born. And it can sometimes happen that only with the
breath of approaching death can the poet breathe life into his poem.

The mood, the imagery and the expression of my poem "Before My
Burning", for example, glowed like live coals inside me and demanded to
be given expression from the autumn of 1941, when I was forced to dance
naked with the 80 year-old rabbi from my street, Rabbi Kosl, around a pile
of burning Torah scrolls. That ghastly image pursued me until the autumn of
the year 1949, in Israel. All those years the poem was struggling to break free,
like a trussed-up bird. But it was not until I saw a cloud over the Carmel that
looked like that rabbi caught in the fire all those years ago that this fertiliza-
tion happened – the tear sparkled and the poem was born.[48]

The tear that created my poem cycle *A letter to the grasses*[49] was – you will
laugh at this – a last remaining plum that by chance – or not by chance – I
noticed in an orchard in the Galilee. The plum had been pecked by a hungry
raven, so that its shining kernel was visible. As soon as I saw it, sounds and
associations welled up in me, and the following four lines [emerged], which
later sparked off the whole poem cycle, with a host of sublimated experiences
stretching from my early childhood until the present day:

> The yellow plum reminds me of myself.
> Between us both there beats a common pulse:
> however much the raven pecks my bones,
> he will not manage to expose my shining kernel.

But finally, having talked so much, I still want to ask: what is poetry after all?
I would like to end with a little story which, though it sounds symbolic, is
indeed the story of one of my deep experiences.[50] This story, or legend, hap-

---

48 In fact Sutzkever wrote an earlier poem about this experience, דער צירק (*Der tsirk*, The circus)
which was not published until 1979 (cf. Sutzkever 1979: 6–9). Sutzkever writes at the end of the
poem: געשריבן אין אַ באַהעלטעניש, אָנהייב יולי 1941 (*geshribn in a baheltenish, onheyb yuli 1941*, written
in a hiding place, beginning of July 1941). For a discussion of the relationship between this and the
later poem cf. Valencia 2012: 109–128.
49 P. 119–123.
50 This experience is the inspiration for one of the prose pieces in גרינער אַקוואַריום (*Griner akvarium*, Green aquarium): דאָס רינגעלע, (*Dos ringele*, The ring) Sutzkever 1955: 98–102; 1963 (II):
246–249; 1975: 24–27.

איבערלעבונגען. און געשען איז די דאָזיקע מעשׂה, לעגענדע, אין 43סטן יאָר, נאָך
דעם ווי איך מיט אַ גרופּע חברים, צוזאַמען מיט מײַן פֿרוי און שמערקען, ע״ה,
זײַנען מיר אַנטלאָפֿן פֿון געטאָ און דערגרייכט דעם נאַראָטשער וועלדער.

אין אַ חודש-אָנדערטהאַלבן נאָך דעם ווי מיר זײַנען געקומען, זײַנען מיר אַרום-
גערינגלט געוואָרן פֿון פּוֹפֿצן טויזנט דײַטשן. ס׳איז געוואָרן אַ בהלה אין וואַלד, די
פּאַרטיזאַנער האָבן נישט געקענט אויפֿנעמען דעם נישט-גלײַכן קאַמף, און זיי האָבן
באַשלאָסן אָפּצוטרעטן, זיך דערשפּרייטן איבער די וועלדער, די דערבײַיִקע. מיר
זײַנען געווען אומבאַהאָלפֿן, נישט געוווּסט ווו זיך צו קערן, וווּהין זיך צו וועסנדן. אונ-
דזערע אָנפֿירער זײַנען אויך נישט געוואָרן.

בין איך צוזאַמען מיט שמערקען און מיט מײַן פֿרוי אַרײַנגעפֿאַרקראָכן אין די זומפּן
און דאָרט געלעגן, דאָרט זיך באַהאַלטן. פֿאָר וואָס אין די זומפּן? דערפֿאָר ווײַל די
דײַטשן פֿלעגן גיין מיט שפּירהינטן און מיט זעגן. די שפּירהינטן פֿלעגן אָבער פֿאַרלי-
רן זיך בײַ די זומפּן, בײַ וואַסערן. די דײַטשן פֿלעגן כאַפֿן דער עיקר אַ ייִדישן פּאַרטיזאַן,
פֿלעגן זיי אים צעזעגן. זײַנען מיר דעמאָלט פֿאַרקראָכן אין די זומפּן. ס׳איז געווען
קאַלט. כ׳געדענק, כ׳האָב זיך אויפֿגעכאַפּט איין מאָל אין דער פֿרי, האָט זיך מיר
געדוכט אַז איך בין צוגעשמידט צו דער ערד. וואָס איז געווען? די וואַסערן פֿון די
זומפּן זײַנען פֿאַרפֿרוירן געוואָרן אַרום מיר און כ׳האָב אַ מאַך געטאָן מיטן קאָפּ,
האָב איך צערבראַכן אַרום זיך די ראַם… אַזוי ווי גלאָז.

זײַנען מיר געלעגן דאָרט אַ דרײַ מעת-לעת און געגעסן די ווילדע יאַגדעס און
עטלעכע נאַסע אַרבעס וואָס זײַנען נאָך געלעגן אין קעשענע. די שטיוול זײַנען
פֿאַרפֿרוירן געוואָרן אויף די פֿיס, האָבן מיר באַשלאָסן, מיר מוזן כאַטש אויף אַ
האַלבער שעה אַרויסקריכן פֿון די זומפּן זיך אָפּטריקענען אין דער זון. האָבן מיר
געקלעטערט, געקראָכן, אַרויסגעקראָכן אויף אַ בערגל און זיך אַוועקגעזעצט אויף
דער זון דערוואַרעמען די גלידער.

מיט אַ מאָל האָבן מיר דערהערט דײַטשע שטימען. האָבן מיר ווידער געצויגן
צוריק אין די זומפּן אַרײַן. און אַזוי קריכנדיק ווײַטער אין די זומפּן ביזן האַלדז, האָט
זיך מיט אַ מאָל דערמאָנט מײַן פֿרוי אַז אויפֿן בערגל פֿריִער ווו מיר האָבן זיך גע-
טריקנט האָט זי איבערגעלאָזן איר רינגעלע וואָס איך האָב איר געגעבן אַ מתנה צו
דער חתונה און וואָס זי האָט זיך אײַנגערעדט, אַז דאָס איז אַ מזל-רינג. מיטן רינגע-
לע איז זי געווען פֿיר מאָל אין געשטאַפּאָ, איז אַרויסגעקראָכן, געווען אין לוקישקער
טורמע, איז שוין געווען אין פּאָנאַר – דער רינגעלע האָט זי גאָראַטעוועט. זאָגט זי:
וואַרט אויף מיר אַ ווײַלע, איך קריך צוריק כ׳וועל געפֿינען און נעמען דעם רינגעלע.
און אײדער מיר האָבן זיך באַוויזן נאָך עפּעס איר צו זאָגן, איז זי שוין ניט געוואָרן. מיר
וואַרטן צען מינוט און צוואַנציק, און אַ שעה און צוויי, און זי איז ניטאָ. מיר הערן
שטימען פֿון דערשאָסענע, […] פֿון געכאַפּטע… קולות, און ס׳ווערט ביטער, מיר

pened in the year 1943 after I together with my wife and Shmerke[51] o"h and a group of comrades, had escaped from the ghetto and reached the Narocz forest[52].

One and a half months after our arrival we were surrounded by fifteen thousand Germans. There was chaos in the forest, the partisans could not engage in such an unequal battle, so they decided to retreat and disperse all around the neighboring woods. We were helpless and didn't know where to turn, in which direction to go. Our leaders had disappeared.

Shmerke, my wife and I crawled into the swamps and lay hidden there. Why did we go into the swamps? Because the Germans had dogs and saws, and when they captured a partisan, especially a Jewish one, they would saw him to pieces. The dogs, however, became disorientated in the swamps, and that's why we crawled there to hide. It was cold. I remember that once when I woke up in the morning, it seemed to me that I was welded to the earth. What had happened? The water in the swamp had frozen round me, and when I moved my head, the frame broke up round me – like glass.

We lay there for about three days, eating the wild berries and a few wet peas we still had in our pockets. Our boots were frozen onto our feet, so we decided that we must scramble out of the swamp for at least half an hour to dry ourselves in the sun. We clambered, crept, climbed onto a hillock and sat there so that the sun could warm our limbs.

Suddenly we heard German voices, so we went back to the swamps, and as we crept further in, my wife suddenly remembered that she had left the ring that I had given her as a wedding present, which she had persuaded herself was a good-luck ring, on the hillock where we had dried ourselves. Wearing that ring she had been in the hands of the Gestapo four times, and had escaped, she had been in the Lukishki prison[53], she had even been at Ponary[54] – and the ring had saved her. So she said: "Wait a while for me, I am going back to rescue my ring." And before we could say anything, she had disappeared. We waited ten minutes, twenty minutes, one hour, two hours, but she did not come back. We heard the voices of people being shot or captured [...]. It was terrible. We tried to crawl back but both Shmerke

51   Shmerke Katsherginski (Kaczerginski, 1908–1954), Vilna left-wing Yiddish poet and activist, one of the founders of the *Yung Vilne* group of poets, worked with Sutzkever in the "paper brigade" (cf. p. 244). He settled in Argentina after the war and died in a plane crash in 1954.
52   Narocz (Narotsh) forest: an area of forests, lakes and swamps to the east of Vilna, where groups of partisans operated. Sutzkever and his wife, and Katsherginski escaped from the Vilna ghetto in September 1943 and joined a Jewish partisan unit (cf. p. 246).
53   The Lukishi (Lithuanian: Lukiškės) Prison, in the centre of Vilna, was used by the Nazis to imprison Jews (cf. Sutzkever 1947: 37 f.) It is still in operation as a prison.
54   Cf. p. 241.

פרוווון קריכן צוריק, פֿאַל איך מיט שמערקען אַריַין אין אַ זומפּ, מיר וווערן שיער
בײַדע ניט דערטרונקען. קוים מיט מאַטערניש, אין אַ פּאָר שעה אַרום, זיַינען מיר
געקומען צוריק צום בערגל, איר געזוכט, קיין סימן, קיין שפּור ניטאָ פֿון איר.

שטעלט אײַך פֿאָר: מיר זיַינען בײַדע געווען פֿאַריִאושט, געמיינט אַז זי איז
געכאַפּט געוואָרן, אַז זי לעבט שוין ניט. און אַזוי זיַינען מיר געלעגן בײַדע אויפֿן
בערגל. די זון האָט זיך געהאַלטן בײַם אונטערגיין. פֿאַלט מיר אַריַין אַ מאַדנע זאַך:
אויפֿן בערגל האָב איך דערזען אַ בוים. אַ פּוסטער בוים. [...] און פֿון פֿאַרצווייפֿלונג
לויף איך צו צום בוים, כאַפּ אונטן אַ שטיין און נעם זעען מיטן שטיין אין בוים
אַריַין, קלערנדיק דערבײַ אַז אפֿשר איז זי ערגעץ פֿאַרפֿלאַנטערט געוואָרן צווישן
די זומפּן, זי וועט דערהערן דעם קלאַפּ, און וועט זי פֿאַרשטיין אַז מיר זיַינען דאָ און זי
וועט אַרויסקריכן.

און איך קלאַפּ מיטן שטיין אין בוים אַריַין, איך קלאַפּ און דער שטיין ווערט
צעבראָכן און איך וועד צעבראַכן, איך פֿאַל אַנידער, אַ מידער, אַ פֿאַרשווייסטער
אונטערן בוים און איך בלײַב ליגן אין האַלבע אָנמאַכט. און אַזוי ווי איך ליג אַזוי
אונטערן בוים, אַ פֿאַרצווייפֿלטער, אַ פֿאַריִאושטער, דערזע איך מיט אַ מאָל צווישן
די ווילדע צווײַגן, ווילדע קוסטן וואָס איבער די זומפּן, באַוועגט זיך עפּעס אַ גע־
שטאַלט. ס׳איז אַ מאַדנע געשטאַלט. די האָר אין גאַנצן פֿונאַנדער געלאָזן, דער קער־
פּער האַלב־נאַקעט, אין פֿאַסן בלוט רינען... רינט איבערן האַלדז, די קליידער צע־
פֿליקט, מיט דערנער, מיט יאַשטשערקעס, מיט שלאַנגען אַרומגעוויקלט. וואָס איז,
אַ באַבע־יאַגע איז אַרויסגעקראַכן צי וואָס? פֿריִער האָב איך געמיינט אפֿשר אַ גע־
פֿענסט, אפֿשר דוכט זיך מיר, נאָר די געשטאַלט איז געקומען נענטער, נענטער...
מיט אַ מאָל האָב איך דערזען ווי עס פֿינקלט אויף איר פֿינגער דער גאָלדענער
רינגעלע. האָב איך לויטן גאָלדענעם רינגעלע פֿאַרשטאַנען אַז דאָס איז מיַין פֿרוי. זי
האָט טאַקע געווען געלעגן אין אַ זומפּ, האָט זיך ניט געקענט געפֿינען, ניט געוווסט
ווּהין, דעם רינגעלע האָט זי פֿריִער יאָ געפֿונען, אָבער גיַיענדיק צוריק האָט זי זיך
פֿאַרבלאָנדזשעט און, הערנדיק מיַין קלאַפּן, איז לויטן קלאַפּ געגאַנגען. האָב איך
דעמאָלט געטראַכט, און איך טראַכט דאָס ביז איצט אַז דאָס בין איצט אַז איַיגנטלער מיטן דיכטער
קומט אויך אַזוינס פֿאָר.

ווען דער דיכטער איז שוין אין גאַנצן פֿאַריִאושט, פֿאַרצווייפֿלט, כאַפּט ער
עפּעס אַ וואָרט און הייבט אָן מיטן וואָרט און מיטן קאָפּ און מיטן האַרץ צו
קלאַפּן אָן אַ טויבער וואַנט און ער קלאַפּט אַזוי לאַנג ביז ער פֿאַלט פֿאַריִאושט,
מיד, צעבראָכן, און דעמאָלט טרעפֿט, אין אַ געבענטשטער מינוט, וואָס ער ליגט
שוין אַ פֿאַריִאושטער, אַז עס באַוויַיזט זיך ערגעץ פֿון דער ווילדעניש זיַין ליד, זיַין
אַרויסגערופֿענע ליד, אויך דערשראַקן, פֿאַרבלוטיקט, אָבער עס פֿינקלט אויפֿן ליד
אַ גאָלדן רינגעלע און דאָס ליד שמייכלט דורך טרערן.

and I fell into a swamp and almost drowned. Finally, after several hours of frantic effort, we managed to get back to the hillock and searched for her, but found no trace of her.

Imagine how we felt: we were both in despair, thinking that she had been captured and was no longer alive. We lay on the hillock as the sun went down. Suddenly I noticed something strange: on the little hill I saw a hollow tree. [...] And in my despair I ran to the tree, grabbed a stone and began striking the tree with it, thinking perhaps that if she had got lost somewhere among the swamps, she would hear the knocking, would realize that we were here and would be able to crawl back.

As I was hitting the tree, the stone broke up and I was broken too; I collapsed in exhaustion, covered in sweat, despairing, and lay there, half-conscious. And while I was lying there in my anguish and despair, I suddenly saw among the undergrowth of branches and bushes, a strange figure moving across the swamp. Her hair was dishevelled, her body half-naked, with blood running down her neck in rivulets... her clothes torn to pieces, spiked with thorns, and she was encircled with lizards and snakes. Was this some sort of Baba-Yaga who had crept out of the swamps? At first I thought it was a ghost, but the figure came nearer and nearer... and suddenly I saw that on her finger sparkled the gold ring. Because of the gold ring I realized that this was my wife. She had indeed been lying in a swamp and had been unable to find her way back. She had found the ring, but had got lost, and hearing my knocking, she had followed it and found her way. I thought then, and still believe to this day, that actually something similar happens with the poet.

When he is completely anguished and despairing, the poet grabs some word or other and begins to beat with the word and with his head and with his heart against a deaf wall[55], and he carries on beating until he collapses in despair, exhausted, broken, and then it happens, in a blessed moment, when he is still lying there in despair, that his poem emerges out of the wilderness, the poem he has summoned. It is also frightened and bloody, but on his poem sparkles a gold ring, and the poem smiles through its tears.

55   In Yiddish, the idiom that means "stone deaf" is טויב ווי די וואַנט (*toyb vi di vant*, as deaf as the wall).

סיביר

(פאלעם)

2: 349

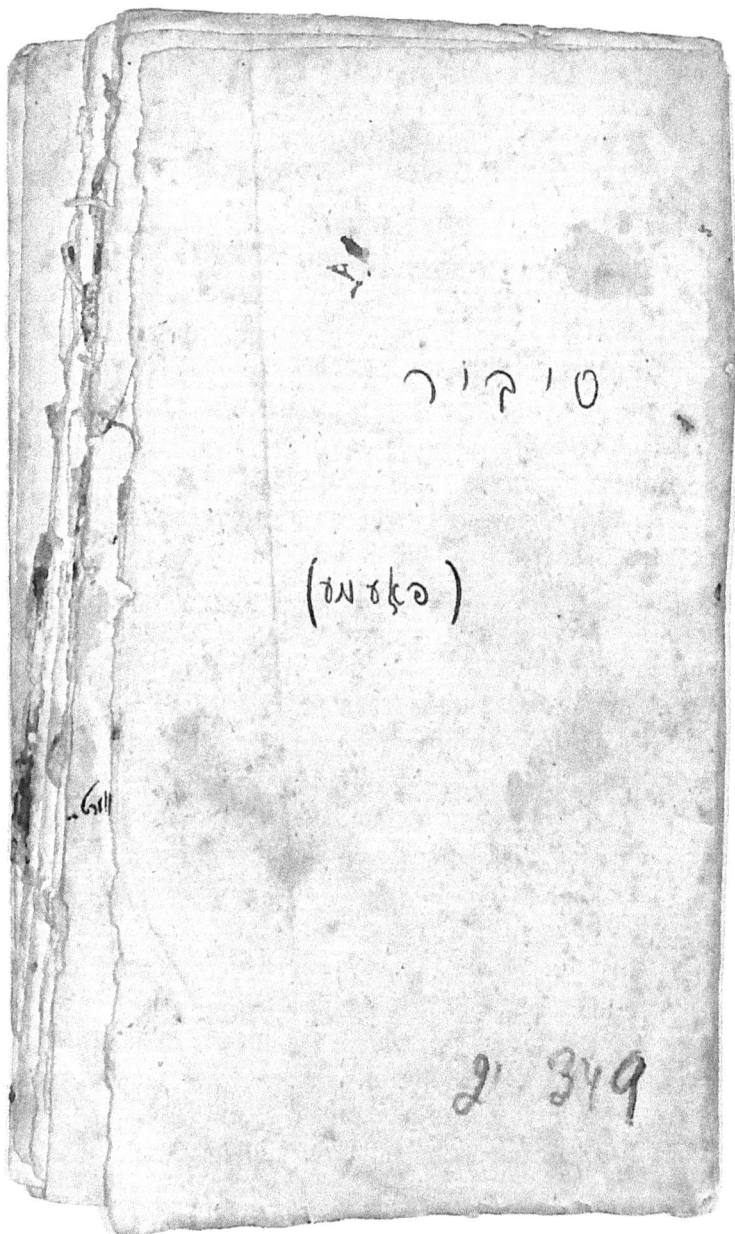

Front-page of the manuscript of *Sibir* (Siberia), copied out by an unknown person in the Vilna ghetto and rescued by Sutzkever after the liberation of Vilna, NLI, ARC 4°1565, 2:349

1935 – 1941

סיביר

אין כּוטער

א

זונפֿאַרגאַנג אויף אייזיק בלאָע װעגן.

זיסע דרעמלפֿאַרבן אין געמיט.

ס׳לײַכט פֿון טאָל אַ שטיבעלע אַנטקעגן

מיט אַ שניי פֿון זונפֿאַרגאַנג באַשיט.

װינדערװעלדער הױדען זיך אױף שויבן,

צױבער־שליטנס קלינגען אין אַ קרײַז.

אויפֿן פּיצל בוידעם װאָרקען טויבן,

װאָרקען אויס מײַן פּנים. אונטער אײַז,

דורכגעשטרײַפֿט מיט בליציקע קרישטאָלן

צאַפֿלט דער אירטיש אין האַלבער װאָר.

אונטער אויסגעשװיגענע קופֿאָלן

בליט אַ װעלט – אַ קינד פֿון זיבן יאָר.

ב

אינעם ליכטיק־טונקעלן, פֿאַרשנייטן

כּוטער פֿון מײַן קינדהייט אין סיביר,

בליִען פֿון די שאָטן־אַפּלען – קװײטן,

קװעקזילבערנע קװײטן אָן אַ שיעור.

אין די װינקלען אָפּגעלאָשן מאַטע

בלאָזט אַרײַן לבֿנה איר געבלענד.

װײַס װי די לבֿנה איז דער טאַטע,

שטילקייט פֿונעם שניי – אויף זײַנע הענט.

ער צעשנײַדט דאָס שװאַרצע ברויט מיט בלאַנקן

רחמימדיקן מעסער. ס׳פּנים בלויט.

און מיט נײַ צעשניטענע געדאַנקען

טונק איך אינעם זאַלץ דעם טאַטנס ברויט.

ג

מעסער. טאַטע. רויביקע לוטשינע.

קינדהייט. קינד. אַ שאָטן נעמט אַראָפּ

ס׳פֿידעלע פֿון װאַנט. און דין־דין־דינע

שנייענקלאַנגען פֿאַלן אויף מײַן קאָפּ.

Siberia

In the Hut

1.

Sunset on the blue and icy pathways.
Sweet slumber colors in my heart.
A little house shines from the valley
covered with the snow of sunset.
Wondrous forests swing across the windows,
enchanted sledges jingle round and round.
In the tiny attic doves are cooing,
tracing out my face. And under ice,
threaded through with glittering crystals
the River Irtysh quivers, – real, or dream.
Under still and silent domes
blooms a world: a seven-year-old child.

2.

In the bright-dark, snowy hut,
my Siberian childhood home,
from the eyes of shadows, blossoms gleam,
quicksilver blossoms, numberless.
Into the dull extinguished corners
the moon breathes out her dazzling light.
Whiteness of the moon is on my father,
silence of the snow upon his hands.
With a merciful, shining knife
he slices the black bread. His face gleams blue.
Then, full of fresh-sliced thoughts, I dip
into the salt my father's bread.

3.

Knife. Father. Smoky fire stick.
Childhood. Child. A shadow takes
the fiddle from the wall. And soft-soft
snow sounds fall upon my head.

שטיל. דאָס שפּילט דער טאַטע. און די קלאַנגען –
אויסגעראַוװירט אין לופֿטן, ווי אין פֿראַסט
זילבערלעך מיט אָטעם בלאָ צעהאַנגען
איבער שניי לעבנדיק באַגלאַזט.
דורך אַן אײַזיק אָנגעפּעלצטן שײַבל
שמעקט אַ װאָלף צום פֿלייש פֿון דער מוזיק.
שטיל. אין אונדזער טויבנשלאַק אַ טײַבל
פּיקט זיך פֿון אַן אייעלע, פּיק-פּיק.

פֿאַר טאָג

די סימנים-לאָפּעס, וואָס אַ חיה
האָט פֿאַרזייט ווי רויזן אינעם שניי,
ווען די זון, אַן אומבאַקאַנטע, נײַע,
האָט דערלאַנגט איר שפּיזיקן געשריי –
זענען קוים באַגילדעט פֿון אויבן. אונטן
פֿינצטערט נאָך. די װאָרצלען פֿונעם װאַלד
קרייצן מיט די צײַן אין טיפֿע גרונטן.
פֿונעם הונט, געשפּאַנט אין שליטן, פֿראַלט
לעבעדיקער דאַמף. דער דאַמף באַגעגנט
שטײַגנדיק אַ קוימענרויך וואָס העלט
און אַ מענטשן-אָטעם פֿון דער געגנט –
ביז אין לופֿט בלײַבט העגנען אַ געצעלט.

דערקענטעניש

א

„זאָג, ווו ענדיקט זיך די וועלט, אָ טאַטע?!“
פֿילאָסאָפֿיש מאָן איך אַ באַשייד.
קומט אַן ענטפֿער: „הינטער יענער כּאַטע
אויפֿן באַרגשפּיץ, ווו די זון פֿאַרגייט.“
אמת טאַקע? אויב אַזוי, – ניט קלערן,
אָניאָגן די שקיעה! און איך לויף
אויבן, דורך אַ זילבערגעץ פֿון טרערן,
ווו די וועלט זיך ענדיקט, באַרג אַרויף.

Silent. Father's playing. And the sounds –
etched on the air, like breath of blue
on silvery frost, hang lingering
over the moon-glazed snow.
Through an ice-furred windowpane,
a wolf can scent the flesh of father's music.
Stillness. In our dovecot a baby dove
pecks and picks its way out of an egg.

Dawn

The pawprints, which some creature
planted like roses in the snow,
when the unknown, new-born sun
cast down her shrieking rays like spears –
now are barely gilded from above. And down below
it is still dark. The forest roots
grind their teeth deep underground.
Harnessed to a sledge, a dog pours out
a cloud of living vapor. And mounting up,
the vapor meets bright chimney smoke
and human breath from near at hand –
till a tent shape hovers in the air.

Realization

1.
"Tell me, father, where does the world end?!"
Like a philosopher, I demand to know.
He answers: "Behind that little hut
up on the mountain, where the sun goes down."
Is this the truth? If so, don't think,
but hunt the sunset! And I run
upwards, through a silver net of tears,
to where the world ends, towards the mountain top.

ביים סיבירער גאָט די אויגן מאַנען,
ס׳זאָל ניט זיין מיין בענקעניש אומזיסט.
אַלע יאָרן ביז־מיר, יאָר־מיליאָנען,
צאַפלען פֿון די שנייען: זיי באַגריסט.

ב

הינטער מיר – אַ פינטעלע אַ טאָטע.
ס׳האַרץ, דער זון אַנטקעגן, אין גאַלאָפּ.
שוין, דערלאָפֿן אויבן צו דער באַטע!
נאָר די שפּאַנונג מאַניעט, לאָזט ניט אָפּ.
מיינע ליפּן ציִען זיך צום שייטער,
וואָס באַשיינט דעם וואָיענדיקן דנאָ.
טאָטינקע! עס ציט די וועלט זיך ווייטער,
און קיין סוף – ניטאָ, ניטאָ, ניטאָ.
טאָטע הערט ניט. שטערן פֿאַלן גרינע.
טאָטע זעט ניט, אַז פֿון העלער הויט
ווער איך פֿון אַ ייִנגל – אַ לאַווינע,
וועמען ליכט און וווּנדער האָט געבוֹיט.

ווי אַ שליטן אין פֿאַרבענקטן קלינגען

אויפֿן שניי דעם דימענטענעם, בלאָען
שרייב איך מיטן ווינט ווי מיט אַ פּען,
בלאָנדזשע אויף די גלימערדיקע דנאָען
פֿון זיין קינדהייט. האָב נאָר ניט געזען
אַזאַ לויטערקייט, וואָס קען באַצווייִנגען
אַלע עלנט־שאָטנס פֿון געדאַנק.
ווי אַ שליטן אין פֿאַרבענקטן קלינגען
גלעקלט דאָ מיין לעבן דין און לאַנג
דורכן אָוונטסטעפּ, וואָס אין זיין שפּיגל,
צוגעטוליעט מיט דער נאָז אַראָפּ,
לויערט די לבֿנה, און צוויי פֿליגל
שלאָגן אָפּ.

To the Siberian God my eyes are pleading,
let not all my longing be in vain.
All the millennia which came before me
rise quivering to greet me from the snows.

2.
Behind me, father – just a tiny dot.
My heart is galloping towards the sun.
Now I have reached the top and found the hut!
But still excitement grips me, drives me on.
My lips are drawn towards the radiant fire
that illuminates the howling depths.
Dear little father! Look, the world goes on,
and has no end – no end, no end at all.
Father does not hear. And green stars fall.
Father does not see, as out of the blue I change
from a young boy to – an avalanche,
created by a miracle of light.

Like a Sledge Jingling with Longing

On the blue, diamond-sparkling snow
I write with the wind as with a pen.
I ramble through the glimmering depths
of the snow's childhood. Never have I seen
such purity, which has the power to banish
every lonely shadow from the mind.
Like a sledge jingling with longing
rings out my life's path, thin and long,
across the evening steppe – and in its mirror,
nestling, peering down, the moon,
is crouching, and two wings
are beating.

פֿײַערדיקער פּעלץ

פֿעלדער – בלאַנקע, בלענדיקע מעטאַלן,
ביימער – אָפּגעגאַסענע מיט פֿעלדז.
שנייען האָבן מער ניט ווּ צו פֿאַלן,
ס׳טראָגט די זון אַ פֿײַערדיקן פּעלץ.
מיט זײַן דימענט־פֿענדזל אויף מײַן שאַרבן
מאָלט דער קינסטלער פֿראָסט ווי אויף אַ שויב
זײַנע שניי־לעגענדעס פֿול מיט פֿאַרבן,
„שרײַבט זיך אונטער" מיט געפֿלי פֿון טויב.
זון פֿאַרגייט אין מיר. ניטאָ די זון מער.
בלויז מע זעט איר פֿײַערפּעלץ אַליין
אויף אַ לאַנגער צוווייג. און איך – אַ שטומער –
אָנטאָן ווויל אים ערבֿ זײַן פֿאַרגיין.

אין אַ סיבירער וואַלד

א

יונגע זון, וואָס אײביקט ניי געבאָרן,
קײַקלט זיך אין שניי מיט מיר באַנאַנד.
זאָגט דער טאַטע: „קינד מײַנס, לאָמיר פֿאָרן
ברענגען האָלץ פֿון וואַלד". און ס׳ווערט געשפּאַנט
אונדזער זילבער־לאָשיק אין אַ שליטן.
ס׳בלאַנקעט די האַק. אין פֿלאַמענשניי דער טאָג
פֿון געשלײַפֿטע זונמעסערס צעשניטן.
פֿונקענשטויב – דער אָטעם! און אַ יאָג
איבער סטעפּ פֿון שלאָפֿנדיקע בערן
דורכן זונגעוועב. דער שניי קלינגט צו.
אַלע נעכטן אָפּגעשיטע שטערן
ליגן איצט פֿאַרפֿראָרענע, אין רו.

ב

וואַלד. אַ פֿרישע בליציקייט אויף צווייגן
אטעמט אויס דעם וואַלפֿישן געהײַל.
אָנגעגליטער עכאָ פֿונעם שווײַגן –
שיסט אין מיר אַרײַן אַ הייסע פֿײַל.
יעדער שניי איז אַ פֿאַפֿראָרן גלעקל,

Fiery Fur

Fields – gleaming, dazzling metal,
trees – forms cast in rock.
Snows have nowhere left to fall,
and the sun is clad in fiery fur.
With his diamond brush the artist frost
is painting on my skull, as on a pane,
his snow legends bright with many colors.
He signs them with the fluttering of a dove.
Sun sets within me. No more sun at all.
Only her fiery fur still hangs
on a long branch. And I – a dumb watcher –
long to put it on before it fades.

In a Siberian Forest

1.
The eternally new-born young sun and I
are rolling round together in the snow.
Father says: "My child, let's ride into the forest
to get wood." And we harness
to the sledge our silver colt.
The axe gleams. Robed in fiery snow,
the day is cut by sharp sun knives.
Our breath is sparkling powder! And we race
across the steppe where bears lie slumbering,
through webs of sunlight. Snow rings out.
Yesterday's fallen stars lie sprinkled everywhere,
frozen and at rest.

2.
Forest. A fresh gleaming on the branches
breathes out the howling of the wolves.
A glowing echo of the silence –
a burning arrow, pierces me.
Every snowflake is a frozen bell,

גיב אַ ריר און ס׳ענטפֿערט מיט אַ קלונג,
און דער קלונג – אויף טויזנט אַ צעברעקל.
פלוצעם ווייזט אַ פֿיקסל מיר די צונג
פֿונעם שנייעצעלט און שוין פֿאַרזונקען.
– „פֿיקסל, האָב ניט מורא!" – און מיַין באַק
וואַרעמט זיך ביַי די הענגענדיקע פֿונקען,
ביז די זון פֿאַרגייט אין טאַטנס זאַק.

ג

ציִען מיר אַהיים צום שטילן כּותער –
בלאָנדזשעט מיַין נשמה נאָך אין וואַלד.
און דער וואַלד אַ גוטער, אַ באַרוטער,
וואַרעמט זי אין בוזעם און באַשטראַלט.
נעמען שטערן מיט געזאַנג מיך קריַינען,
שטערן אויפֿגעבלאָזענע אין ווינט!
און לכּבֿוד שטערן ווילט זיך וויינען...
ביז דער לעצטער בוים פֿון וואַלד פֿאַרשוווינדט,
און עס בליַיבן שטיין אין שנייַ די שניטן.
דעמאָלט וועקט מיך אויף דעם טאַטנס קול.
זע איך: די לבֿנה איז אין שליטן
מיטגעפֿאָרן צו מיַין היים אין טאָל.

צום טאַטן

טאַטע, נאָכן שליטן מיט דיַין אָרון
נאָכגעלאָפֿן בין איך דיר, כּדי
אָנצוויאָגן ערגעץ דיַין זכּרון
מיט אַ טויב אין בוזעם ווייַס ווי שנייַ.
ווען עס האָט אַ כּותער דיר אַ ניַיעם
אויסגעהאַקט אַ האַרצקלאָפֿיקער לאָם,
און פֿאַרשלונגען האָט דיך באַלד אַ תּהום,
ווו דו פֿינקלסט אונטער אייַז עד־היום –
האָב איך דאָרט אַריַינפֿאַלן געוואָלט!
נאָר מיַין טויב איז דעמאָלט גראָד פֿאַרפֿלויגן,
אָוונטזון באַקריינינט מיט וויַיסן גאָלד,
און אַרויף צום לעבן מיך געצויגן...

touch it, and it answers with a ringing sound,
that shatters in a thousand splinters.
A little fox sticks out its tongue at me
from its snow tent, and straightway disappears.
"Don't be scared, little fox!" And now my cheek
is warmed by hovering sparks,
till the sun sets in my father's axe.

3.
Traveling homeward to our quiet hut,
my soul still wanders in the forest.
The forest – kindly, tranquil friend –
shines on it and warms it in his bosom.
Stars begin to crown me with their song,
stars kindled by the wind!
Those stars make me feel like weeping…
Then the last tree disappears from view,
and in the snow our sledge tracks stop.
I'm wakened by my father's voice.
And I see: the moon has travelled with us in the sledge
to my home in the valley.

To My Father

Father, I pursued the sledge that bore your coffin,
running after you, to catch
some memory of you.
A dove was in my bosom, white as snow.
When the crowbar with its pounding heartbeat
hacked out a new home for you,
and a deep chasm swallowed you,
where to this day you sparkle under ice –
O, I wanted to leap in beside you!
But suddenly just then my dove flew up,
crowning the evening sun with her white gold,
and drew me upwards with her, into life…

אירטיש

שטיל! פֿון וואַנען קוואַלט אַזאַ מיַן קלינגען?
ס׳וויל אַנטלויפֿן דער אירטיש פֿון ברעג!
זוכט אין קאַלטע, כוואַליעדיקע ריגגען
אָפּגעפֿלייצטע פּנימער פֿון טעג.
עפֿנט ער די אויגן צו די שטערן
פֿון אַן אויסגעזעגטן ראָד: „ווי לאַנג
וועט דער פֿרילינג מיַן געבעט ניט הערן,
וועט דעם אייז ניט שניַידן מיַן געזאַנג?"
זשומעט נאָכט אין באַרד אַריַין אַ סוד אים:
– „ס׳ווערט שוין אויסגעשמידט אַ זון!" און גליַיך
פֿאַלט אַראָפּ אַ שטערנדל פֿון פֿאָדעם
און – אַ קוש דעם ווינטערדיקן טיַיך.

שניימענטש

א

שניימענטש, דענקמאָל נאָך אַ קינדהייט, היטער
פֿון אַ קאַלטן אוצר! ניט אומזיסט
גליבּן גלייב איך: דו ביסט מיַן געביטער.
זיַי מיר, שניימענטש, טויזנט מאָל באַגריסט!
ביסט דער גאָט פֿון קינדער און פֿון ווינטן,
לעבן דיר מיַן חלום שטייט געקניט.
ס׳קומען וועלף אין גאַנצענע געזינטן
און זיי רופֿן: שניימענטש, היט, באַהיט!
אייביק ביסטו שניימענטש, ניט צעשמאָלצן
ווערט דיַין פֿינקל־פֿאַנצער פֿון קרישטאָל.
אָ, ווי שיין דו טאַנצסט אויף דיַינע שטאָלצן
פֿאַר די שטערנמענטשעלעך אין טאָל!

ב

שניימענטש, אומגעלומפּער, מיט אַ טעפּל
אויפֿן קאָפּ אַנשטאָט אַ קרוין! באַוויַיז
נאָך אַ מאָל דיַין שמייכל פֿונעם נעפּל,
וואָרעם אָן מיַן עלנט מיט דיַין אייז.
אויב מיַן בענקשאַפֿט איז צו דיר דערגאַנגען –

The Irtysh

Hush! What is the source of this strange ringing?
The Irtysh wants to overflow his banks!
Seeking in cold, rippling circles
ebbing faces of drowned days.
From a circle sawn in the ice
his eyes peer out to see the stars: "How long
till the spring hears my prayer,
till my song cuts the ice?"
Night purrs a secret into his beard:
"Already there's a sun being forged!" And suddenly
a little star falls off its string,
and kisses the wintry river.

Snowman

1.

Snowman, monument to a childhood, guardian
of a cold treasure! It's not in vain
that I most steadfastly believe: You are my master.
Snowman, a thousand times I greet you!
You are the God of children and of winds.
My dream is kneeling down beside you.
Packs of wolves are coming, calling out:
"Snowman, save, protect us!"
You are eternal, snowman. Sparkling crystal,
your armor will never melt away.
On your stilts, how beautifully you dance
for the little starfolk in the valley!

2.

Clumsy snowman, with a pot upon your head,
and not a crown! Show me again your smile
that pierces through the mist.
Let your ice warm up my loneliness.
If the longing of my heart has reached you –

אין די זעלבע טריט־סימנים גיי,

וועסטו אין אַ שטיבעלע פֿון קלאַנגען

מיר געפֿינען תּפֿילה טאָן צו שנײַ.

ניט געפֿונען – האָב ניט קיין פֿאַראיבל,

קענטיק, אַז מיר האָבן זיך געמײַדט.

ירשן מײַן געװוֹנקייט פֿון שטיבל

און פֿאַרענדיק אָטעמען מײַן צײַט.

סיבירער פֿרילינג

א

ס׳נעמען פֿאַטשן פֿילקאָלירטע פֿליגל

איבער טײַגע־װילדערניש אין װינט.

ס׳קװאַלט און ריזלט װי צעלאָזטער שפּיגל

מײַל נאָך מײַל און בײַ די ראַנדן גרינט.

נאָסע שנײַען זינגען אַ געזעגנס,

פֿליגלען, שפּיגלען פֿול מיט פֿאַרב און קלאַנג.

מיטן יונגן לײבנברום פֿון רעגנס

פֿלאַקערט אויף דער קינדערשער פֿאַרלאַנג

אָנצװיאָגן אַלע װילדע שטראָמען,

געבן זיך אַ פֿויגלדיקן טראָג

איבער מענטשן, װעלדער, פֿעלדזן, תהומען –

צו דעם נײַעם, יום־טובֿדיקן טאָג!

ב

מיטן שימער פֿון די העלע גרינען

שלײַפֿט זיך דער אירטיש אָן װילד געשטיין.

װײַל די כװאַליעס זײַנע קריק געפֿינען,

װײַלע קריעס האַלטן שוין אין גיין...

און אָנשטאָט צו קוקן שרעקיק־פֿינצטער

דורך זײַן אײַנעם אויסגעזעגטן ראָד –

קוקט ער איצט מיט כװאַליע מיט דער מינדסטער

װי עס גייט די װעלט אַ קאַראהאָד

רונד אַרום דער זון, װאָס אי מיט העזה

װאַרפֿט זי שװערדן, אי זי לעקט אַצינד

ס׳פֿינקלענדיקע אײַזעליכט פֿון בעריאָזע,

װי עס לעקט זײַן צוקערל אַ קינד.

follow in my footprints. Then
you'll find me in a little hut of sounds,
offering up a prayer to the snow.
If you don't find me – bear me no grudge,
we've simply missed each other on the way.
Inherit my former presence in the hut
and finish living out my days.

Siberian Spring

I.
Many-coloured wings have started beating
across the windswept taiga wilderness.
For miles and miles there's gushing, gurgling,
like a melting mirror. At the edges,
green appears. Wet snows sing farewell songs,
wings and mirrors full of sound and color.
With the rain's young lion roar
flares up the longing of the child, to chase
all the wild streams, and, like a bird, to soar
over people, forests, cliffs and chasms –
to the new, festive day!

2.
Amid the shimmer of the bright green places
the Irtysh polishes himself on jagged rocks.
He wants to find his waves again,
as the ice floes drift away…
Instead of peering darkly, fiercely
through his single sawn-out circle –
now he watches with his tiniest wavelet
as the world dances in a ring
round about the sun, which now audaciously
throws swords, now licks
sparkling ice light from the birches,
like a child licking a sweet.

קירגיזן

שלום אײך אין װײַטעניש, קירגיזן,
בײַם אירטיש, פֿון שײַטערן באַגילדט,
װו צעװױשן טאַנצנדיקע שפּיזן
װיקלט איר אַ ניגון און פֿאַרשפּילט
אײַער אומעט, ביז איר פֿאַלט אין דרעמל.
יעדער זופֿט װי בראָנפֿן זײַן געװײן.
און דער אַלטער הױקער פֿונעם קעמל
שמײכלט מיט די קנײטשן, קאָן פֿאַרשטײן
די מוזיק פֿון אײַער געלן פֿיבער.
װען מײַן לעבן צאַנקט װי אַ לאָמטער,
בײַג איך מײַן געזאַנג צו אײַך אַריבער,
עפֿן זיבן אױערן און – הער.

מײַן חבֿרל טשאַנגורי

א

לעבסטו נאָך, מײַן חבֿרל טשאַנגורי,
אָדער ביסט אַ שנײיִקע געשטאַלט?
פֿון די װאָלקנס פֿלעמלט מיר דײַן צורה
מיט די אָפֿלען אױסגעבאַרגט אין װאַלד.
קום זיך שפּילן װידער און געפֿינען
װאָס מיר האָבן קײן מאָל ניט געהאַט.
מיטן ערשטן אָטעם פֿון באַגינען
לאָמיר קושן יעדער גראָז און בלאַט.
לאָמיר זשליאָקען קליאַטשעמילך פֿון לאָגל
און אױף סאָװעס מאַכן אַ געיעג.
לאָמיר, ברודער, נאָכן לאָנגן װאָגל
אײַנשלאָפֿן װי דעמאָלט פֿאַזע װעג.

ב

קום צו רײַטן װידער אױף דער דײַן טױבן,
הױקערדיקן קעמל, און געשװינד
פֿאָרן פֿיצל העמד אַ צי מיך אױבן, –
און אַװעקגעלאָזן זיך אין װינט,
צו באַגעגענען אין שטילע װינקלען

The Kirghiz

Greetings to you, distant Kirghiz
by the Irtysh, gilded by your fires.
There, among dancing spears
you weave a melody to drive away
your sorrow, till you sink in slumber.
You sip your tears like fiery liquor.
The wrinkles of the camel's ancient hump
are smiling. They can understand
the music of your yellow fever.
When my life flickers like a lantern
I bend my song towards you,
open seven ears and – hear.

My Friend Tshanguri

1.

Are you still alive, my friend Tshanguri,
or are you now a snowy form?
From the clouds your face is flickering towards me
with dark eyes borrowed in the woods.
Come and play with me again, and find
all the things we never had before.
With the first breath of dawn
let's kiss each leaf and blade of grass.
Let's gulp mare's milk from a goatskin
and race off, chasing owls.
Brother, after wandering far and wide,
let's go to sleep, as once we did, by the roadside.

2.

Come riding once again upon your deaf
and humpbacked camel; swiftly pull me
up behind you by my scrap of shirt, –
and dash off in the wind,
to meet in quiet corners

דעם געבורט פֿון שאָטנס ערבֿ נאַכט.
אַלע גראָזן צוינבערן און פֿינקלען,
עס דערקענט אַליין זיך ניט די פֿראַכט.
פֿלעקן לעבנס טונקלען אין די װײַטן,
דער אירטיש, אַ װאָלקנדיקער, גליט,
ס'בלויט דער קעמל. און מיר בײדע רײַטן
צו די בלאַנקע פֿעלדזן פֿון גראַניט.

ג

װען די בערג די שטאָציקע פֿאַרשװוינדן –
גיט אַ שוום אַ פֿיאָלעטער װאַלד.
ס'נעמט אַ לאַנגע אָװונטהאַנט פֿאַרבינדן
אַלצדינג װאָס באַזונדער זיך באַהאַלט.
אויף אַ יאָדלע טאַנצט דאָס לעצטע פֿלעמל.
אויף די ליפֿן טאַנצט דאָס לעצטע װאָרט.
אין אַ גראָזן־חלום קניט דער קעמל.
טונקלער. און בלויז די שטילקײט קלאָרט.
פֿײכטן װאָלקן שנײַדט אַדורך אַ בראָנע.
עפֿנט זײַנע סודות. נאַכט קומט אָן.
און מיר עסן בײדע די לבֿנה
װי אַן אויפֿגעשניטענעם קאַװאָן.

בײַם שײַטער

א

בלאָזט די נאַכט פֿונאַנד אין װאַלד אַ שײַטער,
װערן יונגע בײמער גראָ פֿון שרעק.
צװישן קנאָקנדיקע צװײַגן, קרײַטער,
פֿאַלן שאָטנס, װוּ עס בליצן העק.
און קירגיזן – קינדער, פֿרויען, מענער –
שפּיגלען זיך אין זײער שאַרפֿן ראַנד.
ס'קנאַקן צװײַגן מיטן קרײ פֿון הענער.
און װי פּערל פֿון געפֿלאַצטן באַנד
פֿאַלט אַ טוי אויף שטײַגנדיקע פֿונקען,
פֿאַלט אַ טוי אויף בעטנדיקע הענט.
און אַ פֿויגל אין דער נאַכט פֿאַרזונקען –
קומט צו פֿליִען, און זײַן פֿידל ברענט.

the shadows' birth before the night has fallen.
The grasses sparkle, weaving magic spells.
The splendor is still unaware
of itself. Tiny specks of life
darken in the distance, and the cloudy Irtysh glows.
The camel turns to blue. And we two together
are riding to the shining granite cliffs.

3.
When the steep mountains disappear –
a violet forest rises up before us.
A long twilight hand unites
all that was isolated, hidden.
On a fir tree dances the last flame.
On our lips dances the last word.
In a dream of grass the camel kneels.
Darker. Only the silence gleams.
A harrow cuts through a moist cloud,
opening up its secrets. Night is here.
And we eat the moon together,
like an opened watermelon, you and I.

Beside the Fire

1.
Night fans a fire in the forest.
Terror turns the little saplings grey.
Among the plants and crackling branches
shadows fall, where axes flash.
And the Kirghiz – children, women, men –
are mirrored in their sharp and gleaming edge.
Branches crack like cockerels crowing,
and like pearls from a snapped string
dew falls on rising sparks,
dew falls on praying hands.
A bird, from deepest night
soars upwards, and his fiddle burns.

ב

איצט דערלאַנגט אַ פֿלאַטער פֿול מיט גבֿורה
לעבן פֿלאַם אַ בראָנדזענע געשטאַלט.
און אין טאַנץ מיט זילבערנער באַנדורע –
אַ געדריי צוזאַמען מיטן וואַלד.
אַ געדריי. אַ פֿויק. אַ הייסער ניגון.
ביז אין פֿונקען־ריטעם פֿון קאָנצערט –
נעמט די געגנט גלאָקיק זיך צעוויגן,
פֿאַלן לעצטע שטערן אין די בערד.
נעמען שיכּור צוטאַנצן קירגיזן
אין אַ קייט בײַם פֿלאַקערדיקן טיש.
און מיט כוואַליעס, לויפֿנדיקע שפֿיזן,
קיצלט האָריזאָנטן דער אירטיש.

צפֿון־שטערן

צפֿון־שטערן, שפֿאַנסט מיט מיר אין איינעם,
כ׳בין דײַן שנײַמענטש אין אַ קלייד פֿון הויט.
פֿאָר מײַן קעלט צעלויפֿן זיך די שכנים,
בלויז בעריאַזעס בלײַבן לעבן פֿלויט.
צפֿון־שטערן, ביזן טויט געטרײַיער,
וויפֿל מילדקייט וועקסטו און דערמאָנסט!
אַלע זומער שנײַט אויף מיר אַ פֿײַער,
אַלע ווינטער גלינסטו מיר און גלאָנסט.
זאָל די ניט־פֿאַרגאַנגענע דערמאָנונג,
צו דײַן בלאָען שמייכל זײַן געווענדט.
זאָלן אָט די קלאַנגען, זאָל די מאָנונג,
בלײַבן איבער מיר אַ מאָנומענט.

1936

2.

Now, with powerful sinuous movements,
a great bronze figure leaps beside the flames.
A silver lute accompanies his dance –
a dance that whirls together with the forest.
Whirling. Drumbeat. Fiery melody.
To the rhythm of the leaping sparks
the landscape, bell-like, swings and sways.
The last stars fall into their beards, and now
intoxicated, the Kirghiz start to dance,
forming a chain around the flickering table.
And with waves like rippling spears,
the playful Irtysh tickles the horizon.

North Star

North Star, you and I stride along together,
I am your snowman in a cloak of skin.
From my coldness all the neighbors flee,
only the birch trees stay beside the fence.
North Star, faithful unto death,
how many tender memories you revive!
Each summer – fire snows down upon me,
each winter you resound like pealing bells.
May my memory, unextinguished,
always turn its face to your blue smile.
May these sounds, this summons,
remain above me as a monument.

1936

בלאָנדער באַגינען

עס הענגט איבערן טאָל דער מאָרגן־שטערן
ווי אַ גילדן גלעקעלע און – וואַכט.
איבער ווייַסע פֿינגערדיקע צווייַגן
פֿון בעריאָזקעס גייענדיקע ברענט
אין ווייַנענדיקע פֿײַערן די נאַכט.

קוק זיך אײַן אין דעם געבורט פֿון וועלטן!

גראָזן פֿלאַפּלען. וואָרצלען לאָבן. הימלען העלן.
בײַמער זענען שטומע וויאָלאָנטשעלן.
און די טויזנט שטילקייטן באַזונדער
רײַדן אויף דער בלאָנדער שפּראַך
פֿון זאַנגען.
די זאַנגען זענען נאָך מיט ערד פֿאַרדעקט,
נאָר עס שמעקט
פֿון זיי מיט בלאָנדן יום־טובֿ.
שטיל. די טויען קושן זיך. עס פּאַטשן
זילבערדיקע פֿליגל. בלעטער ווייַנען.
אַ פֿאַסטערך זינגט אַ פֿויגלשע מעלאָדיע
דורכן טאָל
און זײַן ליד האָט אָט אַלע זיבן חנען.

איך הייב זיך אויף פֿון שטעבלקלע־געלעגער
און שפּרייַז אַוועק אַ באָרוועסער אויף דעמערדיקע שטעגן.
גראָזן טראָכטן וועגן מיר –
איך פֿלאַטער זיי אַנטקעגן.
שטילקייטן צערײַדן זיך אַלץ העכער.
אַ ווינטל הענגט זיך אויף מײַן האָלדז
און וויל מײַן בענקשאָפֿט רויבן...

מיט מאָרגנטריט אַ וואָנדערער קומט אָן.
איך גיב אים אָפּ מײַן לעצטן שטיקל ברויט
און פֿון זײַן וואָנדער־טאָרבע נעם איך – גלויבן.

דער טאָל ווערט אויפֿגעהילכט,
ס׳איז הױלער קלאַנג.
דער מאָרגן־שטערן וואַכט.
די פֿאַרבן רינען.

Blond Dawn

Over the valley hangs the morning star
like a little golden bell and – watches.
Over the white finger-like branches
of moving birch trees, burns
in weeping fires, the night.

Look and see the birth of worlds!

Grasses chatter. Roots are laughing. Skies are brightening.
Trees are mute violoncellos.
And each of the thousand silences
speaks the blond language
of the ears of corn.
The ears of corn are covered still with earth,
but you can smell
their blond, festive joy.
    Silence. Dews are kissing. Silver wings
    are beating. Leaves are weeping.
A shepherd sings the melody of a bird
all through the valley
and his song has all the seven charms.

I get up from my thorny pillow
and stride out barefoot on the dawning paths.
Grasses are thinking of me –
I fly towards them.
Silences converse more loudly still.
A little breeze drapes itself around my neck
and tries to steal my yearning…

With morning steps a wanderer appears.
I give him my last piece of bread
and from his knapsack I take – faith.

    The valley now resounds
    with a pure sound.
    The morning star is watchful.
    The colors flow.

איך וואָש אַראָפּ אין סאַזשלקע
פֿון זיך די בלאָע נאַכט
און גרייט זיך צו דעם יום־טובֿ
פֿון באַגינען.

אין טאָרבע פֿונעם ווינט

אַ באָרוועסער וואַנדראָווניק אויף אַ שטיין
אין אָוונטגאָלד
וואַרפֿט פֿון זיך אַראָפּ דעם שטויב פֿון וועלט.
פֿון וואַלד אַרויס
דערלאַנגט אַ פֿלי אַ פֿויגל
און טוט אַ כאַפּ דאָס לעצטע שטיקל זון.

אַ ווערבע פֿאַזע טײַך טײַך איז אויך פֿאַראַן.

אַ וועג.
אַ פֿעלד.
אַ צאַפּלדיקע לאָנקע.
געהיימע טריט
פֿון הונגעריקע וואָלקנס.
ווו זענען די הענט, וואָס שאַפֿן וווּנדער?

אַ לעבעדיקע פֿידל איז אויך פֿאַראַן.

איז וואָס זשע בלײַבט צו טאָן אין אָט דער שעה,
אָ, וועלט מײַנע אין טויזנט פֿאַרבן?
סײַדן
צונויפֿקלײַבן אין טאָרבע פֿונעם ווינט
די רויטע שיינקייט
און ברענגען זי אַהיים אויף אָוונטברויט.

אַן עלנט ווי אַ באָרג איז אויך פֿאַראַן.

1935

In a pond I wash off
the blue night.
And prepare for the festival
of dawn.

In the Knapsack of the Wind

A barefoot wanderer upon a stone
in the gold of evening
casts off the dust of the world.
Out of the wood
a bird soars into flight
and snatches the last particle of sunlight.

And there's a willow by the stream.

A path.
A field.
A quivering meadow.
Secret footsteps
of hungry clouds.
Where are the hands that can create such miracles?

And there's a living fiddle.

So what is left to do at this very hour,
o, my world of a thousand colors?
Except
to gather in the knapsack of the wind
all the red beauty
and take it home for supper.

And there's a loneliness, as heavy as a mountain.

1935

גֵעשרײַ

מיט דער נאַקעטער ברוסט צו דער ערד,
מיטן פּנים אין גראָזן פֿאַרגראַבן, –
אַזױ ליג איך און שרײַ, ביז עס װערט
מײַן ברײטבֿרוסטיקער שרײַען דערהערט
פֿון בעריאָזעס, פֿון שטערן און ראָבן:

פֿאַרװאַנדל מיך אין לופֿט,
פֿאַרװאַנדל מיך אין רױם
און װילסטו – אין אַ פֿױגל
אױף דײַן שענסטן בױם.

איבער מיר טוט אַ פֿלײץ דער באַגין
מיט אַ האַרדע גרצונדענע שטראָמען.
מײַן גֵעשרײַ, װי אַ בליץ אַזױ דין,
פֿאַלט אַראָפּ אױפֿן פֿעלדישן גרין,
װוּ עס יאָגט אַ גֵעשטאַלט אָן אַ נאָמען:

באַפֿרײַ מיך פֿון מײַן גוף,
װאָס איז צעבראָכן, מיד,
און איך װעל דיך באַגלײטן
מיט מײַן שענסטן ליד.

די גֵעשטאַלט װערט אַ רעגן פֿון פֿרײד,
נעמט מיר צוזאַמען די ערדענע גלידער
און אַנטהילט פֿון איר װינטיקן קלײד,
און מיט װאַרעמע װאָלדיקע רײד,
לײגט זי העל בײַ מײַן זײַט זיך אַנידער:

פֿון שרײַיִקן גֵעבעט
זאָל װערן אַ גֵעבאָט – – –

אָבער װען איך דערזע, איך דערשפּיר
די פֿאַרװאָרונג פֿון מײַנע גֵעבעטן,
זײַער װאַרעמען פֿינגער־באַריר
אין מײַן גײַסט, אין מײַן לעבן, אין מ י ר, –
װאַרף איך װידער גֵעשרײַען־ראַקעטן:

Scream

With my naked breast pressed to the earth,
with my face buried deep in the grass, –
here I lie and I scream, till at last
my mighty screaming is heard
by the birches, the ravens, the stars:

> "Change me into air,
> change me into space,
> or if you will – into a bird
> on your loveliest tree."

Above me surges the dawn
with streams of burning light.
My scream, as thin as a lightning flash
falls on the green of the fields,
where a nameless figure roams:

> "Free me from my body
> that's broken, tired and worn,
> and I will delight you
> with my loveliest song."

The figure turns into a joyful rain,
that soaks my earthen limbs,
then, freed of her airy clothes,
murmuring warm forest-words,
and shining, she lies down beside me:

> "Your screaming demand
> shall become my command – – –"

But when I see, when I feel
the fulfilment of my prayers,
the warm touch of their fingers
on my spirit, my life, and my *self*, –
then once more I hurl my screams:

באַשאַף מיר אויף דאָס נײַ
מיט אויגן, האַרץ און צײַן,
פֿאַרוואַנדל מיך צוריק
פֿון אַ ל ץ אין מיר אַליין.

1937

*

אַלץ איז ווערדיק פֿאַר מײַן אויגס געוואָגל,
אַלץ איז חשוב, טײַער פֿאַר מײַן סטראַף:
גראָזן, ביימער, ערד, אַ קוואַל, אַ לאָגל
און די ווײַטע פֿאַרביקייט פֿון שלאָף.
און אין אַלץ באַגעגן איך אַ שפּליטער
פֿון אין־סוף.

כ׳זע מײַן לײַב אין ווײַס פֿון דער בעריאָזע,
כ׳פֿיל מײַן בלוט אין בלויונג פֿון אַ רויז,
און אויס דער נאַטורס מעטאַמאָרפֿאָזע
וועב איך פֿון דערקענטעניש אַ הויז.
און אין אַלץ אַנטפּלעקט זיך מײַן געביטער
טיף און גרויס.

פּראָסטע שטויבן רײדן פֿון פֿאַרגיבשאַפֿט,
שטילער טוי – פֿון לײַכטנדיקן גנאָד.
עפֿל זאָגן אָן פֿון קלוגער ליבשאַפֿט
צו דעם ווײַסן, אָפּגעשיידטן סאָד.
און ס׳איז יעדע רגע אָן אַ הימען –
מיר אַ שאָד.

אַלץ, וואָס ווערט פֿון מיר דערפֿילט, איז מײַניק.
ווו נאָר ס׳גרייכט מײַן וואָרט, בין איך פֿאַראַן.
ווי אַ קוואַל אין מידבר שלאָגט דער תענוג
און ער לאָקט מײַן לעבנס קאַראַוואַן.
און אין אַלץ, אין אַלץ איז דאָ דער סימן
פֿון מײַן שפּאָן.

"Create me now anew
with eyes and heart and teeth,
transform me once again
from *all* into my self."

1937

*

Everything is worthy of my roaming eye,
everything is good and precious for my verse:
grass, trees, earth, a drinking vessel and a spring,
and the distant colors of kind sleep.
There is a splinter of infinity
In everything I meet.

I see my body in the whiteness of the birch,
feel my blood throb in the blossoming rose,
and from nature's transformations,
my understanding weaves a dwelling place.
    And in everything my Master is revealed –
deep and great.

Simple specks of dust speak of forgiveness,
quiet dew – of shining grace.
Apples tell of their wise love
for the white orchard, out of sight.
    To me each moment where no hymn rings out
 brings no delight.

Everything I feel belongs to me entirely.
Wherever my word reaches, there I stand.
My pleasure gushes like a desert spring,
drawing with it my life's thread.
    And in everything I see the imprint
 of my tread.

לאַנדשאַפֿט

דער הימל – ווי דער חלום פֿון אַ דולן,
ניטאַ אין אים די זון. זי בליט און קוועלט
מגולגל אין אַ הייסן, פֿולן
און ווילדן רויזנביימל אויפֿן פֿעלד.
דער ווינט איז אַ מכשף. ער פֿאַרקנעפֿלט
דעם טאָג מיט נאַכט.
אַ וואָרצל צו אַ וואָרצל עפּעס פּרעפּלט.
אַ וואָלקן לאַכט
פֿון שלאָף. עס ווינקט פֿון וואַלד אַ בליציק אייגל.
ווי פֿאַלנדיקע שטערן פֿליִען פֿייגל.

אַ צווייִגל קאַרשן

כ'האָב געבראַכט פֿאַר דיר אַ צווייִגל קאַרשן,
צייטיק, צאַפֿלדיק, ווי מייַן געדאַכט.
הער, ווי ס'אָטעמט נאָך. פֿאַרנעם און ירשן
זייַנע ליניעס, פֿאַרבן, צייכנס, – ביזקל
זייער גלי פֿאַראַשיקט ניט די נאַכט.

קוק עס אָן! אין יעדער קאַרש באַזונדער
עקבער־אינין דעם נייַגעריקן בליק,
און דערפֿיל, ס'גייט אויף אַ קליינע זון דיר
פֿון דער זאַפֿט וואָס קרייַזט אין אַ געריזל,
אונטער הייַטל, פֿול מיט פּייַן און גליק, –

פּייַן פֿון אויפֿשפּראָץ, בליִעכץ און באַבלעטער,
וואָרצלדיקער שטראָם דורך טעג און נעכט;
פֿרייד פֿון זון אין פֿרילינגדיקן וועטער
און דאָס גליק בייַם זען אַ פֿרי העַנגען,
אין געבליץ און שטורעמדיק געפֿעכט.

ס'איז פֿאַראַן אין דעם אי מוט, אי גלויבן,
זון־פֿאַרליבטקייט, אימפּעט און געיאָג,
גבֿורהשאַפֿט אַרויסצוטאָנצן אויבן,
פֿון די טיפֿעענישן, און זיך ברענגען
צו דער לופֿט, צום רעגן און צום טאָג.

Landscape

The sky is like a madman's dream, without a sun.
Instead, the sun is blossoming and swelling,
transformed into a hot
wild rosebush in the field.
The wind's a sorcerer. He buttons
    day and night together.
A root is muttering something to another root.
    A cloud is laughing in its sleep.
    In the wood a bright eye beckons from afar.
    Birds fly like falling stars.

A Bunch of Cherries

I have brought for you a bunch of cherries,
ripe and trembling like my thoughts.
Hear – it's still breathing. O, perceive, inherit
    its lines and signs and colors, –
till their glow turns the night to ash.

Gaze at it! and let your curious eye
pierce into the cherries, one by one,
and feel a small sun rising up inside you
    from the juice that's trickling and pulsing,
full of pain and joy, under the fragile skin, –

The pain of growing, blossoming and greening
streams from the roots through days and nights together;
the joy of sunshine in the warm spring weather,
    the happiness of seeing a fruit hang safely,
despite the lightning of a clashing storm.

In such a thing there is both faith and courage,
sun adoration, eagerness and haste,
the mighty power to rise up
    from the depths and dance out merrily
to greet the air, the gentle rain, the day.

קוק עס אָן – און פֿיל, ווי זויבער, זוניק
ס׳בייגט זיך דאָס פֿאַרווייינטע צווייגל. שפּיר
זײַן געצייטער – דין, באַהאַרצט און סטרוניק,
ווייך און שטיל ווי אָטעם אויסגעברענטער, –
און זײַן גלוסט אַרײַנצוגיין אין דיר.

איצטער איז שוין דײַנ ס דאָס צווייגל קאַרשן:
האָסט דערקענט דעם ווונדער פֿון זײַן שטאַם.
האָסט דערקענט – אַצינד זײַן שיינקייט ירשן!
בייג צו אים די צײַנער דײַנע נענטער
און פֿאַרזוך פֿון אייביקייט דעם טעם!

מוראַשקע־נעסט

מוראַשקע־נעסט, דו וואַלדס אונטערבאַוווסטזײַן,
צעגישטערט פֿון אַ נײַגעריקן שטאָק, –
מיט לאַבירינטן דײַנע, שטאָק נאָך שטאָק
צעפֿאַלענע אין שטויב, זאָל דיר באַוווסט זײַן:
ווי דו בין איך. מײַן שאַרבן פֿאַלט. אָט ווערט ער
צעטראָגן פֿון מוראַשקעלעך – פֿון ווערטער.

און יעדער וואָרט וואַרט – אַרויף, אַראָפּ, אַריבער,
פֿון נערוו צו נערוו, דורך רוקן און קוויל.
און אַלע יאָגן פֿון די שטיבער
מיט ווייַסן אייעלע אין מויל.

י. ל. פּרץ

גלייך אַ קוואַל וואָס שלייפֿט זיך אָן דעם חושך אונטערערדיק,
יעדער מאָל אַלץ קלערער קלינגט אַרויף צו אונדז דײַן קול.
האָסט פֿאַרוואַנדלט אין אַ באַרג אַ יאַמערדיקן טאָל,
און אַהין גערוף אַ רוף געטאָן דאָס פֿאָלק דערפֿרייט און ווערדיק.

Gaze at it – and feel how pure and sunshine-bright
the bunch of cherries bends, weeping with joy.
Sense its trembling – thin, bold, violin-string-taut,
    soft and still like a spent breath, –
and its desire to enter into you.

Now it's entirely *yours*, the bunch of cherries.
You've recognized the wonder of its being.
This you have recognized – inherit now its beauty!
    Bend your mouth towards it, nearer, nearer,
and try the taste that is eternity!

Anthill

Anthill, subconscious of the forest,
demolished by a curious, poking stick, –
those labyrinths of yours, floor upon floor
crumbled to dust. This you should know:
I am like you. My skull disintegrates. And see: its shards
are borne away by little ants – by words.

And every word – going up and down, criss crossing
from nerve to nerve, past bullets and through smoky fog.
Each one rushes from its home,
in its mouth a tiny pure white egg.

1940

I. L. Peretz

Like a subterranean spring that hones itself on darkness,
your voice rings up to us more clearly every day.
You changed a vale of tears into a mountain,
and called the people to it, dignified and glad.

נאָר דאָס פֿאָלק איז מיד געווען פֿון דורותדיקן קלעטער.
וויפֿל מאָל איז עס געבליבן שטעקן אין דער מיט!
האָסטו פֿון פֿאַרגאַנגענקייט אַ ליכט אַזאַ געשמידט
וואָס פֿאַרקניפֿט זי ווי אַ רעגן־בויגן מיטן שפעטער.

און פֿון קונצן־מאַכערס, פֿון משוגענע בטלנים
האָסטו אויסגעשטאַלטיקט אונדזער לעבן, אונדזער מיין,
ווי דער סקולפּטאָר, וואָס פֿון ווילדן גליווערדיקן שטיין
קנעט ער אויס אַן אויסגעטרוימטן גלייבנדיקן פנים.

אונדזער ביסטו. פֿייגל צירלען דיין געזאַנג אויף דעכער.
קינדער מאַכן לעבעדיק דיין וואָרט מיט זייער הויך.
און בשעת מיר פֿרעגן: וועלן מיר דערגיין דיין הייך?
ענטפֿערט אונדז אַ יום־טובֿדיקע שטים: אויב ניט נאָך העכער!

1941

But the people, tired from struggling through the generations,
kept stumbling while climbing up to reach you!
From the chains of their past you forged a light
that joins it to the future like a rainbow.

From pranksters and from crazy dreamers
you fashioned us: our life and meaning,
like the sculptor, who from raw hard stone
kneads out a trusting face that he has dreamed.

You are ours. Birds trill out your song on roofs.
The breath of children brings your word to life.
And even as we ask: will we ever reach your heights?
A joyful voice gives answer: If not higher!

1941

"In khuter" (In the hut), from the Vilna ghetto manuscript of *Siberia*, with an alteration to the first line in Sutzkever's handwriting, NLI, ARC 4°1565, 2:349

1941 – 1944

איך ליג אין אַן אָרון

איך ליג אין אַן אָרון,
ווי אין הילצערנע קליידער,
איך ליג.
זאָל זײַן, ס׳איז אַ שיפֿל
אויף שטורמישע כוואַליעס,
זאָל זײַן, ס׳איז אַ וויג.

און דאָ,
וווּ עס האָבן זיך גופֿן
געשיידט מיט דער צײַט,
רוף איך דיך, שוועסטער,
און דו הערסט מײַן רופֿן
אין ווײַט.

וואָס טוט זיך אין אָרון אַ צאַפּל
אַ לײַב אומגעריכט?
דו קומסט.
איך דערקען דײַן שוואַרצאַפּל,
דײַן אָטעם,
דײַן ליכט.

אזוי איז אַ פּנים דער סדר:
הײַנט דאָ,
מאָרגן דאָרט,
און איצט אין אַן אָרון,
ווי אין הילצערנע קליידער,
זינגט אַלץ נאָך מײַן וואָרט.

ווילנע
30סטן אויגוסט
1941

I Lie in a Coffin

I lie in a coffin
as in clothes made of wood,
here I lie.
Let it be a boat
on wild stormy waves,
let it be a cradle.

And here,
where bodies have
parted with time,
I call you, sister,
and you hear my voice
from afar.

Suddenly, here in the coffin,
a body is moving. How can it be?
You approach.
And I know you: your eyes
and your breath
and your light.

This, it seems, is the order of things:
here today,
there tomorrow,
and now, in a coffin,
as in clothes made of wood,
still my word sings.

Vilna
August 30
1941

גלוסט זיך מיר צו טאָן אַ תּפֿילה

גלוסט זיך מיר צו טאָן אַ תּפֿילה – ווייס איך ניט צו וועמען,
דער, וואָס האָט אַ מאָל געהערט מיך, וועט זי ניט פֿאַרנעמען,
ווייס איך ניט צו וועמען –
האַלט זי מיך אין קלעמען.

אפֿשר זאָל איך בעטן ביי אַ שטערן: „פֿריינד מיין ווייטער,
כ׳האָב מיין וואָרט פֿאַרלוירן, קום און זיי אים אַ פֿאַרבייטער!"
אויך דער גוטער שטערן
וועט עס ניט דערהערן.

נאָר אַ תּפֿילה זאָגן מ ו ז איך, עמעץ גאָר אַ נאָנטער
פֿייניקט זיך אין מיין נשמה און די תּפֿילה מאָנט ער, –
וועל איך אָן אַ זינען
פלאַפּלען ביז באַגינען.

ווילנער געטאָ
17טן יאַנואַר
1942

צום קינד

צי פֿון הונגער,
צי פֿון גרויסער ליבשאַפֿט, –
נאָר אַן עדות איז דערביי דיין מאַמע:
איך האָב געוואָלט דיך איינשלינגען, מיין קינד,
ביים פֿילן ווי דיין גופֿל קילט זיך אָפּ
אין מיינע פֿינגער,
גלייך איך וואָלט אין זיי געדריקט
אַ וואַרעמע גלאָז טיי,
פֿילנדיק דעם איבערגאַנג צו קאַלטקייט.

ווייל דו ביסט ניט קיין פֿרעמדער, ניט קיין גאַסט,
אויף אונדזער ערד געבוירט מען ניט קיין צווייטן, –
זיך אַליין געבוירט מען ווי אַ רינג,
און די רינגען שליסן זיך אין קייטן.

I Long to Say a Prayer

I long to say a prayer – to whom, I do not know.
He who used to comfort me will not hear it now,
   and so I do not know –
    it fills my heart with woe.

Perhaps I'll pray to a star: "Hear, my distant friend,
I have lost my word; oh, come and take its place!"
   But even the good star
    will not hear my prayer.

But I must say a prayer. In my soul some being,
my closest friend, in torment, demands that I should pray, –
   so I'll babble senselessly
    until the break of day.

Vilna ghetto
January 17
1942

To My Child

Whether from hunger,
or my great love for you
– only your mother can bear witness to it –
I wanted to devour you, my child,
when I felt your little body cooling down
between my fingers,
as if I'd clasped them
round a glass of warm tea
and felt its slow transition into coldness.

For you are not a stranger, not a guest.
On our earth one gives birth not to another
but to oneself – that self is like a ring,
the rings linking together to form chains.

קינד מײַנס,

וואָס אין ווערטער הייסטו: ליבשאַפֿט,

און ניט אין ווערטער ביסטו עס אַליין,

דו – דער קערן פֿון מײַן יעדער חלום,

פֿאַרהוילענער דריטער,

וואָס פֿון די וועלטישע ווינקלען

האַסטו מיטן ווּנדער פֿון אַן אומגעזעענעם שטורעם

צונויפֿגעבראַכט, צונויפֿגעגאָסן צוזוויען

צו באַשאַפֿן דיך און צו דערפֿרייען: –

פֿאַר וואָס האַסטו פֿאַרטונקלט דעם באַשאַף,

מיט דעם וואָס דו האַסט צוגעמאַכט די אויגן

און געלאָזט מיך בעטלערדיק אין דרויסן

צוזאַמען מיט אַ וועלט אַן אויסגעשנייטער,

וואָס דו האַסט אָפּגעוואָרפֿן אויף צוריק?

דיך האָט ניט דערפֿרייט קיין וועג,

וואָס יעדער איר באַוועגונג

באַהאַלט אין זיך דעם ריטעם פֿון די שטערן.

עס מעג די זון צעברעקלען זיך ווי גלאָז –

ווײַל קיין מאָל האַסטו ניט געזען איר שײַן.

אַ טראָפּן סם האָט אויסגעברענט דײַן גלויבן,

דו האָסט געמיינט:

ס׳איז וואַרעם-זיסע מילך.

– – – – – – – – – – – – –

איך האָב געוואָלט דיך אײַנשלינגען, מײַן קינד.

כדי צו פֿילן דעם געשמאַק

פֿון מײַן געהאָפֿטער צוקונפֿט.

אפֿשר וועסטו בליִען ווי אַ מאָל

אין מײַן געבליט.

נאָר איך בין ניט ווערט צו זײַן דײַן קבֿר.

וועל איך דיך אַוועקשענקען

דעם רופֿנדיקן שניי,

דעם שניי – מײַן ערשטן יום-טובֿ,

און וועסט זינקען

ווי אַ שפּליטער זונפֿאַרגאַנג

My child,
in words your name is love.
But not in words alone:
you are the kernel of my every dream,
that third person concealed.
From the corners of the world,
through the miracle of an unseen storm,
you brought together, fused two human beings
to create you and rejoice.

Why have you darkened all Creation
by closing your eyes
and leaving me outside, a beggar,
together with a snowed-up world,
which you have cast behind you?

No cradle has delighted you,
its every rocking movement
concealing in itself the rhythm of the stars.
Let the sun smash itself like glass
since you have never seen its light.
A drop of poison has burnt out your trust.
You thought:
it's warm sweet milk.
– – – – – – – – – – – – – –
I wanted to devour you, my child,
to experience the taste
of my hoped-for future.
It might be you would blossom in my blood
as once you did.

I am not worthy, though, to be your tomb,
so I will part with you
and give you to the calling snow,
to the snow – my first delight –
and you will sink
like a splinter of the sunset

אין זײַנע שטילע טיפֿן
און אָפּגעבן אַ גרוס פֿון מיר
די אײַנגעפֿרירטע גרעזלעך – – –

ווילנער געטאָ
18טן יאַנואַר
1943

ווי אַזוי?

ווי אַזוי און מיט וואָס וועסטו פֿילן
דײַן בעכער אין טאָג פֿון באַפֿרײַונג?
ביסטו גרייט אין דײַן פֿרייד צו דערפֿילן
דײַן פֿאַרגאַנגענקייטס פֿינצטערע שרײַונג
ווו עס גליווערן שאַרבנס פֿון טעג
אין אַ תהום אָן אַ גרונט, אָן אַ דעק?

דו וועסט זוכן אַ שליסל צו פֿאַסן
פֿאַר דײַנע פֿאַרהאַקטע שלעסער.
ווי ברויט וועסטו בײַסן די גאַסן
און טראַכטן: דער פֿריִער איז בעסער.
און די צײַט וועט דיך עקבערן שטיל
ווי אין פֿויסט אַ געפֿאַנגענע גריל.

און ס׳וועט זײַן דײַן זכרון געגליכן
צו אַן אַלטער פֿאַרשאָטענער שטאָט.
און דײַן דרויסיקער בליק וועט דאָרט קריכן
ווי אַ קראָט, ווי אַ קראָט – –

ווילנער געטאָ
14טן פֿעברואַר
1943

into its still depths
and greet for me
the frozen blades of grass…

Vilna ghetto
January 18
1943

How?

How and with what will you fill
your cup on the day of deliverance?
Are you ready to feel in your joy
the dark screams of your past,
where the skulls of the days petrify
in a bottomless, limitless pit?

You will search for a key which would fit
the jammed locks of your doors.
For bread you will gnaw on the streets
and will think: the past times were better.
And time will drill silently through you
like a cricket trapped in a fist.

And your memory will come to resemble
an ancient buried city.
And your gaze will creep all around there,
like a mole, like a mole – –

Vilna ghetto
February 14
1943

קערנדלעך ווייץ

הייליק, דערלאַנגט זיך אַן עפֿן,
צעשפּאַלט זיך פֿון אונטער מײַן האַק!
אײדער די קױל וועט מיך טרעפֿן –
איך ברענג אײַך מתּנות אַ זאַק.

אַלטינקע, תּכלתּנע דפֿן
מיט פּורפּור אױף זילבערנע האָר,
ווערטער אױף פּאַרמעט, געשאַפֿן
דורך טױזנטער גרױזיקע יאָר.

ווי בײַם באַשיצן אַן עופֿל –
איך לױף מיטן ייִדישן וואָרט,
נישטער אין איטלעכן הײפֿל,
דער גײַסט זאָל ניט ווערן דערמאָרדט.

שטערק אינעם שײַטער די אָרעמס
און פֿרײַ זיך: דער עיקר איז דאָ!
מײַנס איז נאָך אַמסטערדאַם, וואָרעמס,
ליװאָרנע, מאַדריד און יזוואָ.

אָ, ווי מיך פֿײַניקט אַ שײַמע
פֿאַרטראָגן אין רױכיקן ווינט!
ס׳וואָרגן מיך לידער געהײמע:
– באַהאַלט אונדז אין דײַן לאַבירינט!

גראָב איך און פֿלאַנץ מאַנוסקריפּטן,
און גיט מיר דער ייִאוש אַ פֿלײץ,
קומט מיר אין זינען: עגיפּטן,
אַ מעשׂה מיט קערנדלעך ווייץ.

דעמאָלט די שטערן דערצײיל איך:
אַ מאָל האָט בײַם ים נילוס געבױט
זײַן פּיראַמידע אַ מלך,
צו קיניקן דאָרט נאָכן טױט.

Grains of Wheat

Caves, open up quickly,
split apart under my axe!
Before I am killed by a bullet –
I bring you gifts in a sack.

Ancient azure pages
purple on silvery hair,
words on parchment, created
over thousands of years of despair.

As if protecting a baby – ,
I run with the Yiddish word,
digging in every courtyard,
that the soul may not be destroyed.

I stretch my hands into the bonfire
and rejoice, for the essence is saved!
I still possess Amsterdam, Worms,
Livorno, Madrid and YIVO.

How I grieve to see one sacred page
carried off by the smoky wind!
Secret poems choke me; they whisper:
"O, hide us in your labyrinth!"

I dig and plant manuscripts deep,
and my heart is flooded with grief;
then I suddenly think of Egypt,
and a story of grains of wheat.

Once a king built a pyramid high
– to the stars I tell the story –
by the banks of the River Nile,
after death to reign there in glory.

זאָל מען אין גילדענעם אָרון

אָנשיטן, האָט ער באַפֿעלט,

קערנדלעך וייץ – לזכּרון

פֿון אונדזער, דער ערדישער וועלט.

ניַין טויזנט יאָר האָבן זונען

געביטן אין מידבר דעם גאַנג,

ביז מ׳האָט די קערנער געפֿונען

אין דער פּיראַמידע ניט לאַנג.

ניַין טויזנט יאָר שוין פֿאַרגאַנגען!

נאָר ווען מ׳האָט די קערנער פֿאַרזייט, –

האָבן אין זוניקע זאַנגען

צעבליט זיך אַ בייט נאָך אַ בייט.

– – – – – – – – – – – – – –

אפֿשר אויך וועלן די ווערטער

דערוואַרטן זיך ווען אויף דעם ליכט –

וועלן אין שעה אין באַשערטער

צעבליִען זיך אויך אומגעריכט?

און ווי דער אוראַלטער קערן

וואָס האָט זיך פֿאַרוואַנדלט אין זאַנג, –

וועלן די ווערטער אויך נערן,

וועלן די ווערטער געהערן

דעם פֿאָלק, אין זיַין אייביקן גאַנג.

ווילנער געטאָ

מאַרץ

1943

"Pour into my golden coffin,"
– thus his command was heard –
"grains of wheat, for a memory
of this, our earthly world."

For nine thousand years the suns
in the desert would come and go,
till the grains of wheat were discovered
in the pyramid, not long ago.

Nine thousand years had passed,
but when the grains were sown, –
sunny ears of wheat
blossomed, row upon row.
– – – – – – – – – – – – – – – –
Perhaps these words will also
live to see the light –
and in the destined hour,
will blossom again, shining bright?

And like the ancient grain
transformed into wheat once more,
these words will also nourish
these words will also belong
to the people, for evermore.

Vilna ghetto
March
1943

יעדער שעה, יעדער טאָג

יעדער שעה, יעדער טאָג, –
איז מער ניט קיין שעה,
איז מער ניט קיין טאָג,
ס׳איז א גרייטער מזבח ביי דיר אין געביין,
וווּ פֿאַרשלונגען ווערט אַלץ, וואָס דו פֿילסט, וואָס דו זעסט,
און דו זינגסט נאָך דערביי, ווען דו פֿרעסט
זיך אַליין.

ווילנער געטאָ
27סטן אפּריל
1943

פֿאַרברענטע פּערל

ניט דערפֿאַר וווייַל מייַנע ווערטער וואַרפֿן זיך
גלייַך ווי הענט צעבראָכענע נאָך רעטונג,
ניט דערפֿאַר, וווייַל צייַנערדיק זיי שאַרפֿן זיך
צו א לייַב אין פֿינצטערניש, – נאָך זעטונג, –
בלאָזסטו אויף די קוויל פֿון מייַן גרימצאָרן,
דו געשריבן וואָרט, – מייַן וועלטס פֿאַרבייַטער;
נאָר דערפֿאַר, וווייַל דייַנע קלאַנגען גלימצערן
ווי פֿאַרברענטע פּערל
נאָך אַן אויסגעצאַנקטן שייַטער,
און קיינער – אויך ניט איך – דורך טעג צעריבענער,
דערקענט שוין ניט די פֿרוי אין פֿלאַם געוואַשן,
וואָס פֿון אַלע פֿריידן איז געבליבן איר
גראָ-פֿאַרברענטע פּערל אין די אַשן – –

ווילנער געטאָ
28סטן יולי
1943

Every Hour, Every Day

Every hour, every day, –
is no longer an hour,
is no longer a day,
it's a sacrificial altar prepared in your bones,
where all that you feel, that you see, is consumed,
yet still you sing, as you devour
yourself.

Vilna ghetto
April 27
1943

Burnt Pearls

It's not because my words are trembling
like broken hands, yearning for rescue;
it's not because, like teeth, they hone themselves
on flesh in darkness, – craving satisfaction, –
that you fan up the flames of my great rage,
you written word – my alternative world;
but it's because your sounds are glimmering
like burnt pearls
in a pyre that has died down,
and none – not even I – crushed by the days
can recognize the woman washed in flames,
whose only remnant now of all her joys
are grey burnt pearls in the ashes – –

Vilna ghetto
July 28
1943

די בלייענע פּלאַטן פֿון ראָמס דרוקעריי

מיר האָבן װי פֿינגער געשטרעקטע דורך גראַטן
צו פֿאַנגען די ליכטיקע לופֿט פֿון דער פֿרײַ –
דורך נאַכט זיך געצױגן, צו נעמען די פּלאַטן,
די בלייענע פּלאַטן פֿון ראָמס דרוקעריי.
מיר, טרױמער, באַדאַרפֿן איצט װערן סאָלדאַטן
און שמעלצן אױף קױלן דעם גײַסט פֿונעם בלײַ.

און מיר האָבן װידער געעפֿנט דעם שטעמפּל
צו עפּעס אַ היימישער אײביקער הײל.
מיט שאָטנס באַפֿאַנצערט, בײַ שײַן פֿון אַ לעמפּל –
געגאָסן די אותיות – אַ צײל נאָך אַ צײל,
אַזױ װי די זײדעס אַ מאָל אינעם טעמפּל
אין גילדענע יום־טובֿ־מנורות – דעם אײל.

דאָס בלײַ האָט געלױכטן בײַם אױסגיסן קױלן,
מחשבֿות – צעגאַנגען אַן אות נאָך אַן אות.
אַ שורה פֿון בבֿל, אַ שורה פֿון פּױלן,
געזאָטן, געפֿלײצט אין דער זעלביקער מאָס.
די ייִדישע גבֿורה, אין װערטער פֿאַרהױלן,
מוז אױפֿרײַסן איצטער די װעלט מיט אַ שאָס!

און װער ס׳האָט אין געטאָ געזען דאָס כּלי־זײן
פֿאַרקלאַמערט אין העלדישע ייִדישע הענט –
געזען האָט ער ראַנגלען זיך ירושלים,
דאָס פֿאַלן פֿון יענע גראַניטענע װענט;
פֿאַרנומען די װערטער, פֿאַרשמאָלצן אין בלײַען,
און זײַערע שטימען אין האַרצן דערקענט.

ווילנער געטאָ
12טן סעפּטעמבער
1943

The Lead Plates of Romm's Printing House

Like fingers stretched out through the bars of a prison
to capture the bright air of freedom –
so we ran through the night, to capture the plates,
the lead plates of Romm's printing house.
We dreamers must now become soldiers, and melt
into bullets the soul of the lead.

And now once again we have broken the seal
to enter a cavern, familiar, eternal.
Armed only with shadows, by the light of a lamp
we poured out the letters – line after line,
just like our grandfathers once in the temple
poured into golden menorahs the oil.

The lead shone as from it we poured out the bullets,
thoughts melted together – letter by letter.
One line from Babylon, one line from Poland
seethed, flooded into identical moulds.
And now Jewish valor, concealed in these words
must with a gunshot, tear open the world!

And he who has seen, in the ghetto, a weapon
grasped in courageous Jewish hands –
then it's Jerusalem's struggle he's witnessed,
the fall of those great granite walls;
he can hear all the words that were forged into bullets,
and their voice he has recognized deep in his heart.

Vilna ghetto
September 12
1943

זינג ניט קיין טרויעריקס

זינג ניט קיין טרויעריקס,
טו ניט פֿאַרשעמען
דעם טרויער.
ווערטער פֿאַרראַטן.
עס שטעלן זיך נעמען
קאַפויער.

קוק אויפֿן סניי
און באַלײַכט מיט זײַן רו
דײַן זכּרון:
ליכט איז די שפּראַך פֿון דײַן האַרצן.
און דו –
נײַ־געבאָרן.

שטרעק דײַנע פֿינגער צום סניי,
צו די קאַלטע
געוועבן.
אויסלײַזן וועסטו אין זיי
דאָס באַהאַלטענע
לעבן.

נאַראָטשער וועלדער
5טן פֿעברואַר
1944

פֿאַרפֿרוירענע ייִדן

האָסטו געזען איבער פֿעלדער מיט סניי
פֿאַרפֿרוירענע ייִדן, אַ רײַ נאָך אַ רײַ?

זיי ליגן אָן אָטעם, פֿאַרמירמלט און בלאָ,
נאָר טויט איז אין זייערע קערפֿערס ניטאָ.

ווײַל ס׳פֿינקלט אויך ערגעץ פֿאַרפֿרוירן דער גײַסט,
ווי אַ גילדענער פֿיש, אין אַ כוואַליע פֿאַראײַזט.

Sing no Sad Songs

Sing no sad songs,
do not shame
sorrow.
Words only deceive.
Names turn themselves
upside down.

Gaze at the snow.
Let your memory shine
with its peace:
light – your heart's language,
and you –
are reborn.

Let your fingers reach out to the snow,
to its icy cold
webs.
And your touch will release
the life that awaits there,
concealed.

Narotsh woods
February 5
1944

Frozen Jews

Have you seen, across fields full of snow
frozen Jews lying, row upon row?

They lie, marbled and blue, without breath
and yet in their bodies there is no death.

For somewhere still their spirit gleams,
like a golden fish, in a frozen stream.

זיי ריידן ניט. שווײַגן ניט. יעטוועדער ט ר אַ כ ט.
און די זון ליגט פֿאַרפֿרוירן אין שניי אויך בײַ נאַכט.

עס גליט אויף אַ ראָזלעכער ליפ אין געפֿריר
אַ שמייכל און קען זיך ניט געבן קיין ריר.

אַ טראָט לעם דער מאַמען ליגט הונגעריק ס׳קינד
און מאָדנע: זי קען עס ניט זייגן אַצינד.

און ס׳גליווערט אַ פֿויסט בײַ אַ נאַקעטן גרײַז
און קען ניט זײַן כּוח באַפֿרייען פֿון אײַז.

כ׳האָב אַלערליי טויטן פֿאַרזוכט ביז אַהער
און ס׳קען מיך שוין קיינער ניט וווּנדערן מער.

נאָר אַצינד אין דער יוליקער היץ אויף אַ גאַס
באַפֿאַלט מיך אַ פֿראָסט ווי ס׳באַפֿאַלט משוגעת:

עס גייט מיר אַנטקעגן דאָס בלאָע געביין –
פֿאַרפֿרוירענע ייִדן אויף שניייִקן פּלייין.

מײַן הויט ווערט באַצויגן מיט מירמלנער שיכט,
און אָפּשטעלן נעמט זיך דאָס וואָרט און דאָס ליכט.

און אויך מײַן באַוועגונג פֿאַרפֿרירט, ווי בײַם גרײַז,
וואָס קען ניט זײַן כּוח באַפֿרייען פֿון אײַז.

מאָסקווע
10טן יולי
1944

They speak not. Are not silent. *Thoughts* fill each head.
By night, frozen in snow, the sun lies dead.

Glowing on rosy lips in the frost
there's a smile, that can't move, and is lost.

A hungry child lies by its mother, quite near
but, strangely, the mother can't suckle it here.

The fist of a naked old man, petrified,
can't free its strength and escape from the ice.

I've experienced all kinds of deaths from before,
and none can surprise me or shock any more.

But now in July, in the city's heat,
frost attacks me, like madness, here in the street.

And all the blue corpses come toward me again –
frozen Jews on a snowy plain.

A layer of marble spreads over my skin,
and slowly the word and the light start to dim.

My limbs freeze, like the old man, petrified,
who could not free his strength and escape from the ice.

Moscow
July 10
1944

A page from Sutzkever's ghetto diary, dealing with the liquidation of the ghetto and the planned escape of the Jewish partisans, NLI, ARC 4°1565

1945 – 1948

צום דינעם אָדערל אין קאָפּ

צום דינעם אָדערל אין קאָפּ פֿאַרטרוי איך זיך אין גאַנצן.
מייַן וואָרט זיך נערט אין זייַן קרישטאָליק-זינגענדיקן שטויב.
און אַלע זיבן חכמות, וואָס דער ווירבל וויל פֿאַרפֿלאַנצן –
זיי פֿאַלן אָפּ אַנטפֿליגלטע ווי האָגל אָן אַ שויב.

איך ליב דאָס וואָרט פֿון אייַן געשמאַק, וואָס זאָל אין זיך ניט פֿאַלשן,
און ניט קיין זיס-און-זויערן היבריד מיט פֿרעמדן טעם.
אַלץ איינס, צי שטייַג איך הויך אויף מייַנע ריפֿן צי איך פֿאַל שוין –
דאָס וואָרט איז מייַנס. אין שוואַרצאַפּל פֿון טויט – אַ שטיקל פֿלאַם.

ווי גרויס עס זאָל ניט זייַן מייַן דור – איז גרעסער נאָך זייַן קליינקייט.
נאָר אייביק איז דאָס וואָרט מיט גאָר זייַן מיאוסקייט און פּראַכט.
צום דינעם אָדערל אין קאָפּ פֿאַרטרוי איך לעצטע שייַנקייט:
אַ ווינט. אַ בינטל גראָז. דעם לעצטן שטערן פֿון דער נאַכט.

1945

*

ווען כ'וואָלט ניט זייַן מיט דיר בייַנאַנד,
ניט אָטעמען דאָס גליק און ווי די דאָ, –
ווען כ'וואָלט ניט ברענען מיטן לאַנד,
וווּלקאַניש לאַנד אין חבֿלי-לידה;
ווען כ'וואָלט אַצינד, נאָך מייַן עקדה,
ניט מיטגעבוירן מיטן לאַנד,
וווּ יעדער שטיינדל איז מייַן זיידע –
געזעטיקט וואָלט מיך ניט דאָס ברויט,
דאָס וואָסער ניט געשטילט מייַן גומען.
ביז אויסגעגאַנגען כ'וואָלט פֿאַרגוי'ט,
און בלויז מייַן בענקשאַפֿט וואָלט געקומען...

1947

To the Thin Artery in My Head

To the thin artery in my head I entrust myself entirely.
My word is nourished by its singing crystal dust.
And all the seven wisdoms, which the whirlwind tries to plant –
They lose their wings and fall, like hail on window panes.

I love the word that has one single flavor, – pure, not false,
no sweet and sour hybrid with a foreign taste.
It matters not if I rise high or if I fall –
The word is mine. In the pupil of death's eye – a little flame.

However great my generation – greater still its smallness.
But the word with all its ugliness and splendor, is eternal.
To the thin artery in my head I entrust the final beauty:
a wind. A tuft of grass. The last star of the night.

1945

*

Had I not been here with you
breathing in your joy and pain, –
had I not burned together with the land,
volcanic land in her birth pangs;
had I now, after my *akeyde*,
not been born together with the land,
where every little stone is my grandfather –
then bread would not have satisfied my hunger,
water not have quenched my thirst.
I would have perished as an exile,
and only my yearning would have reached its home…

1947

דער שניי אויפֿן חרמון

מאי קא משמע לן דער שניי, וואָס אויפֿן חרמון אויבן?
ער אַנטפּלעקט מיר אַ באַשנייטע, אָוונטיקע כאַטע,
ווען באַגאַרטלט מיט אַ זעג עס קומט אַריין מײַן טאַטע,
און די זון, וואָס בלאַנדזשעט אינעם וועלדל אויף די שויבן,
פֿינקלט אין זיין באַרד זײַן אָנגעאײַזיקטע, אין כאַטע.

ער דערמאָנט מיר אָן די יידן, וואָס ווי שנייען קלאָרע,
זענען זיי ג ע פ אַ ל ן שטומערהייט אַ גאַנצן ווינטער
און זיי ליגן הינטער מײַנע שוואַרצאַפּלען, – אַהינטער,
בענקען אַז אַ פֿרילינג זאָל זיי מאַכן אַ הזכרה.
נאָר איז דען פֿאַראַן אַזאַ מין פֿרילינג אַ צעגרינטער?

פֿויגל פֿונעם חרמון! וואָס איך האָב געשלאָסן קאַנטשאַפֿט
נאָר אין א ל ה צ פ ו ר מיט דיין האַרציקער נגינה, –
ברענג אַ שניי אַ קינדישן אויף דײַנע פֿליגל דײַנע
פֿון מײַן היים, דער עיר וואם, – ועט ליבער זיין די לאַנדשאַפֿט.
אָנעם שניי וועט קאַלט זיין אין דער פֿלאַמיקער מדינה.

1948

הירשן ביים ים־סוף

דער זונפֿאַרגאַנג האָט זיך פֿאַרעקשנט מיט העזה
צו בלײַבן אין ים־סוף ביי נאַכט, ווען עס קומען
צום פּאַלאַץ פֿון וואַסער – די אומשולדיק ראָזע,
די איידעלע הירשן צו שטילן דעם גומען.

זיי לאָזן די זײַדענע שאָטנס ביים ים באַרטן
און לעקן אין ים־סוף די רינגען פֿון קילקייט
מיט פֿידלענע פֿנימער לאַנגע. און דאָרטן
געשעט די פֿאַרקנסונג ביי זיי מיט דער שטילקייט.

געענדיקט – אַנטלויפֿן זיי. רויזיקע פֿלעקן
באַלעבן דעם זאַמד. נאָר עס בלײַבן פֿול יאָמער
די זונפֿאַרגאַנג־הירשן אין וואַסער און לעקן
די שטילקייט פֿון יענע, וואָס זענען ניטאָ מער.

The Snow on Mount Hermon

What means to me the snow upon Mount Hermon?
It reveals to me a snowed-in hut at evening,
when my father, girdled with his saw, comes in,
and the sun, wandering through the forest on the windows,
sparkles in his frosted beard, in our hut at evening.

It reminds me of the Jews, who, like pure flakes of snow,
silently *fell* all winter long,
and they lie behind the pupils of my eyes,
yearning for a spring to come and give them a memorial.
But can such a verdant spring exist upon the earth?

Bird of Mount Hermon! It was in *El hatzipor*
that I first met you and your joyful song. –
Bring me back some childhood snow upon your tiny wings
from my home, my *ir veeym* – and I will love this landscape more.
Without that snow it will be cold in this hot fiery land.

1948

Deer at the Red Sea

The sunset has boldly and stubbornly lingered
in the Red Sea at evening, till the hour when they come
to the palace of water – the rosy and innocent
noble deer, eager to soothe their parched throats.

On the shore they abandon their shadows of silk
and lap in the Red Sea the circles of coolness
with long slender violin faces. And there
the betrothal takes place between deer and the stillness.

They finish – and flee. And flecks of rose color
give life to the sand. But the sunset deer linger
alone in the water, lamenting,
and lapping the silence of those that are gone.

פֿעלדזענע שפּיגלען

אויב זען ווילסטו איין מאָל די אייביקייט
פּנים־אל־פּנים,
און, אפֿשר, ניט שטאַרבן –
די אויגן באַהאַלט,
דרייַ אַראָפֿ זיי
ווי קנויטן אין שאַרבן.
און דעמאָלט
אַן איין־זיך־געצונדענער,
גיי, ווו עד־היום
דײַן וואַנדערשאַפֿט איז ניט מסוגל געווען זי צו טרעפֿן –

און גיב זיך אַן עפֿן
אַנטקעגן די פֿעלדזענע שפּיגלען פֿון ירושלים.

1947

פֿון: קאָמענטאַרן צו אַ פּנים אין שפּיגל

און וועסטו פֿאַרמאָלן דאָס בילד פֿון דער ייִדישער גאַס,
מיט פֿענדזל געטונקט אין דײַן זוניק, נייַעם פּאַלעטער, –
זייַ וויסן: די פֿאַרבן די איצטיקע וועלן זיך שיילן.
דאָס געוועזענע בילד מיט אַ האַק וועט באַפֿאַלן דיך שפּעטער,
פֿאַרווונדן אַזוי, אַז דאָס נייַע וועט קיין מאָל ניט היילן.

1949

פֿון: אַ בריוו צו די גראָזן

1.

מיר איז אומעטיק און גוט,
ווי ערבֿ מייַן געבאָרן.
אָפֿגענאָפּלט פֿון זכרון,
ווי אַ רויז אין וואַזע,

Mirrors of Stone

If you yearn to look once on eternity
face to face,
and, perhaps, not die –
cover your eyes,
turn them down
like wicks in your skull.
And then,
with the light burning inside yourself,
go, where till now
your wandering has never been able to find it –

And open your eyes
face to face with Jerusalem's mirrors of stone.

1947

From: **Commentaries on a Face in the Mirror**

And if you paint over the picture of past Jewish life,
with a brush that you've dipped in your sunny new palette, –
then know that these colors, now glowing, will peel.
The past image will later take hold of an axe and attack you,
and will wound you so badly, the new one can never more heal.

1949

From: **A Letter to the Grasses**

1.
I feel sad and happy,
like a baby in the womb.
Severed from my memory,
like a rose in a vase,

קושט זיך מיטן זונפֿאַרגאַנג צונויף
מיַין עולם־הזה.
היַינט האָב איך צעשניטן זיך אומישנע
מיט אַ שטיקל גלאָז מיַין האַנט,
געוואָלט זיך איבערציַיגן,
צי דער גאָלדשמיד פֿון יסורים
האָט נאָך זיַין טאַלאַנט.
געזען אַז יאָ –
האָט ביזן סאַמע דנאָ
אַ זעלטן גליק באַצעוווּנגען מיַינע גלידער:
גוט נאָוונט גראָזן, אַ גוט נאָוונט ווידער!

5.

די ליפן קניַין פֿאָרן וואָרט דעם אָפּגעזוּנדערטן און מאָנען:
„הלמאי געלאָזן אוּנדז אַליין, מיר זאָלן זינגען מער ניט קאָנען?
צו וואָס די פֿליִעניש צו גאָט? אַז אָן דיַין זוּניק ליכט – ווי בלעטער
פֿאַרוועלקן מיר און וועפֿן אויס אין גאָרנישטקייט אין פֿיאַלעטער!
אַ קיניגין פֿון בינשטאָקס מויל, אַרויסגעפֿלויגן און ניטאָ מער –
אַזוי ביסטו פֿון אוּנדז אַוועק אין רעגנס תּאָווהדיקן יאָמער.
אין ווינקלען אוּנדזערע ווי אַש, – די מענטשנקינדער צאָנקען, צאַנקען:
באַאָטעם זיי מיט דיַין געפֿלאַם, באַלעב דאָס לעבן מיט געדאַנקען!
דיַין היים, וואָס בלאָנדזשעט אויף דער ערד, ווי דו – איז קיין מאָל ניט געשטיגן,
מיר וועלן זינגען שטומערהייט, זאָלסט קומען וועדליק אוּנדזער ניגון“.

די ליפן אָפּגעשיידט פֿון וואָרט, – זיי מאָנען, זוכן אין דער פּוסטקייט
אַ מינדסטן פֿליגלפֿאָר אין ווינט, און צאַנקען אויס אין אומבאַוווּסטקייט.

9.

עס האָט געלוינט, אָן ספֿק,
איבערשוווימען דעם סמבטיון
צו זען די געלע פֿלוים.
נאָר וואָלט, למשל,
אַ פֿעלדוזנראָב ניט אָפּגעפּיקט פֿון איר
אַ פּיצל שאַרבן,
און ס׳וואָלט ניט אָפּגעקלאַפּט פֿון איר
אַ בלישטשענדיקער יאָדער –
וואָס זשע וואָלט מיר אָנגעגאַנגען
יענע געלע פֿלוים,
אַפֿילו ווען דער גאַנצער בוים

the sunset and my sensual delight
meet in a kiss.
Today, deliberately, I cut my hand
with a shard of glass,
to ascertain
whether the goldsmith of pain
still retains his talent.
When I found he does indeed –
then to the very depths of me,
great joy took possession of my limbs:
good evening, grasses, I greet you once again!

5.
The lips kneel down before the separated word, demanding:
"Why have you deserted us, so we can sing no more?
Why did you fly to God? Without your sunny light – like leaves
we wither, and fade to purple nothingness!
A queen has flown out from the beehive's mouth and disappeared –
thus you left us for the passionate lamentation of the rain.
In our ashy corners – human beings flicker, dying:
Breathe your flames into them, bring life alive again with thoughts!
Your home, that wanders on the earth like you – has never risen up.
We will sing mutely. Come, respond now to our melody."

Separated from the word, the lips demand, and search the emptiness
for the slightest wingbeat in the wind, then fade into unconsciousness.

9.
It was worthwhile, without a doubt,
to swim across the Sambatyen,
to see the yellow plum.
But if, for instance,
a raven had not pecked from it
a tiny piece of skull,
and had not exposed
a shining kernel –
what would it have meant to me,
that yellow plum,
even if the tree itself

אויף איר איז אָנגעהאַנגען,

ווי אַ גרינער בגד אויף אַ נאָגל?

ס׳וואָלט דעמאָלט ניט כּדאי געווען דער וואָגל.

די געלע פֿלוים דערמאָנט אָן מיר אַליין,

עס קלאַפֿט צעווישן ביידן אַ צוזאַמענדיקער אָדער:

וויפֿל ס׳זאָל דער פֿעלדזנראַב ניט פּיקן מײַן געביין,

וועט ער ניט קאָנען אויפֿזיגלען מײַן בלישטשענדיקן יאָדער.

.12

איידער כ׳וועל מיט שאָטן זיך באַהעפֿטן –

ענטפֿערט, גראָזן, אויף אַ קליינע שאלה:

צווישן אַלע אײַערע געשעפֿטן,

קלערט איר וועגן מענטשן אויך אַ ווײַלע?

.14

אַז איר זאָלט קאָנען ענטפֿערן,

אַז איר זאָלט קאָנען פֿרעגן, –

מוז איך קודם זיך פֿאַרוואַנדלען אין אַ ווילדן רעגן,

דעמאָלט וועט איר אײַנזאַפּן ביז ווײַטיק מײַנע טראָפּנס.

צום ווידערזען

אין צימערל,

אין חלום מײַנעם, גראָזן.

צום לידערזען

אין שימערל,

וואָס איך האָב אײַך געלאָזן –

און פֿאַרגעסט ניט אויפֿבליִען אַ מאָל בײַ מײַן צוקאָפֿנס.

1948

had been attached to it,
hanging like a green garment on a nail?
The journey then would not have been worthwhile.

The yellow plum reminds me of myself.
Between us both there beats a common pulse:
however much the raven pecks my bones,
he will not manage to expose my shining kernel.

12.
Before I am united with the shadows once again –
answer, grasses, just a little question that I ask:
though you're busy with so many tasks
do you also think about us humans now and then?

14.
So that you can answer,
so that you can ask, –
I must first transform myself into torrential rain,
and then you will drink in my raindrops till you ache.

Till we meet again
in my dream,
in my own room, grasses.
Till we sing again
in the gleam
that I have left you, grasses –
And don't forget to blossom some day beside my bed.

1948

Manuscript of Sutzkever's lecture on Young Vilna, NLI, ARC 4°1565, 2:337

1950–1959

אָדע צו דער טויב

I

זעלטן, אַ מאָל אין דער קינדהײט, באַװײזט זיך קאָליריק און בלענדיק
אונטער די שטערן אַ מלאך, זײַן ניגון װעט נאָכשפּילן שטענדיק.
האָט זיך באַװיזן – אַנטרונען אױף יענער זײַט װעלטישן גדר,
איבערן הײמישן קוימען אַ סימן געלאָזן – אַ פֿעדער.

גאָר ניט קײן פּשוטער מלאך, װי קומט אים אַ ייִנגל אין זינען?
װוּנדער! אַ טױב איז די פֿעדער אין שנײיען-מאַגנעט פֿון באַגינען.
פֿלאַטערט די טױב ערשט-געבױרן, צו לערנען זיך – ניט קײן סעקונדע,
בײַזקל זי פֿאַלט בײַ זײַן גאָניק אין זילבערנע שװעבונגען רונדע.

פֿינגערשע נעסטן פֿון ייִנגל דערװאָרעמען זי און זיי קושן.
װאָרקען מיט זוניקן אָטעם אױף ס׳נײַ אירע שנייִקע פּליושן.
לערנט דער ייִנגל זי פֿליִען, אַ פֿיק טאָן װי אַרבעס דעם נעפּל.
– האָסט מיך גערעטעװעט, ליבער, – דערלאַנגט זי אַ קניטיש מיטן קעפּל –

װאָסער מתנה פֿאַרלאַנגסטו, נאָר שלאָג זיך ניט לאַנג מיט דער דעה,
אַפֿשר דעם סוד פֿון מײַן װײַסקײט, אַן אײביקן שניי, אַ קמיע?
ענטפֿערט דער ייִנגל בגילופֿן: מײַן ליבינקע, בין איך דיר טײַער,
קום, אַז אַ מאָל כ׳װעל דיך רופֿן אין רעגן אין שניי און אין פֿײַער.

II

קלאַנגען אין ליפּן געפֿאַנגען, װי פּערל אין ימיקע שלעסער,
שטומען שױן טױזנטער יאָרן, און איבער דער שטומקײט – אַ מעסער.
– טײַבעלע, קינד פֿון דער קינדהײט, גיב לשון די ליפּן, גיב לשון,
הער דאָס געװײן פֿון די קלאַנגען, אַניט איז אַ חלום פֿאַרלאַשן...

פּלוצעם – אַ קוש מײַנע ליפּן. װער בין איך, װוּ בין איך? די שלעסער
שליסן אַלײן זיך פֿונאַנדער. די שטומקײט – צעשניטן פֿון מעסער.
פּערל און פּערל און פּערל, מיט ימיקע רױשן געהײמע,
רעגענען שױן פֿון די ליפּן, ס׳באַפֿאַלט מיך אַ פּערלענע אימה.

Ode to the Dove

I.

Seldom, but sometimes in childhood, appears brightly colored and shining
under the starlight an angel, his melody lingers for ever.
Then he escapes and flies off to the regions beyond the horizon,
leaving behind, floating over my chimney, a sign that he's been here – a feather.

Not just an ordinary angel, what would put him in mind of a boy?
A miracle! His feather's turned into a dove in the snow-white magnet of dawn.
The baby dove, fluttering, endeavors to fly – but in less than a second
she sinks down in silvery circles beside the boy's threshold.

The boy's finger nests encircle the dove and they warm her with kisses.
Her snowy soft feathers coo once again, with a breath warm as sunshine.
He teaches the dove how to fly, and to peck through the mist with her beak.
"You have saved me, my dearest" she says to him, graciously bowing her head.

"What gift would you have? You must answer me swiftly, don't ponder too long;
an amulet? Snow everlasting? Or the secret, perhaps, of my whiteness?"
Drunk with delight the boy answers: "My dear one, if truly you love me,
then come, if sometimes I should call you, in rain and in snow and in fire."

II.

Sounds imprisoned in lips, like pearls in undersea castles,
have been mute for thousands of years, and above their muteness – a knife.
"Little dove, child of my childhood, give words to these lips, let them speak,
hear how the captive sounds weep; if you don't, then a dream is extinguished…"

All at once there's a kiss on my lips. Who am I, where am I? The castles
open up all by themselves. The silence – cut by the knife.
Pearls upon pearls upon pearls, with mysterious sounds of the sea,
rain suddenly down from my lips, and a pearly terror invades me.

... גרילן, ווי שוסטערלער, קלאָפן די גראָזן אַרײַן אין מײַן שטערן,
ס'קומט אויפן בוידעם אַ לאַנקע און לאָזט אויף מײַן באַק אירע טרערן.
ס'קרייען געקוילעטע הענער לכּבֿוד אַ רגע פֿון טרויער.
שנייען צעגאַנגענע גיסן געצונדענעם ספּירט אין מײַן אויער.

ווער האָט פֿאַרשיכּורט די פֿינגער, זיי זאָלן באַשאַפֿן אַ שורה:
„אַלע וואָס ענדיקן לעבן פֿאַרזייען אין מיר זייער גבֿורה?"
– טײַבעלע, האָסט געשאָנקען אַ בלעטל פּאַפּיר ווי אַ שפּיגל,
האָסט מײַנע ווערטער וואָס בלאַנקען מיר איבערגעשפּרייט מיט די פֿליגל!

III

בלעטל פּאַפּיר, ביסט אַ דענקמאָל, אַ נעסט די ווייט אין דײַן חומר,
בלעטל, אין דיר, ניט אין מאַרמאָר, איז אייביק דאָס פּנים פֿון טרוימער.
דאָ, צווישן אָפּקלאַנגען רויע, פֿאַרזונקענע, ליימיקע פֿאָרמען,
זאַמל איך זילבערנע זילבן, צו קענען מײַן טײַבעלע קאָרמען.

זונפֿאַרגאַנג זינגט אין אַ לעמפּל. און אונטערן מאַגישן לעמפּל
בוי איך פֿון בײַנערנע קלאַנגען, באַגאָסן מיט בלוט מײַנס, – אַ טעמפּל.
ער האָט דאָס וואָרט ניט דערזונגען, אַזוי איז דאָס וואָרט ניט־דערשליפֿן!
גליט דער וווּלקאַן פֿון פֿאַעזיע פֿאַרזיגלט אין בראָנדזענע טיפֿן.

דאָ, מיט דער פּען, דיריזשיר איך אַן אייגענע, שטילע קאַפּעליע:
קומען אין רעגן נשמות און טריפן אַרײַן דורך דער סטעליע.
קאַרשן, פֿאַרמוירערט אין בײַמער, באַפֿאַל איך צו בײַטן די ערטער,
קומען אויף פֿורפורנע פֿיסלער צו לעבן ווי קאָרשן אין ווערטער.

ווײַזט זיך אין טעמפּל אַ וואָרעם. אַזאַ צוייבעריי איז אים פֿרעמדעלעך.
אמתע קאָרשן אין ווערטער צעראַצן זײַן גומען ווי זעמדעלעך.
וואָרקעט די טויב ווי אַ שוועסטער: באַפֿאַל, זאָלן קומען די קאָרשן,
דו ביסט די מאָס און דער מעסטער, פֿאַרשוווּנדענע זעונגען ירשן!

... Crickets, like cobblers, are tapping the grasses right into my forehead,
in the attic a meadow is growing, its tears fall onto my cheeks.
Slaughtered cockerels are crowing to honor a moment of sadness.
Snows, disappearing, now pour burning spirits right into my ear.

Who has made these fingers so drunk, that they have created a verse:
"All those who are dying have planted in me their great valor?"
"A white sheet of paper you've given to me, little dove, as a mirror
and over my lost, wayward words you protectively spread out your wings!"

III.

Paper, you are a monument, the dove builds a nest in your body.
Oh, paper, in you, not in marble, the dreamer's face lives on forever.
Here, among harsh unripe echoes, and sunken amorphous clay forms,
like a hunter, I catch silver syllables, food for my own little dove.

The sunset sings in a lamp. And under this magical lamp
from sounds made of bone, and doused with my blood, I am building a temple.
The word, still raw and unformed, was not perfectly sung by the sunset!
Poetry, a glowing volcano, lies sealed within caverns of bronze.

Now, with my pen, I conduct my own silent orchestra here:
souls appear in the rain; see how they drip through the ceiling.
Cherries are walled up in trees, I command them to move from their prison,
to come on their small crimson feet to a new life as cherries in words.

There appears in the temple a worm. To him all this magic is alien.
Real cherries in words are scratching his palate like sand grains.
My little dove coos like a sister: "Command the cherries to come.
You are both potter and vessel – the vanished visions inherit!"

IV

טענצערין מײַנע, ווער ביסטו, צי האָט דיך געבוירן אַ פֿידל?
אונטער דײַן טאַנץ ווערט צעגראַבן מײַן גאָרטנדיק לײַב מיט אַ ריידל.
קראַנק איז די קלײנע, לונאַטיש, אין זילבערנעם נאַכטהעמד, ניט זעלטן
שווימט זי אַוועק ווי אַ כוואַליע אין קאַלטע, צעפליעסקעטע וועלטן.

פֿול איז מײַן קאָפּ מיט רעצעפּטן צו הײלן איר הימלישן פֿיבער –
האָט אַ לעבנדיק יִינגל פֿאַרליבט זיך דערווײַל אין מײַן ליבער.
וואַרף אין אים שפּיזן ווי שאָול – באַהאַלט זיך דער יִינגל אין צווײַגן,
ווילסטו אים בינדן אין לידער – באַווײַזט ער דיר זילבערנע פֿײַגן.

טאָפּעלע שוויבן באַשטעל איך צו שיצן מײַן גליק פֿון די מענער...
בלײַבן זיי גאַנץ ווי מײַן ליבע און זויבער און טאָפּל, נאָר י ע נ ע ר
שלינגט זי אַרויס פֿון די שויבן, פֿאַרנאַרט מיט אַ שײַנער מתּנה,
אײדער צו טאַנצן אין טעמפּל שוין טאַנצט זי בײַם ראַנד פֿון לבֿנה.

– טײַבעלע, זאָג דער לבֿנה, זי זאָל זיך ניט צו פֿיל צעברענען,
לערן די טענצערין פֿליִען, אַרומפֿליִען מוז מען דאָך קענען!
כ׳וועל דיך באַלוינען מיט קערנער, וואָס יעדער צו דעם איז אַ בעלן,
זאָל זי ניט פֿאַלן אויף דערנער, אויב יאָ – אויף מײַן ברוסט זאָל זי פֿאַלן.

V

בוין און בוין דעם טעמפּל, מיט זוניקן שֹכל אים בוין!
קומט אין אַ פֿײַער דער טײַוול צו ברענגען מײַן טויב צום נסיון.
גראָ איז די זון. אַלע פֿאַרבן פֿאַרשפּינט ער מיט גראָע לישײַעס,
איבערגעברענט איז דער טעמפּל, ס׳אַנטלויפֿן די זײַלן ווי חיות.

קינדער, ווי גאָלדענע פֿייגל, צעלייגט ער אַצינד אין סקעלעטן,
סם אויף די ליפּן פֿון קלאַנגען, זיי זאָלן פֿאַרסמען פֿאַעטן.
פּנימער שטעקן אויף העלדזער ווי שאָטנס פֿון העק אין דער נידער.
גליקלעכע זענען די טויטע ווען אײַגן און פֿלײש זענען ברידער.

זומפּיק די ערד און דער הימל, און איך בין זיזן האַלדז בין געזונקען.
פֿײַער – און מיר אַזוי פֿינצטער. אַ שטײן מיט פֿאַרלאָשענע פֿונקען,
בלויז אין די גליביקע פֿינגער דאָס בלעטל פּאַפּיר דאָס פֿאַרהיטע,
מוזן די פֿײַערן קניִען, זיי האָבן דעם אויף דעם ניט קײן שליטה.

IV.

My dancer, beloved, who are you, were you born from a violin?
Your dance delves into my body, like a spade preparing a garden.
The little one's ill, she is moonstruck; in her silvery nightdress she often
ebbs away like a wave, into cold, watery worlds.

My head's full of remedies – cures for her heavenly fever –
but meanwhile a moon youth has fallen in love with my darling.
If you pelt him with spears like King Saul – this cunning lad hides among branches,
if you try to bind him with verses – he gives you the silvery finger.

Double windows I buy to protect my beloved from men…
Intact are the panes like my love, and immaculate, double, but he
sucks her out through the windowpanes, lures her with beautiful presents,
and rather than dance in my temple, see her dance at the edge of the moon!

"Little dove, speak to the moon, it should not blaze up too fiercely.
Teach the dancer to fly, she should master this wonderful art!
I shall reward you with seeds of the kind that every dove longs for,
only may she not fall upon thorns; if she falls, may it be on my breast."

V.

Keep building and building your temple, with sunlit reason you'll build it!
In the midst of a fire comes the devil, to lead my dove into temptation.
He turns the sun grey and spins over all colors a grey web of lichens,
the temple is burned to the ground, its columns flee off like wild creatures.

Children, like pure golden birds, he dissects and reduces to skeletons.
Poison there is on the lips of the sounds, to poison the poets.
Faces stick out on necks in the depths, like shadows of axes.
Only the dead are happy, when metal and flesh meet like brothers.

The earth and the heavens are swamps, and I am sunk up to my neck.
Fire – but for me there's such darkness. A stone with its sparks all extinguished.
But there in the faithful fingers the leaf of white paper is rescued.
The fires are forced to kneel down. Over it they have no dominion.

ווייס איך: די טויב איז דאָס בלעטל, וואָס לאָזט ניט פֿאַרגליווערן פֿינגער,
ווערטער, ווי אייניקלעך, זאָלן געדענקען די צײַט פֿון באַצווינגער.
טעג אָן דער טויב זענען מילבן, אַ לויב צו די לויטערע פֿאָרמען!
זאַמל איך זילבערנע זילבן צו קענען מײַן טײַבעלע קאָרמען.

VI

– יאָ, איך בין שולדיק, בין שולדיק, אַ זינד איז געווען צו פֿאַרלאַנגען,
זאָלסט מיר די טענצערין ברענגען צוריק צו די ערדענע זאַנגען.
תּהומיקער בראַנד האָט פֿאַרשלונגען איר יונגע איינמאָליקע בלאָקייט,
זידן אַצינד מײַנע שלייפֿן מיט פּערל אין אַש – מיט איר גראָקייט.

– ניין, ביסט ניט שולדיק, ניט שולדיק, די טענצערין טאַנצט מיטן זעלבן
וואַרעמען טאַנץ פֿון דער יוגנט אין שמייכלענדיק־בלאָע געוועלבן.
וואַנדער פֿון איין לאַנד אין אַנדער, שנײַד אָפּ מאַמע־ערד פֿונעם נאָפּל,
אויבן דער טאַנץ וועט דיר העלפֿן אַ נעם טאָן די וועלט אויף אַ גאָפּל.

– אויבן דער טאַנץ איז אַ חלום, ווּוהין זאָל איך, טײַבעלע, וואָגלען?
אויגן פֿון טויטע ווי נעגל באַשלאָגן מײַן גוף און זיי נאָגלען
צו מײַן נשמה צום גאָרניט. מײַן ברויט און מײַן זאַלץ – אַ רוִינע.
אונטער די טריט איז מײַן היימלאַנד, באַשימלט מיט גראָז – מײַן מדינה.

– כ׳וועל מײַנע פֿליגל דיר אָנטאָן, אַרויסציִען וועל איך די נעגל,
אָנבלאָזן וועט זיך מיט פֿרײַהייט אַ ווײַסער געדאַנק ווי אַ זעגל.
ביסט ניט בײַם טויט אין אַרענדע, די טעג וועלן קרײַזן און קרײַזן,
אייביק איז בלויז די לעגענדע און זי וועט אַ שמייכל באַווײַזן.

VII

וועלט. וואָס איז וועלט? בלויז איר ניגון איז כוואַליק און וואַלדיק און וועלטיק,
יאָמערט איר געטלעכער ניגון אין אָדערן מײַנע: געוועלטיק!
לעש איך דעם יאָמער מיט ימען, ס׳באַגריסן מיך שטעט אומבאַקאַנטע.
שטיי! מיט אַ רעגן טערצינען האָט דאָ זיך אַ שפּיל געטאָן דאַנטע.

– מײַסטער פֿון גיהנום, צי ווילסטו זיך בײַטן אַ ווײַל מיט די גיהנומס?
איך וועל אין דײַנעם שפּאַצירן, און דו – אין די פֿײַערן יענעמס...
מינערן וועט עס ניט, מײַסטער, דײַן אייביקע, מאַרמאָרנע גלאָריע,
דו ביסט נאָך אַלץ אַליגיערי, דײַן גיהנום – נאָך אַלץ אַלעגאָריע.

I know then – the dove is the paper, which does not let fingers grow rigid,
so that the words, like descendants, shall remember the time of the tyrant.
Doveless days are like dust mites; a hymn of praise to pure forms!
Like a hunter, I catch silver syllables, food for my own little dove.

VI.

"Yes, I am guilty, am guilty; for it was a sin to demand
you should bring me the dancer to dwell once again among earth's ears of corn.
Chasms of fire have devoured her young and unique shining blueness,
and now my temples are seared by pearls in ashes – her grayness."

"No, you're not guilty, not guilty, the dancer is dancing as ever
the same warm dance of her youth in the smiling blue arch of the heavens.
Wander abroad, and cut your umbilical cord from the earth,
the celestial dance will help you confront the whole world without fear."

"The celestial dance – a vain dream. O, where, little dove, should I wander?
The eyes of the dead are like nails, they are piercing my body, and nailing
my soul to the void. My bread and my salt – just a ruin.
My homeland is trampled to death, moldy with grass is my country."

"I will fasten my wings to your shoulders and pull out the nails from your body.
And a white thought will fill up with freedom, like a sail blowing out in the wind.
You are not in death's clutches, your days will keep soaring and soaring.
The legend alone is eternal, and it will smile graciously on you."

VII.

World. What is world? Its melody only is wave-like and wood-like and world-like.
Its heavenly melody weeps in my veins and commands: be the master!
I quench her lamenting with oceans; I am greeted by cities unknown.
Wait! Here is Dante, who's playing a game with a shower of tercets.

"Master of Hell, will you swop our two hells for a while?
I shall go walking in yours, and you – in the fires of the other…
O Master, it will not detract from your marble, eternal glory,
you will always remain Alighieri – but your hell will remain allegory."

מענטשן... וואָ זענען זיי, מענטשן! מקנא זיין דאַרף מען די שטויבן,
בלויז אין די ווערטער פֿון אַ י י ַ נ ע ם איז דאָ זייער גייסט, זייער גלויבן.
ס׳קלינגען בית־עלמינס – מע הערט ניט... פֿאַר מיר זענען זיי אַן אַכסניא.
שטיי! ווי אַ לייב האָט הלוי מיין בענקשאַפֿט געזונגען פֿון שפּאַניע.

היי, איר פֿאָעטן, פֿאָעטן, אָן אייַך איז דאָס לעבן אַ דרעמל,
ס׳וואָלט דאָך שוין לאַנג אָן פֿאַעזיע געקניט פֿאַרן טויט ווי אַ קעמל.
ס׳וואָלטן סיי מענטש און סיי חיה געפֿייניקט זיך עלנטער, פֿרעמדער,
ס׳וואָלט ניט מיין טויב געטרייע באַגלייט מיט אַ פֿלייט איבער לענדער...

VIII

טענצערין, זאָג מיר וווּ ביסטו? די האָר מיינע פֿילן דיין פֿלאַטער...
ענטפֿערן קאָן מיר די טויב ניט: אַוווּ איז דיין היים, דיין טעאַטער?
ס׳ברענגט מיר אַ מאָל דיינע אויגן אַ סאַרנע אין זוניקע טויען,
וווער איז דער ציטער אין גאָרטן ווי ס׳בליִען שאַאַלישע בלויען?

הינטערן וואַלד אין אַ רעגן וווער אָטעמט מיך אײַן רעגנבויגיק?
וווער איז די נאַקעטע כוואַליע – אָן גלידער און דאָך אַזוי בויגיק?
וווער איז די שנייען־לאַווינע צעגליט איבער פֿעלדזענע ראַנדן?
קושן די בריסט ווייל אַן אָדלער, באַשיט זי אים באַלד מיט גירלאַנדן.

וווער איז דער שפּיגל אין טרערן? וווער זענען די פֿנימער נייע?
וווער איז די פֿרוי אינעם אָרון, די רויזן־באַדעקטע לוויה?
ס׳דרייען זיך, דרייען די רעדער און שלינגען און וויקלען מיין שאָטן,
היינטיקן טאָג האָט אַ רידל אַליין זיך אין קבֿר פֿאַרשאָטן.

וווער איז די ווייסע פֿאַרוואַנדלונג, וואָס קאָן ניט אַרויס פֿון בעריאָזע?
וווער איז דער אָפּהילך פֿון שטיליקייט און ווער איז די שטילקייט די ראָזע?
וועט מיר ניט ענטפֿערן קיינער? צי ברענען אין מיר משוגעתן?
היינטיקן טאָג האָבן שטיינער אַליין זיך פֿאַרשטיינט אין די גאַסן!

IX

ווייַט אין דער וועלט איז געפֿאַלן אַ שטיין־מעטעאָר און זיין ניגון
האָט מיך געצויגן דורך דזשונגלען, ביז איין מאָל דערזע איך אים ליגן
פֿול מיטן ריח פֿון שטערן. דערבייַ האָט אַ לייב אויף אַ סקאַלע
ברומענדיק אויסגעשמידט גלעקער און פֿלאַם האָט צעשמאָלצן זיי אַלע.

Human beings... where are they, these humans! Indeed one should envy the dust.
There is only *one* whose words can encompass their spirit, their faith.
Graveyards ring out – no one hears them. For me they're a refuge.
Wait! Like a lion, Halevi has sung of my longing from Spain.

Listen you poets, you poets, without you our life is a sleep.
Without poetry, life would already have knelt before death like a camel.
Humans and animals both would be still more tormented and lonely,
and my dove could not come with me over the lands and accompany me on her flute.

VIII.

Dancer, o tell me, where are you? The hairs on my head feel your fluttering...
Even my dove cannot tell me: where is your home and your stage?
Sometimes a little doe brings me your eyes in the sunny bright dew,
who trembles here in the garden, where the blues of Chagall are in bloom?

Behind the wood, in rain, who breathes me in like a rainbow?
Who is the naked wave – that is limbless and yet is so supple?
Who is the snow avalanche, incandescent, beyond the cliff's edge?
An eagle is longing to kiss her breasts, but she showers him with garlands.

Who is the mirror in tears? Who are the new, unknown faces?
Who is the woman in the coffin, the funeral covered with roses?
The wheels are turning, turning; they envelop and swallow my shadow.
Today was the day that a spade came and buried itself in a grave.

Who is the white transformation, which can't free itself from the birch tree?
Who is the echo of silence, and who is the rose-colored silence?
Will no one give me an answer? Is madness burning within me?
Today was the day that stones stoned themselves in the street!

IX.

Far, far away a meteor fell to the earth, and its melody
drew me, searching, through jungles. At long last I found it lying,
still full of the fragrance of stars. On a cliff nearby roared a lion
and his roaring forged bells. They all were melted in flames.

ווער איז דער שטײן? איז מיר קענטלער. מוזיק אונטער גאָלדענע ריפּן.
ס׳הימלקינד רופֿט מיך בײַם נאָמען. עס צישען זיך ליפּן צו ליפּן.
– א י ך בין די טענצערין, פֿרעג ניט... אַ לויב צו דעם לײַב מיט זײַן ברומען!
אָנגעזאָגט האָט מיר דער קיניג דײַן קומען, דײַן קומען, דײַן קומען.

ס׳גליווערן גלידער. ביז וואַנען מײַן גוף, דער אין ליבע פֿאַרברענטער,
אויסלעשן וועט זיך אין גאַנצן – אָ, שטיל מײַנע ליפּן, קום נענטער!
לאָזן איך וועל דיר אַ סימן: די לעצטע, דרײַ בלוטיקע טראָפּנס,
איידער עס וועט די לבֿנה זײַן מיר אַ מצבֿה צוקאָפּנס.

א י ך בין די שנײען־לאַווינע, די ווײַסע בעריאָזע, דער שפּיגל,
א י ך בין דער אָפּהילך פֿון שטילקייט, וואָס נעמט דיך אַרום אין אַן עיגול.
זאָמל די קלאַנגען, די בילדער, אַ הונגער וועט צינדן דײַן געזאנג...
לעב זיי, באַלעב זיי און שילדער!
אַזוי האָבן מיר זיך געזעגנט.

X

אונטער אַ בוים לעבן ים־סוף. די כוואַליעס דערקלינגען מײַן אָדע.
שטיל. אין זײַן שאָטן – אַ מילשטיין, געדרייט פֿון דער זון מיט התמדה,
אָטעם איך הײַשעריק־דיונעס – די היטער פֿון צײַט און זכרון.
דאָ האָט דאָס פֿאָלק זיך געצויגן דורך פֿערציק תנכּישע יאָרן.

מײַליקע טריט אונטער זאַמדן, און גרויס ווי דער מידבר די ציפֿער.
זאָלן די הײַשעריק־דיונעס אנטפּלעקן די זעונגען טיפֿער!
ווי זענען מ ײַ נ ע פֿיר צעגנדליק, אין מידבר, צוזאַמען מיט יענע?
בײַנער געבליבן, בלויז בײַנער – גענאָד פֿון אַ בלינדער היענע?

וואָרקעט די טויב אויף מײַן אַקסל: גוט־מאָרגן! און איך וועל דיך פֿרעגן –
יאָרן דאָס זענען דען בײַנער? אַ בלאַז און זיי שפּילן אַנטקעגן.
זאָנגען מיט קינדערשע אויגן באַוועגן זיך אונטער די דיונעס,
תחית־המתים פֿון זאַנגען, און אויבן – אַ וואָלקן מיט סטרונעס!

– טײַבעלע, ביסטו די זעלבע, די פֿליגל ניט גראָ, איז דאָס מעגלעך?
זאָל איך דאָ בויען מײַן טעמפּל, ווי איך האָב געבויט אים טאָג־טעגלעך?
זאָל איך מײַן צוויבערדיק לעמפּל צעגרינען אויף ס׳נײַ און צעבלויען?
– בויען און בויען דעם טעמפּל, מיט זוניקן שכל אים בויען!

1954

Who is the stone? Yes, I know it. Music plays under golden ribs.
The heaven's child calls out my name. Lips are drawn to lips.
"*I* am the dancer, don't ask any more. All praise to the lion:
the roar of the king announced it to me: you are coming, are coming!"

Limbs stiffen. Until my body, that's burning with love,
is about to be wholly extinguished – "Oh, come and quench my lips' thirst!
Before I lie with the moon as a tombstone over my head
I shall leave you a sign: my last three droplets of blood.

I am the snow avalanche, the silver birch tree, the mirror,
I am the echo of silence, which encompasses you in a circle.
Gather the sounds and the images – your world will be lit by your hunger – ,
Live them, depict, give them life!"
                            Thus we parted, one from the other.

X.

Under a tree by the Red Sea. The waves ring out with my ode.
Still. In its shadow – a millstone, which the sun is carefully turning.
I breathe in locust dunes – the guardians of memory and time.
Here my people wandered for forty long biblical years.

Miles of steps under the sands, their number as huge as the desert.
Let the locust dunes show me these visions more deeply, more clearly!
Where are *my* four decades – in the desert, together with those?
Bones they remain, only bones – thanks to a sightless hyena?

My little dove coos on my shoulder: "Good morning! I just want to ask you –
years are just bones?" One breath, and they come to perform here before me.
Cornstalks with children's eyes are moving under the dunes,
A resurrection of corn, and above them – a cloud violin!

"Little dove, are you still as you were, and your wings are not grey, can that be?
Shall I build my temple here, as I built it day after day?
Shall I make my magic lamp shine green again, and blue?"
"Keep building and building your temple, with sunlit reason you'll build it anew!"

1954

פֿון: העלפֿאַנדן ביַי נאַכט

אין אָנהייב

אין אָנהייב איז געווען אַ שוואַרצער העלפֿאַנד.
זיַין העלפֿאַנדביין איז אויך געוועזן שוואַרץ
ווי ער אַליין.
פֿאַרן שטאַרבן האָט ער אין אַ טיַיך
אַ העלפֿאַנדביין פֿאַרלוירן.
און אַזוי ווי ס׳האָט אין טיַיך
געבאָדן זיך אַ רעגן־בויגן –
האָבן זיַינע פֿינגער
אָנגעכאַפֿט דעם העלפֿאַנדביין, וואָס איז געווען זיַין רעטער.

אויס דאַנקשאַפֿט האָט דער רעגן־בויגן
אים געטאָן אַ קוש.
דעמאָלט האָט דער העלפֿאַנדביין
באַקומען אויגן, ציינער,
און איז געוואָרן מ ע נ ט ש –
דער עלטסטער פֿון די מענטשן.

און ווי דער עלטסטער מענטש
אַזוי בין איך:
שוואַרץ, ווי יענער העלפֿאַנדביין,
און רעגן־בויגן־ליכטיק.

העלפֿאַנדן ביַי נאַכט
יעגערליד

העלפֿאַנדן ביַי נאַכט, ווי שווערע גיַיסטער
וואָס קומען איינער נאָכן צווייטן
באָדן זיך אין טיַיך,
זענען ניט קיין העלפֿאַנדן,
זיי טראָגן בלויז אַ מאַסקע.
איך, דער יעגער פֿון די נעכט,
וואָס האָב געזען ווי שטערן

From: **Elephants at Night**

In the Beginning

In the beginning was a coal-black elephant.
His tusks were also black
like him.
Before he died, he lost
one tusk in a river.
Just then there was a rainbow
bathing in the river –
its fingers
grabbed the tusk, which saved the rainbow.

Gratefully the rainbow
kissed it.
And then the tusk
got eyes, and teeth,
became a *human being* –
the oldest of the human race.

And like that oldest man
am I:
black, like that tusk,
and shining like a rainbow.

Elephants at Night
A Hunter's Song

Elephants at night, like heavy spirits
walking along in single file
to bathe in the river
are not elephants,
they're simply wearing masks.
I, the hunter of the night,
I, who have seen stars

פֿאַרוואַנדלען זיך אין אַנטילאָפּן –
האָב אַ מאָל בײַם וואַסער
נאָכגעלויערט, צווישן גראָז, אויף זיבן
לעבנדיקע העלפֿאַנדן
וואָס ציִען זיך צום ברעג.

יעדער האָט אַ ווייַל באַטראַכט דעם טייַך
צי קיינער זעט ניט,
און אויסגעטאָן די העלפֿאַנדישע מאַסקע.
אויסגעטאָן די אויערן, די ציין, די לאַנגע נעזער –
און ס׳האָבן זיך אַנטפּלעקט פֿאַר מייַנע אויגן
זיבן מיידלעך.
זיבן מיידלעך שנייַדן אויף דאָס וואַסער מיט די בריסט,
בייגן זיך ווי רייצנדיקע שטראַלן,
שווימען, שווימען.

כ׳האָב געוווּסט: זיי וועלן באַלד צוריקשווימען, און אָנטאָן
די אויערן, די נעזער – ווערן העלפֿאַנדן אויף ס׳נייַ.
און שטילער פֿון אַ שלאַנג בין איך דערקראָכן צו די מאַסקעס,
מיטגענומען איינע און באַהאַלטן זיך צוריק.
און ווען די זיבן מיידלעך, אין אַ הילעניש פֿון פֿערל,
האָבן זיך גענומען אָנטאָן אין די העלפֿאַנדקליידער –
האָט פֿאַר איינער אויסגעפֿעלט אַ מאַסקע, און פֿאַרבליבן
איז זי נאַקעט אויף אַ שטיין, מיט ציטעריקער הויט,
אָן אַ פֿרייַנד, אָן צערטלעניש, אָן לאַסקע.

און איך, דער יעגער,
האָב חתונה געהאַט מיט איר – אַ מיידל אָן אַ מאַסקע.

בית־עולם פֿון העלפֿאַנדן

ווי שיף־סקעלעטן אויפֿן דעק פֿון ים –
ליגן דאָ די העלפֿאַנדן מיט ברייט צעפֿראַלטע בייַכער,
אין וועלכע די לבֿנה קומט געבוירן אירע קינדער...

די שוואַרצע פֿעלדזן אַרום זיי – מצבֿות
מיט עפּיטאַפֿן זילבערנע, אין קלוגן העלפֿאַנד־לשון.

change into antelopes,
once lay in wait beside the water,
in the grass, to spy on seven
moonlit elephants
walking to the river bank.

Each one gazed upon the river for a while
to make sure no one saw,
then they took off their elephant disguise.
Took off their ears, their teeth, their long, long trunks –
and before my eyes appeared
seven girls.
Seven girls cleave the water with their breasts,
bending like charming rays of light,
swimming, swimming.

I knew that they would soon swim back, and put on
their ears, trunks – and turn into elephants again.
And so, more silent than a snake, I crept up to the masks,
snatched one and hid again.
And when the seven girls, all covered in a spray of pearls,
started putting on their elephant clothes again –
one lacked a mask, and sat there,
naked, trembling, on a stone,
without a friend, or tenderness, or a caress.

And I, the hunter,
married her – a girl without a mask.

The Elephants' Graveyard

Like ship skeletons on the bottom of the sea,
the elephants lie, with bellies split wide open,
where the moon comes to bear her children.

The black cliffs that surround them are tombstones
with silver epitaphs, in wise elephant language.

קיינער ברענגט זיי ניט אַהער. זיי שפּאַנען
אײַנציגװײַז דורך װײנענדיקע װעלדער
חדשים, יאָרן, װען עס קומט די צײַט פֿון זײער שטאַרבן.

אָט אָ שפּאַנט אַ העלפֿאַנד.
זײַנע פֿיס – פֿיר דומפּע דונערן –
פּױקן אױס דעם שטױב פֿון זײַנע יאָרן די צעקנײַטשטע.

נאָר אױפֿן רוקן רײַט שױן די געשטרײַפֿלטע היענע.
און װען ער װעט זיך אױסקלײַבן בשלום זײַן געלעגער –
װעט זי אים די אײגעלעך די קינדערשע פֿאַרצוקן,
און ס׳װעלן אים אַראָפֿזױגן דעם העלפֿאַנדבײן –
די זעגער.

דימענט־מײדל

ערגעץ אין דער טיפֿעניש פֿון קימבערלי,
אין קראַטערס,
און װוּ נאָר ס׳בליצט די מאַמע־ערד
מיט כּישופֿדיקן צוזאָג –
טאַנצט אַ דימענט־מײדל הינטער פֿענצטער פֿון איר פֿאַלאַץ.

טאָג און נאַכט, װי דאָרשטיקע טערמיטן,
צִיִען זיך צו איר פֿאַרליבטע מענער,
בלאָנדזשען צו איר שמײכל רױט צעפֿלאַקערטע פֿון תּאװה,
זעצן מיט די האַמערס אין איר פֿאַלאַץ,
טוען תּפֿילה:

דימענט־מײדל,
יונגינקע לבֿנה אין דער ערד,
לאָז קושן דײַנע פֿיס
די מידע שקלאַפֿן.
עס װאַקלען זיך די טױערן צו דיר פֿון שװערן האַמער
און דײַן פֿאַרליבטער איז שױן טױט פֿון ליבע.

נאָר די װאָס טוען תּפֿילה מיט די שװײס־באַדעקטע האַמערס –
פֿאַלן מיט געפּלאַצטע הערצער
בײַ די שװאַרצע טױערן.

No one brings them here. They walk
in single file through weeping woods
for months, for years, when the time comes for them to die.

Just now an elephant is walking.
His feet – four muffled thunderclaps –
drum out the dust of all his wrinkled years.

But already on his back the striped hyena rides.
And when he has calmly chosen the place where he will lie –
it will devour his childlike eyes,
and men with saws will plunder
his ivory tusks.

Diamond Girl

Somewhere in the depths of Kimberley,
in craters,
wherever mother earth is flashing
with enchanting promise –
dances a diamond girl behind the windows of her palace.

Day and night, like thirsty termites
besotted lovers journey to her,
wander to her smile, inflamed with fiery lust,
attack her palace with their hammers,
praying:

> Diamond girl,
> lovely young moon that's buried in the earth,
> let your weary slaves
> now kiss your feet.
> Your gates are shaking from our mighty hammer blows,
> and your beloved has already died of love.

But they who pray with hammers drenched in sweat –
fall down, their hearts burst open,
by the black gates.

און זי טאַנצט ווײַטער
מאַניעט אַ געפֿאַנגענע אין היכל.

טאָג און נאַכט, ווי דאָרשטיקע טערמיטן,
ציִען זיך פֿאַרליבטע צו איר שמייכל.

דאָס זעלבסטמאָרדליד פֿון די הערעראָס

דעם רעגן־בויגן גייט ניט אָן. זײַן פֿיל־קאָלירטע שווערד
פֿאַרהאַלט דעם רעגן. זאָגט אים: בלײַב אין הימל.
און מיר באַגייען זעלבסטמאָרד אין די קנייטשן פֿון דער ערד,
עס אײַלט שוין די היִענע גרין ווי שימל.

דעם רעגן־בויגן גייט ניט אָן.

די ביקסן־טרעגער מיט די ווײַסע שקלאָפֿערישע הינט
פֿאַרנאַראַן אונדז אין גאָלדמינעס מיט אַלע סאָרטן דרײַדלעך.
דעם רעגן־בויגן גייט ניט אָן, אַז אונדזער בלוט צערינט,
און אַז עס קוילען זיך אַליין די מיידלעך.

דעם רעגן־בויגן גייט ניט אָן.

אַ, פֿויגל אינסינגיזי, וואָס ביסט קלענער פֿון אַ צאָן,
דערצייל פֿון אונדזער זעלבסטמאָרד אין דײַן קיניגרײַך די געטער.
דעם רעגן־בויגן גייט ניט אָן. גייט שוידערלעך ניט אָן.
דערלויבן וועט ער גיין דעם רעגן – שפעטער.

דעם רעגן־בויגן גייט ניט אָן.

צו אַ טיגער

מיר האָבן פלוצעם זיך דערזען. די צײַט איז ניט געוואָרן.
האָסט באַוואַכט דעם טויער פֿון גן־עדן.
איבער דיר צוויי וואַסערפֿאַלן –
שטראָמענדיקע פֿליגל.

She dances on,
seductive, a prisoner in her temple.

Day and night, like thirsty termites
besotted lovers journey to her smile.

Suicide Song of the Hereros

The rainbow does not care. Its many-coloured sword
holds back the rain. Commands it: stay in heaven.
And we commit suicide in the deep folds of the earth,
while swiftly, the hyena – green as mould – approaches.

The rainbow does not care.

The gunmen with their slavish white dogs lure us
into goldmines by all kinds of evil tricks.
The rainbow does not care, though we are bleeding,
though young girls kill themselves.

The rainbow does not care.

Oh insingizi bird, even smaller than a tooth,
tell the gods in your kingdom how we died.
The rainbow does not care. Horribly – does not care.
It will allow the rain to fall – but later.

The rainbow does not care.

To a Tiger

Suddenly we saw each other. Time disappeared.
You were guarding the gates of Paradise.
Above you, two waterfalls –
cascading wings.

ברודער! האָסט מײַן בליק פֿון שווערן בלײַ
צעשמאָלצן אין דײַן פֿײַערדיקער מילדקייט.
פֿחדנות האָט מיר אָפּגעטאָן אַ שפּיצל, –
ניט דערלאָזן דײַנע ליפֿן זאָלן מיך פֿאַרזוכן.

אָנשטאָט צו ליגן נאַריש אין דער ערד –
וואָלט מײַן בלוט געריזלט אין אַ טיגער!

צו שפּעט. איך בין פֿון דיר דערווײַטערט
צען טויזנט מײַל.
צוריק צום וואָרט דעם אויסטערליש ניט־זאָטן.

און כאַטש מיר זענען ביידע פֿרײַ – גייען מיר אין קראַטן.

עלזע לאַסקער־שילער

געבויגענע ווײַנען די אייזלען אין ירושלים,
ניטאָ מער די הייליקע זקנה, די זינגערין עלזע.
ניטאָ ווער ס׳זאָל קאָרמען די אייזלען מיט בליציקן צוקער
און העלפֿן זיי שלעפֿן די ווונדיקע שטיינער פֿון קאַסטעל;
די שטיינער, וואָס פֿאַלן אַראָפּ מיט אַן „אויַ" פֿון די הערצער
בײַ אַלע וואָס קומען אין לאַנד – אַ מאָמענטעק מיט שטיינער! –
צו בויען אַ היים פֿאַרן היימלאָזן מלך משיח.

אַ מאָל האָט פֿון באַרג זיך אַראָנטערגעקוליעט אַן אייזל,
פֿאַרלאָרן אַ פֿאַדערשטן צאָן. האָט די זקנה צעשמאָלצן
איר חתונה־רינג בײַ דעם גאָלדשמיד ר׳ ניסים פֿון אַלטשטאַט,
און ס׳האָט שוין דער אייזל אַ גאָלדענעם צאָן אַ מתנה.

און ווער האָט באַנומען ווי זי דאָס געוויין פֿון באַשעפֿער? –
שוין אַלצדינג באַשאַפֿן! די אייביקייט איז אים שוין אייביק
אַ קייט אויפֿן האַלדז, און קיין צווייטער איז מער ניט בנימצא...
זי שפּילט אין האָטעל אויף איר בלויען קלאַוויר זײַן דערמאָנונג,
ווען ער איז געוועזן דער מײַסטער פֿון טריילערס און לייבן,
געשריבן מיט אַ גרימער בײַמער זײַן פֿרישע גן־עדן־פֿאָעמע,
אַ ווײַבלעכן גראָם פֿון אַ מענערשן ריפּ אויסגעקנאָטן.

Brother! My heavy leaden gaze
you melted in your fiery mildness.
Cowardice played a trick on me –
did not allow your lips to taste me.

Instead of lying, dumb and useless, in the earth –
my blood could have been flowing through a tiger's veins!

Too late. I went away from you
ten thousand miles.
Back to the word that's weirdly never satisfied.

And though we both are free – yet both of us are circled round with bars.

Else Lasker-Schüler

Donkeys, bowed down with grief, are weeping now in Jerusalem,
Else the singer, that saintly old lady, is dead.
Now there's no one to feed them with crystals of sparkling sugar,
and help them to carry the wounded stones of the Kastel,
the same stones that roll with an "oy" from the hearts
of all who enter the land – How many thousands of stones! –
to build for the King, for the homeless Messiah, a home.

One of the donkeys once stumbled and fell down the hillside,
and lost a front tooth. Straightaway the old lady
had her wedding ring melted by Nisim the Old City goldsmith,
and the donkey received as a present a new golden tooth.

And who heard as she did the weeping of God the Creator? –
For He has already created all things! And eternity seems to Him now
like a chain round His neck for eternity. And no one exists
                                        any more but Himself...
But in her hotel room, on her blue piano, she plays His memory,
how He once was the Master of larks and of lions,
how He once wrote with trees his brand-new Paradise poem,
and sculpted a feminine rhyme from a masculine rib.

עס גוסטן רויק ביים שפילן די אשיקע פֿינגער.
זי טאָר נאָך ניט שטאַרבן! אַ יונגע, פֿאַרליבטע מוראַשקע,
ביז בלוט אַ צעביסענע, האָט אין איר צימער פֿאַרבלאָנדזשעט
און שפּילט מיט דער זקנה באַנאַנד אויף די אַלטע קלאַװװישן.

זי טאָר נאָך ניט שטאַרבן! געפֿאַלן אין גאָרטן אַ זונרויז –
אַ װעלט איז געפֿאַלן! די קערנער – גאָלדהױטיקע מענטשן.
מען װעט זיי פֿאַרקויפֿן אין מאַרק, און זיי שינדן די הױטן...
און אויסלײזן דאַרף זי די קנעכט – די גאָלדהױטיקע מענטשן.

זי טאָר נאָך ניט שטאַרבן! אין ים זענען קװאַליעס געבױרן.
זיי קאָנען ניט רײדן. זיי מאָנען מיט קינדערשע הענטלעך!
ס׳געבעט פֿאַר די זױגלינגען־קװאַליעס מוז װערן דערזונגען,
דער שטורעם זאָל היַנט ניט פֿאַרשלינגען די ראָזע נשמות.

אַװװ איז דער אָנהײב פֿון הימל? – אין ירושלים.
אַצינד איז איר די זקנה אַ שטערן און שװעבט איבער מױערן.
אַ בלויער קלאַװװיר איז די שטאָט. אַ פֿאַרשלייערטע כּלה.
איך שפּאַן אויפֿן שטיינערנעם טעפּעך צוזאַמען מיט עלזען,
פֿאַרשיכּורט פֿון בלויען קלאַװװיר און צעשניטן פֿון העלזען.

ירושלים
27סטן פֿעברואַר
1957

פּרץ מאַרקיש

מיר האָבן ביידע זיך געזעגנט
ביַי פּושקינס דענקמאָל, ביַי די טרעפּ;
און מאָסקװע האָט צו לאַנג באַרעגנט
מיט רויטע שטערן אונדז די קעפּ.
און װי מיר נעמען זיך פֿונאַנדער
און ליפֿן צוקן: זיַי געזונט! –
האָסטו דערזען װי אַלעקסאַנדער
פֿאַרשטעלט אין בראָנדז אַ הייסע װוּנד.

Peacefully, while she is playing, her ashen fingers are fading.
She must not die yet! A young, lovesick ant, its heart pierced and bleeding,
has wandered by accident into her chamber, and with the old lady
it plays a duet on the ancient piano keys.

She must not die yet! A sunflower's collapsed in the garden –
A world has collapsed! The seeds – they are golden-skinned humans.
They'll be sold in the market. They will be skinned…
She must save the slaves – these golden-skinned humans.

She must not die yet! Little waves have been born in the sea.
They are still unable to speak. They plead with their small children's hands!
The prayer for the tiny wave babies must be sung loudly
so that the storm will not swallow these rosy young souls.

Where is the beginning of Heaven? – it is here in Jerusalem.
The old lady now is a star floating over the walls.
The city – a blue piano. A bride with a veil.
I stride on the carpet of stone together with Else
drunk with the blue piano, and pierced by my visions.

Jerusalem
February 27
1957

Perets Markish

We met once more to say goodbye
at Pushkin's monument, beside the steps;
and Moscow had rained down red stars
too long, too long, upon our heads.
And as we parted from each other
with trembling lips: be well my friend! –
you looked and saw how Alexander
concealed in bronze a burning wound.

און נאָר אַ מאָל דיין האַנט אין מיינער
און דיינע אויגן גרוי פֿון גרויל.
– איך וויל ניט ווערן אַ ציגיינער –
האָסטו געזאָגט מיט קרומען מויל.
פֿאָעט! אין אייביקייט דיין וואָנדער,
וווּ ס׳גיט זיך אונדזער שטויב אַ צונד!...
און איבער דיר האָט אַלעקסאַנדער
פֿאַרשטעלט אין בראָנדז אַ הייסע ווּנד.

איך האָב געזאָגט: אַ שוואַרצע חופה,
פֿון טויט געשפּונען, איז מיין שטאָט.
מיר זענען טעקסטן צו דיין „קופּע"
און אויסדערוויילט צום עשאַפֿאָט.
אַוודאי איז דער שניי מיר אייגן
און קיין מאָל וועט ער ניט צעגיין...
נאָר מיר צוקאָפֿנס וויל איך לייגן
אַ ייִדישן, אַ ווייכן שטיין.

עס האָבן פּלוצעם די טרומייטן
זיך אויסגעלאָשן אויפֿן סקווער.
און כ׳האָב דערזען דיין טרער אין קייטן,
ווען ס׳איז אַוועק אַהיים דיין טרער. –
וווּ ביסטו, חבֿר? – זינג דעם אמת!
פֿון קבֿר זינג מיט פֿרייען מויל:
איך האָב דיר, לאַנד, געשאַלט פֿאַמעמעס
און האָסט צוריקגעשאַלט אַ קויל.

1956

פֿאָעזיע

אַ טונקל-פֿיאָלעטע פֿלוים
די לעצטע אויפֿן בוים,
דיין-הייטלדיק און צאַרט ווי אַ שוואַרצאַפּל,
וואָס האָט ביי יאַ נאַכט אין טוי געלאָשן
ליבע, זעונג, צאַפּל,

One last time your hand in mine,
but grey with terror were your eyes.
"I will not be a homeless wanderer" –
Your mouth was twisted as you spoke.
Poet! Eternally you wander,
everywhere our dust flares into life!
And above you, Alexander
concealed in bronze a burning wound.

I said to you: my town is now a *khupe*,
woven by death itself in cloth of black.
We are the text to your great poem "Di kupe",
the scaffold is our destined fate.
It's true, the snow is still my own,
and never will it melt away,
yet at my head I yearn to lay
a soft and kindly Jewish stone.

As we stood, the trumpets suddenly
fell silent on that mighty square.
And I saw your tear, in chains,
as your eyes turned towards your home – –
Where are you, friend? – sing out the truth!
Sing with a mouth that now is free:
I sent forth poems to you, my country,
a bullet you sent back to me.

1956

Poetry

A ripe, dark purple plum
the last one on the tree,
thin-skinned and tender as the pupil of an eye,
which has by night extinguished in the dew
love, vision, trembling,

און מיטן מאָרגן־שטערן איז דער טוי
געוואָרן גרינגער –
דאָס איז פֿאָעזיע. ריר זי אָן אַזוי
מען זאָל ניט זען קיין סימן פֿון די פֿינגער.

1954

אויסדערוויילטער בוים

ווען סטראַדיוואַריוס האָט דערפֿילט: באַשערט איז אים צו שניצן
די לעצטע פֿידל – איז ער אין אַ שטורעמנאַכט, אַ גרויער
אַוועק אין וואַלד, געבויגן אויף אַ שטעקן.
ווי ברענענדיקע סמיטשיקעס באַפֿאַלן אים די בליצן.
ער קניט פֿאַר יעדן בוים, לייגט צו זיין אָטעמדיקן אויער:
אָ, וועלכער אויסדערוויילטער בוים אַצינד וועט אים אַנטפֿלעקן
די גרויסע הערונג, אַז פֿון זיין געהילץ די לעצטע פֿידל
זאָל שניצן סטראַדיוואַריוס ערבֿ גסיסה?
עס וויינט אין אים דער צער פֿון מינדסטן זאַמען־קלאַנג. צער־גידול־
מוזיק, ווי ער אַליין וואָלט פֿון אַ תּפֿיסה
באַפֿרײַט זיין טויט באַנאַנד מיט ריינסטע קלאַנגען.
מחילה בעט ער בײַ די שאַטנס, וואָס ער האָט גזלניש
אַראָפּגעזוגגט די קעפּ, כדי צו פֿאַנגען
דעם נאַכטיגאַל, ער זאָל אַרײַן אין פֿידל און סימפֿאָניש
מגלה זיין דעם טרויער פֿון אַ בוים נאָך ערשטן רעגן,
בשעת אַנטלויפֿן קאָן ער ניט ווען אים באַפֿאַלן זעגן...

מיט אײַזערנער און קאַלטער הענטשקע וואַרפֿט אים אום דער שטורעם.
אַ וואָלקן שטײַט צוקאָפֿנס מיט אַ רידל.
און סטראַדיוואַריוס קוים
ער שעפּטשעט: אויסדערוויילטער בוים,
צעזוג מײַן גוף – דעם וויינענדיקן פֿורעם,
און שניץ פֿון מיר, און מיט מײַן בלוט באַמאָל – די לעצטע פֿידל.

and with the morning star, the dew
grew lighter, did not linger –
that is poetry. Touch it so gently
that not a trace remains there of your finger.

1954

The Chosen Tree

When Stradivarius sensed the appointed time had come
to carve his final violin – he went, one grey and stormy night,
into the forest, leaning on his stick.
Like burning violin bows the lightning strikes him down.
He kneels and presses to each tree his breathing ear:
O, which chosen tree will now reveal its resonance,
that Stradivarius from its wood may carve
the final violin, before he dies?
Within him weeps the sadness of the tiniest seed of sound.
Music fathered in pain, as if he, from a prison
had freed his death, together with the purest sounds.
He asks forgiveness of the shadows for murderously
hacking off their heads to catch the nightingale,
that it should fly into his violin, revealing through its music
the sadness of a tree after the early rain,
that cannot flee away when saws attack it…

With a cold iron glove the storm fells Stradivarius.
Holding a spade, a cloud stands at his head.
And with his last breath, Stradivarius whispers: "Chosen tree,
saw up my body – that weeping form,
and carve from me, paint with my blood – the final violin."

Dedication to the present writer on a copy of the book *Di fidlroyz* (The Fiddle Rose), 1985

1962 – 1972

דער קוש

דער ווונדער איז געשען אזוי נאטירלעך:
אראפגעלאזט זיך האט א דיכטער אין א ים – נאך פערל,
וואס ציטערן און בענקען אומבאריירלעך.
און קוים האט ער א קוש געטאן א פערל,
זענען אים פארשווונדן זיינע גלידער.
ניטא מער ס׳פנים זיינס.
ניטא קיין טרערן.
דער דיכטער איז אריין אין זיינע לידער.

דריטע שטילקייט

צוויי שאלן זע איך זע אנטקעגן מיר אנטקעגן:
אויף איינער שטילקייט פֿונעם ים. אויף צווייטער –
די מידבר־שטילקייט. עמעץ דארף זיי וועגן.
און זייער אורגעוויין איז מיין באגלייטער.

דאס צינגל ציט אהער – אהין. דערווייל ניט
באשטימט נאך סאראַ שטילקייט ציט ארונטער.
אנטלויף ניט, האַרץ מיינס, בלייב א רגע. אייל ניט.
פֿאראן א דריטע שטילקייט, הער זיך אונטער:

זי האט געבוירן ס׳לעבן. איז אומשטערבלעך,
ניטא א זאמד ווו ניט פֿארזייט איר זאמען.
די שערבל־יעגערס קושן אירע שערבלעך,
מע רופֿט זי טויט, נאר אנדערש איז איר נאמען.

ביי נאכט, ווען שאַרפֿער זילבערן די שאלן
מיט ים־ און מידבר־שטילקייט בלוי צעגליטע,
דאס צינגל דרימלט איין אן קלאַנג, אן קול – און
די דריטע שטילקייט רעדט פֿון שלאָף. די דריטע.

The Kiss

The miracle occurred so naturally:
a poet dived into a sea to hunt for pearls
that tremble there, and yearn, untouchable.
No sooner had he kissed a pearl
than his limbs disappeared.
His face had gone.
There were no more tears.
The poet had been transformed into his words.

The Third Silence

Two pans hang before me on these scales:
on one the silence of the sea. And on the other
the desert's silence. Someone must weigh them.
Their ancient weeping is my true companion.

The pointer wavers to and fro. It's not yet clear
which silence is the heavier.
Don't flee, my heart. Just wait a little while.
A third silence exists. O, listen carefully:

It gave birth to life. It is immortal.
There is no grain of sand without its seed.
The fragment hunters kiss its fragments,
and though men call it death, it has a different name.

At night, the scale pans gleam with silvery light,
glowing blue with sea and desert silence,
the pointer falls asleep, without a voice or sound –
and that third silence speaks out from its slumber.

*

דאָס אויג פֿון דער נשמה וויינט מיט בילדער,
פֿאַר זיך אַליין ווי פֿאַר אַ צוווייטן,
פֿאַר אַ צוווייטן ווי פֿאַר זיך אַליין.
דאָס אויג פֿון דער נשמה וויינט מיט בילדער,
ווי זונפֿאַרגאַנג מיט וואָלקנס:
ווו און וועמען זיך פֿאַרטרויען?

איך האָב פֿאַרברענט מײַן שרײַבטיש. אַ בזיון
צו בײַגן זיך פֿאַר האַלץ, און אים פֿאַרביטן אויף אַ ווילדער
געראַנגל־נאַכט אין מידבר, בײַ אַן אָדלער אין געצעלט,
ווו ס׳אויג פֿון דער נשמה וויינט מיט בילדער
ערשטמאָליקע, וואָס מאָנען: שילדער, שילדער
פֿאַר זיך אַליין, ווי פֿאַר אַ צוווייטער וועלט.

1968

באַאַחרית־הימים

אַ טיגער מיט אַלף־בית־פֿלעקן, אַ נאָכטיגאַל איבער אַ קראָטער,
דאָס מענטשלעכע וואָרט וועלן הערן פֿון קעלער, פֿון בוידעם.
אויף אַקסלען פֿון שטיין וועלן אָנוואָקסן פֿליגל און לאַכן אין זוניקן פֿלאַטער,
אַ שטערן וועט אָפֿרײַסן זיך פֿון דער נאַכט און אַ פֿאַל טאָן, צו אָנקומען קודם.

פֿאַרזונקענער שאַרבן אין ים. אַן אַכסניא פֿאַר פּערל. דערלאַנגען
וועט עמעץ אַ הייב מיט די פּערל צוזאַמען פֿון תהום אים.
און ברענגען דעם שאַרבן צו קעלער און בוידעם, צו מענטשלעכע ווערטער און קלאַנגען:
אַזוי וועט געשען מיט דער דיכטונג באַאַחרית־הימים.

1969

*

The eye of the soul weeps pictures,
for itself and for another,
for another and for itself.
The eye of the soul weeps pictures,
like sunset with clouds:
where and whom to trust?

I have burned my writing desk. What an indignity
to bow down to wood. I have replaced it with a tempestuous night
of struggle in the desert, in an eagle's tent,
where the eye of the soul weeps pictures,
unparalleled. And they demand: depict, depict
for yourself, and for another world.

1968

In the Last Days

A tiger with alphabet patches, a nightingale over a crater,
will hear the human word from attic and cellar.
Wings will grow on shoulders of stone. They will laugh as they fly in the sunlight.
A star will tear itself off from the night and plunge, to arrive there before them.

A skull that is sunk in the sea, an inn for pearls. And someone
will reach down and bring it up out of the depths, and the pearls within it,
and will carry the skull into attic and cellar, to human words and sounds:
thus it will happen with poetry, in the last days.

1969

די פֿידלרויז

פֿון תחית־המתימדיק װאַרעמען רעגן
פֿאַװאָלינקע נעמט זיך צעבליִען, באַװעגן
(בײַנאַנד מיט דער קינדהײט אין אַלטן זכּרון)
די פֿידלרויז אינעם שוואַרצערדיקן אָרון.

די פֿידלרויז דאַרף שוין אַצינד ניט קיין פֿידלער,
ניטאָ מער קיין לויבער, ניטאָ מער קיין זידלער.
זי שפּילט אָן אַ שפּילער מיט פֿרייד און אמונה
לכּבֿוד אַ װידערגעבױרענער סטרונע.

לכּבֿוד אַ סטרונע, לכּבֿוד איר ציטער,
לכּבֿוד אַ בין װאָס איר האָניק איז ביטער
נאָר זיס איז איר שטאָך, אַזױ זאַפֿטיק און קװײטיק –
לכּבֿוד אַ װידערגעבױרענעם װײטיק.

The Fiddle Rose

Brought to life by the rain, resurrectively warm,
she cautiously, slowly begins now to blossom, to move
(together with childhood in ancient remembrance)
the fiddle rose inside her black earthen tomb.

The fiddle rose now has no need of a fiddler,
there is no one who praises her, no one who scorns.
She plays by herself, with faith and with joy,
to honor a string that has just been reborn.

To honor a string, and its gentle vibration,
to honor a bee whose honey is bitter
though sweet is its succulent, blossomy sting –
to honor a pain that has just been reborn.

ההסתדרות הכללית של העובדים בארץ־ישראל

גאָלדענע קייט

רבעון לספרות ולבעיות חברתיות
פערטליאָר־שריפֿט פֿאַר ליטעראַטור
און געזעלשאַפֿטלעכע פּראָבלעמען

DI GOLDENE KEYT, Quarterly Periodical for Literature and Social Problems
Tel-Aviv, Rechov Weizman 30, Israel, Tel. 268846

תל־אביב: 4 יאַנואַר 1974
רח' ויצמן 30, טל. 268846

טײַערער מלך ראַוויטש

אַ דאַנק, אַ דאַנק. פֿון די דרײַ
לידער וואָס איר האָט געשיקט
האָב איך אויסגעקליבן... אַלע
דרײַ. דאָס זענען דרײַ
גרויסע לידער, גרויס
אין זייער טיפֿקייט און
פּשטות. דער טרויער
ווערט דאָ סובלימירט
אין געגײַסטיקטער פּאָעטישער
פֿרייד.

מיט ליבשאַפֿט און [illegible]
אײַער

Letter to Meylekh Ravitsh, January 4th 1974, NLI, ARC 4°1540

1974–1984

*

די רויטע ציגל פֿון דיַין ליַיב – געדענקסט ניט זייער בנין,
געדענקסט ניט מער דיַין גאַס און ביַים לאַמטערן־שיַין דעם נומער.
אַ וואָלקן איז געבליבן אין אַ פֿאָרעמען זיך, ליניען,
געבליבן איז אַ געלער בלאַט אין אָנדענק פֿון אַ זומער.

געדענקסט ניט מער דעם יונגן פֿנים פֿונעם ערשטן רעגן,
דעם אַדרעס פֿון דיַין טויב און איר קעמיע אינעם שנעבל.
די לאַנקע, וווּ איר זענט צוזאַמען זאַלבע איינס געלעגן
צעפֿרעסן איז אַצינד פֿון פֿער און פֿון שוועבל.

געדענקסט ניט מער דיַין טאַטע־מאַמע. ווער האָט דיך געבוירן?
דער זעלבער אַש פֿון פֿיַיער און זיַין קרבן, וויַיסט ניט וועמעס.
נאָר אינעווייניק וויַיסטו יאָ: עס הערט ניט אויף צו יוירן
דאָס טונקלסטע און קלאָרסטע וואָרט פֿון אַלע ווערטער: אמת.

נאָר אינעווייניק וויַיסטו יאָ: דער פֿינקלענדיקער עיקר
איז דימענטיקער ווי געוועזן און קאַנסט מיט אים צעשניַידן
די שאָטנוועלט, אַז פֿידלען זאָלן שפּילן פֿון די שטיקער
און לינדערן אין דיר אַ צווייטנס ליַידן.

1974

*

באַשעפֿעגישן אויפֿן גרונט פֿון ים, אַן זון, אַן שטראַלן,
שפּאַצירנדיקע צמחים אין אַ יענוועלטיקער לאַנדשאַפֿט,
געבוירט פֿון טויט און לעבן, בבֿל־טורעמס פֿון קאָראַלן,
קאָפֿריזן געטלעבקע, שוין צייַט מיר זאָלן שליסן קאַנטשאַפֿט.

שוין צייַט אַרויסאייַלן פֿון צירק מיט זייַנע ליצים, הוידעס,
אַהין ווו עס געוועלטיקט נאָך דער פֿערל אין זייַן גלאַריע.
שוין צייַט אַרויסצוקניַיפֿן פֿון דער פֿינצטערניש די סודות
ווו ס'קלאַפֿן הערצעלעך פֿון שלים אין ימס לאַבאַראַטאָריע.

שוין צייַט צו טרינקען וויַין מיט לאַנג־דערטרונקענע מאַטראָסן
אין וואַסער־קרעטשמע אויפֿן דעק פֿון ים, אין אַ קאַיוטע
און הערן זיי דערצייַלן פֿון פֿיראַטן, אַלבאַטראָסן
און ליבעס פֿון פֿאַר טויזנט יאָר, און אַלץ נאָך ניט־באַרוטע.

*

The red bricks of your body – you've forgotten how they're built,
forgotten where your street is, and the number in the lamplight.
Only a cloud remains, taking shape, then fading,
a yellow leaf remains as a memento of a summer.

You've forgotten the young face of the first rain,
the address of your own dove, the amulet in its beak.
The meadow where you two lay joined as one
has now been gobbled up by pitch and sulphur.

You've forgotten father, mother. Who gave birth to you?
The fire and its victim – ash: you don't know which is which.
But deep within, you do know: the darkest and yet brightest
word of all words is still fermenting: truth.

But deep within, you do know: the glittering essence
is more diamond-sharp than ever, and with it you can slice
the world of shadows, so that fiddles play out from its shards,
soothing in you the sufferings of another.

1974

*

Creatures on the seabed, deprived of light and sunshine,
ambulating plants in an other-worldly landscape,
birthplace of death and life, coral Towers of Babel,
divine caprices, now it's time for us to get acquainted.

Time to hurry from the circus with its swings and clowns,
to where the pearl still reigns in all its glory.
Time to prize the secrets from the darkness,
where hearts of slime are beating in the sea's laboratory.

Time to drink wine with sailors drowned long, long ago,
to sit in the cabin of their sea bed inn,
and hear them tell of pirates, albatrosses, and lost loves
not yet at peace, although a thousand years have gone.

באַפֿרייען וויל זיך יעדער קלאַנג פֿון מעש און האַלץ און סטרונע,
געפֿאַנגען איז דאָס מענטשן-לשון הינטער שווערע שטייגן.
שוין ציִט זיך אײַנצוהערן און דערזען דורך אַ שפּאַרונע
ווי שטומע שטילקייט לערנט זיך דעם אַלף-בית פֿון שווײַגן.

1974

*

ווער וועט בלײַבן, וואָס וועט בלײַבן? בלײַבן וועט אַ ווינט,
בלײַבן וועט די בלינדקייט פֿונעם בלינדן וואָס פֿאַרשווינדט.
בלײַבן וועט אַ סימן פֿונעם ים: אַ שנירל שוים,
בלײַבן וועט אַ וואָלקנדל פֿאַרטשעפּעט אויף אַ בוים.

ווער וועט בלײַבן, וואָס וועט בלײַבן? בלײַבן וועט אַ טראַף,
בראשיתדיק אַרויסצוגראָזן ווידער זיין באַשאַף.
בלײַבן וועט אַ פֿידלרויז לכבֿוד זיך אַליין,
זיבן גראָזן פֿון די גראָזן וועלן זי פֿאַרשטיין.

מער פֿון אַלע שטערן אַזש פֿון צפֿון ביז אַהער,
בלײַבן וועט דער שטערן וואָס ער פֿאַלט אין סאַמע טרער.
שטענדיק וועט אַ טראָפּן וויין אויך בלײַבן אין זיין קרוג.
ווער וועט בלײַבן, גאָט וועט בלײַבן, איז דיר ניט גענוג?

1974

*

פֿון ביכער-טאָוולען צוויי און צוויי, געאַרעמט און געווינקלט,
כ'האָב אייגנהאַנטיק, אייגנהאַרציק אויסגעבויט אַ קאַמער
פֿון אומבאַקאַנטע ווערטער, קוים באַלויכטן און באַשפּרינקלט,
און אויסער דעם רשות פֿון טויזנטאויגיקן פֿאַרסמער.

אַ קרעטשמעלע אין ווילדן וואַלד... פֿון זיך אַליין באַהאַלטן,
באַהאַלטן אויך פֿון מעשענעם אָרקעסטער אין די בוינעס.
אַהער גענענען אײנציקווײַז די טײַערסטע געשטאַלטן,
פֿאַרלוירן אין דער אייביקייט, און זייערע זכרונות.

Each sound longs to free itself from brass and wood and string,
human language is imprisoned in strong cages.
It's time to listen carefully, and, spying through a crevice,
to see mute stillness learning the alphabet of silence.

1974

*

Who will remain, what will remain? A breath of wind will stay,
and the blindness of the blind man, even though he goes away.
A fleck of foam will stay as a reminder of the sea,
and a wisp of cloud, caught in the branches of a tree.

Who will remain, what will remain? A syllable remains,
to bring forth grasses in a new Creation once again.
A fiddle rose will still remain, alone and in command,
her nature only seven of those grasses understand.

Of all the stars spread out between the farthest north and here,
there will remain only the star that falls into a tear.
A drop of wine will always remain within its cup.
Who will remain? God will remain. Is that not enough?

1974

*

From right-angled book covers, two by two and arm in arm,
single-handed, single-hearted, I've built a little room
of unknown words. Dimly lit and speckled,
it's well-protected from the poisoner with a thousand eyes.

An inn in the wild forest... hidden even from itself,
hidden from the brass band of the slaughterhouses.
One by one my dearest people, lost in eternity,
lost in their memories, approach my inn.

פֿאַראַן אין וואַלד אַזעלכע ביימער וואָס געבוירן פֿייגל,
אַ רעגן איז פֿאַראַן מיט בריוו צו מתים אין דער נידער.
פֿאַראַן אַ בלום וואָס רייטלט זיך ווען עמעץ וואַרפֿט אַן אייגל
פֿון צווישן לופֿט־און־גראַז אויף אירע לייכט־אַנטבלויזטע גלידער.

זיי אַלע קומען אין מיין פֿיצל קרעטשמעלע און ברענגען
באַגלייטנדיקע בשמים פֿון אַ נאַכטיקן מהלך.
און ס'בלייבט נאָך אַלץ אַ פּוסטעניש פֿאַר ברייטן און פֿאַר לענגען
און ס'וועט זיך נאָך געפֿינען אַ געלעגער פֿאַר אַ מלאך.

1976–1975

*

די ליים פֿון ציַיַט איז וויַיך געוואָרן. ס'גייט שוין אויף די קנעטעניש
פֿון זונפֿאַרגאַנג נאָך זונפֿאַרגאַנג. עס ווערט שוין באַלד געשפּאַלטן
אַ זעמדעלע אין חלום צו צעטרייבערן אַ רעטעניש,
און בלויז די סאָווע פֿלאַנקעט פֿון אַ זילבערלעכן קאַלטן.

די מתים זענען לאַנג שוין אויפֿגעעשטאַנען! זענען האַסטיק
אַנטרונען דאָ פֿון יענער וועלט, פֿון הויקערדיקער משׂא
און מאַכן יאָגאַ, שפּילן שאַך און זענען פֿריַי און גאַסטיק,
באַלעגערן די אָפּערע און פּיקן אויס איר קאַסע.

געדענקט נאָך עמעץ ווער עס האָט צעריסן זייַנע גלידער?
צו וואָקלדיק און שוואַך די ציַין זאָל אַזוינס צעקיַיען.
די מתים האָבן ליב אַבסטראַקטע קונסט און קידער־ווידער,
אַנשטאַט אַ קין־צייכן טראָגט אַ הבֿל־צייכן קין.

און בלויז אַ בלינדער זעער ביזן אָפֿגרונט אַ צעשונדענער,
אַ קדמונדיקער נבֿיא וואָס איז קיין מאָל ניט געשטאָרבן
און קיינער וויים ניט: קיַיקלט ער דעם חושך, איז די זון דען ער? –
לויפֿט אויסליַיזן פֿון תהום צו תהום די שמייכלען פֿונעם קרבן.

1976–1975

In the forest there are trees that give birth to birds,
there is a rain that carries letters to the dead below.
There is a flower that blushes when someone dares to peep
at her half-uncovered body, between the air and grass.

They all come to my tiny inn and bring Havdala spices
from their nocturnal journeying. Yet inside there remains
an empty space, both long enough, and broad,
where an angel still may find a place to lay his head.

1975–1976

*

Time's clay has softened. And the dough of sunset after sunset
has already risen. Soon a sand grain in a dream
will split, and tear apart a puzzle,
and only the owl still wails alone from a silvery thicket.

The dead have long since risen! Hastily
they fled from the Other World, their humpbacked burden;
they're doing yoga, playing chess – they're sociable and free;
they besiege the opera and plunder all the tickets.

Does anyone remember who tore his limbs asunder?
Too wobbly and weak their teeth to chew on such a mouthful.
The dead love abstract art and hefty arguments;
instead of the mark of Cain, Cain bears the mark of Abel.

Only a blind seer, whipped into the abyss,
a prophet since the dawn of time, who has never died,
and no one knows: does he roll away the dark, is he the sun? –
runs through every chasm, to release the victims' smiles.

1975–1976

*

אַ שלאַנג אַן אומגעזעענע האָט סם אַ פֿולע דאָזע
אַרײַנגענאָדלט זיס אין מײַנע אָדערן לאַנגזאַמיק,
אַז איבער מיר די שטערן זאָל ניט שלײַפֿן מער שפּינאָזע
און תמיד זאָל אַ טראָפֿן גאַל זיך בלעזלען אין מײַן האָניק.

נאָר דעמאָלט האָט אַ קעגן־סם, אַן עליקסיר פֿון קלאַנגען,
אַ לאָז געטאָן זיך אינעווייניק צו באַהערשן יענעם,
אַז בעטלען זאָל דער שונא גנאָד בײַם ים געפֿאַנגען
און אױפֿהייבן די לאָפֿעס אונטערטעניק זאָל דאָס גיהנום.

פֿאַרלוירן צי געוווּנען? ס'איז געבליבן לזכּרון
אַ נעדעלע אין מיר; און ווען עס גיט אַ שטאָך, אַ גראַבל,
פֿאַרוואַנדלען זיך אין אוירן די אויסגעצאַנקטע יאָרן
און הערן פֿון אַן אײלבערטבלעטל דאָס געוויין פֿון מבול.

פֿאַרוואַנדלען וועל איך צײַט אין רוחניות, אָט איז מײַן אידעע!
פֿאַרוואַנדלען וועל איך טויט אין לעבן; איך, דער לאַנג פֿאַרלענדטער.
פֿאַרוואַנדלען וועל איך גראָזן אין אַ קאָסמישער אַלעע,
פֿאַרוואַנדלען וועל איך זיך אַליין, אין מענטש וואָס איז נעעטער.

1976–1975

*

דער פֿידלשפּילער שפּילט און ווערט אַלץ דינער, דין און דינער,
שוין דינער פֿונעם פֿידל־בויגן, דינער פֿון אַ סטרונע.
אַנשטאָט איר האָר, די פֿידל שפּילט אַליין אַלץ דינער, דינער,
און אויף אַ ווײַסן שײַטער ברענט איר האָר פֿאַר זײַן אמונה.

די פֿידל שפּילט אַצינד אַליין אַלץ דינער, דין און דינער,
דער פֿידלשפּילער קאָן איר קיין טרונק וואַסער ניט דערלאַנגען.
אַליין די קלאַנגען שפּילן און זיי שפּילן דינער, דינער,
ביז וואַנען אויפֿן שײַטער גליִען קלאַנגען, גליִען קלאַנגען.

עס גליִען קלאַנגען אויפֿן שײַטער, גליִען דין און דינער,
שוין שפּילט אַליין די פֿינצטערניש אָן פֿידל און אָן בויגן.
זי שפּילט אָן קלאַנגען און איר שפּילן – דינער, דינער, דינער,
ביז וואַנען מיר צעפֿינקלען זיך אין אירע שוואַרצע אויגן.

*

An unseen serpent long ago injected
into my veins a full dose of sweet poison,
so that Spinoza should no longer polish stars above me,
and a drop of gall should always bubble in my honey.

But suddenly an antidote, an elixir of sounds,
streamed into my body to defeat the other poison,
so that my enemy should plead for mercy when I hold him captive
and hell itself retract its claws, submitting to my will.

Have I lost or won? Inside me there's a needle
to act as a reminder. When it stabs and tears me
then all the vanished years change into ears,
which hear the weeping of the Flood in an olive leaf.

I shall change time into spirit – that is my idea!
I shall change death into life; I, the long-destroyed one.
I shall change grasses into a cosmic avenue,
I shall change myself into a person closer to my self.

1975–1976

*

The fiddler plays, becoming thinner, thinner, thinner,
now thinner than his fiddle bow, thinner than a string.
Without her master now the fiddle plays, alone. Her sounds grow thinner,
and on a white pyre, for his faith, her master burns.

Now the fiddle plays alone, her sounds grow thinner, thinner,
the fiddler cannot quench her thirst with water.
The sounds play on their own, becoming thinner, ever thinner,
until, upon the pyre, sounds are glowing, sounds are glowing.

Sounds glow on the pyre, becoming thinner, ever thinner,
till the darkness plays alone – with neither bow nor fiddle.
Playing soundlessly, its music – thinner, thinner, thinner,
till we start to sparkle in its deep black eyes.

אָ, פֿינצטערניש, פֿאַר וועמען שפּילסטו דינער, דין און דינער,
פֿאַר אונדז, די קליינע טרערן? איז באַשערט אונדז דײַנע גנאָדן?
מוזיק פֿון טרערן. קליינע טרערן. דינער, דינער, דינער,
צוזאמען מיטן ווייסן שייטער און דעם שוואַרצן באָדן.

1976–1975

*

פֿון ביימער מאַכט מען ווונדערלעך פּאַפּיר. און איך – ס׳פֿאַרקערטע:
פּאַפּיר פֿאַרוואַנדל איך אין אין ביימער, אין דעם בוים פֿון לעבן.
איך וועל זיך צוווואַרצלען צו אים ביז וואַנען עס וועט אויפֿגיין
ס׳געזאַנג פֿון זײַנע פֿייגל.

זיי וועלן זיך צעבליִען און אַרויסבלאָזן די ערשטע
געבענטשטע קלאַנגען; אומפֿאַרבײַטלעך, אײנציק איז מײַן שליחות:
פֿאַרוואַנדעלן די פֿאַרוואַנדלונגען אין זייער ערשטן מקור,
פֿאַרוואַנדעלן זיך אַליין אין פּראָטאָפּלאַזם פֿון מײַן חלום.

פֿאַרוואַנדלען וועל איך גרודעס לייַם אין זייער מענטשלעך פּנים,
פֿאַרוואַנדלען אײדלשטיינער אין אַ לעבעדיקן גאָלדשמיד.
און סודות אָפּגעזונדערטע און מײַלן־ווײַט פֿון ווערטער,
פֿאַרוואַנדלען וועל איך אין אַ שטראַלונג ביזן דנאָ פֿון טרערן.

איך טונק אין זון מײַן זיגלירינג און שטעל אים אין דער פֿינצטער
צו היטן די פֿאַרוואַנדלונגען. מײַן קומענדיקער יורש,
דער קאָסמישער פּאָעט, זאָל קאָנען זוכן און געפֿינען,
און מײַן געבײן זאָל שמייכלען.

1976

For whom, oh darkness, do you play – thinner, ever thinner,
for us, the little tears? Do you bestow on us your favor?
Music of tears. Little tears. Thinner, thinner, thinner,
together with the white pyre, the black earth.

1975–1976

*

From trees, miraculously, we make paper. But I – the opposite:
I transform paper into trees, into the Tree of Life.
I shall entwine my roots with his, till there arises
the song of his birds.

They will blossom and send forth their first,
their blessed sounds; immutable, unique is my vocation:
to transform the transformations into their origin,
to transform myself into the protoplasm of my dream.

I shall transform lumps of clay into their human face,
I shall transform jewels into a living goldsmith.
And secrets, cut off miles away from words,
I shall transform into a radiance that reveals the depths of tears.

I dip in sun my signet ring and place it in the darkness
to guard the transformations. So that my future heir,
the cosmic poet, shall seek and find them,
and my bones shall smile.

1976

*

איך האָב אַ בריוו דערהאַלטן פֿון מײַן היימשטאָט אין דער ליטע
פֿון איינער וואָס איר יוגנט־חן האָט ערגעץ נאָך אַ שליטה.
אַרײַנגעלייגט האָט זי אין אים איר ליבשאַפֿט און איר צער:
אַ גרעזל פֿון פֿאָנאַר.

דאָס גרעזל מיט אַ צאַנקענדיקן וואָלקנדל, אַ גוסס,
האָט אָנגעצונדן אות נאָך אות די פֿנימער פֿון אותיות.
און איבער אותיות־פֿנימער אין מורמלענדיקן זשאַר:
דאָס גרעזל פֿון פֿאָנאַר.

דאָס גרעזל איז אַצינד מײַן וועלט, מײַן היימיש־מיניאַטורע,
וווּ קינדער שפּילן פֿידל אין אַ ברענענדיקער שורה.
זיי שפּילן פֿידל און דער דיריגענט איז לעגענדאַר:
דאָס גרעזל פֿון פֿאָנאַר.

איך וועל זיך מיטן גרעזל פֿון דער היימשטאָט ניט צעשיידן,
מײַן אויסגעבענקטע גוטע ערד וועט מאַכן אָרט פֿאַר ביידן.
און יעמאָלט וועל איך ברענגען אַ מתנה פֿאָרן האַר:
דאָס גרעזל פֿון פֿאָנאַר.

1981

*

פֿאָר יאָסל בערגנער

אַ פֿרוי ווײַזט אָן איר יִנגעלע: דער דאָזיקער בײַם טישל,
אין ווײַסן הוט, איז ניט קיין מענטש. – טאָ וואָס זשע? – אַ לעגענדע.
דאָס יינגעלע דרייט אום דאָס קעפֿל. מאַמע, קינד, פֿאַרשווינדן.
און ס׳הוידעט זיך אויף אירע לאַנגע אויירינגען די שקיעה.

דער דאָזיקער בײַם טישל, זאָגט די פֿרוי, איז אַ לעגענדע.
אַ פֿעניקס־מענטש געבוירן פֿונעם אש פֿון שײַטער־הויפֿן
איז טאַקע אַ לעגענדע. נאָר פֿאַר וואָס איז די לעגענדע
כּסדר דאָרשטיק נאָך דער יונגער מורמלעניש פֿון קלאַנגען?

*

From my home town in Lithuania I received a letter,
sent by one whose youthful charm still retains its power.
And in it she enclosed her love and all her sorrow:
a little blade of grass from Ponar.

Together with a flickering, dying cloud, the grass ignited
the faces of the letters, letter after letter.
Above their faces in the murmuring embers of the fire:
the little blade of grass from Ponar.

Now this blade of grass is my miniature world of home,
where children play the fiddle in a burning row.
They play, and their conductor is a legend near and far:
the little blade of grass from Ponar.

No more will I be parted from this grass of my home town,
my yearned-for kindly earth shall make for both of us a place.
And then I'll bring to the Lord a present from afar:
the little blade of grass from Ponar.

1981

*

For Yosl Bergner

Says a woman to her little boy: "That man at the next table
in the white hat – he's not a man – " "What is he then?" "A legend."
The child turns round to look. Then child and mother disappear,
the glow of sunset swaying in her dangling earrings.

"That man at the next table," says the woman, "is a legend."
A phoenix man, born from the ashes of a pyre,
is indeed a legend. But why does that legend
thirst constantly for the young murmuring of sounds?

פֿאַר וואָס איז די לעגענדע איבערצײַטיק און אײנצײַטיק
אין וווּנדן, עלעהײ אין אַ שפּיטאָל בשעת אַ מעסער
שפּאַצירט אַרום אין לײַב און ס׳זוכט אַנטרינונג אָן אַ קאָמפּאַס
דורך לאַבירינט פֿון אָדערן אַ פֿינקלענדיקער עיקר?

די שפּאָגל נײַע נאַכט איז לינד און צערטלעך ווי אַן אָקערשט
געלייגטע אײַ. דער מילכוועג – מיטן פֿוס אים צו דערלאַנגען.
דער פֿעניקס־מענטש בײַם טישל האָט אַ חשק אײַנצובײַסן
זײַן שרײַבנדיקע האַנט. ער וויל פֿאַרזוכן זײַן לעגענדע.

1981

*

אַ פֿויגל האָט געשפּילט אין אָוונט אויף אַ סטראַדיוואַריוס
און כ׳האָב געפֿרעגט אַ נײַגעריקער זיך אַליין: צו וועמען?
אַ פֿויגל שפּילט ניט אָן אַ זינען אויף אַ סטראַדיוואַריוס,
מסתמא איז פֿאַרטײַעט אַ געהער, ס׳איז דאָ צו וועמען.

געווען די גרייס אַ פֿינגערהוט, און סאָראַ וווּנדער: נעמען
און שפּילן אויף אַ סטראַדיוואַריוס. ווי אַזוי? צו וועמען?
אַכיבע שפּרינג אַרײַן אין פֿײַער־מושל פֿון אַ קראַטער
און דאָרטן פֿרעג דעם לאַבעדיקן אַשמדאַי: צו וועמען?

צו וועמען האָט געשפּילט אַ פֿויגל אויף אַ סטראַדיוואַריוס,
דערבאַרעמדיקער גאָרנישט, זאָג צו וועמען?
אַ פֿויגל שפּילט ניט אָן אַ זינען ביזן לעצטן פֿלאַטער,
אַ נאָמען וויל איך הערן, אָדער נעמען.

און אַז איך האָב געפֿרעגט בײַם ים פֿויגל מיטן סטראַדיוואַריוס,
געבעטן רחמים האָט ער: ניטע, זאָלסט מיך ניט פֿאַרשעמען.
צעשיטן זיך אין אַש און פֿאָרער וועט מײַן סטראַדיוואַריוס
בשעת איך וועל דערוויסן זיך צו וועמען.

1983

Why is that legend beyond the reach of time, but at the same time
full of wounds, as if in hospital, and all the while a knife
wanders about his body, and, without a compass,
through the labyrinth of veins a glittering essence seeks escape?

The brand new night is mild and tender like a new-laid egg.
The Milky Way is near enough to reach on foot.
The phoenix man at the table has an urge to bite
into his writing hand. He wants to taste his legend.

1981

*

A bird was playing one evening on a Stradivarius
and, curious, I asked myself: to whom?
A bird does not play aimlessly on a Stradivarius,
There must be someone hiding here. There is a listener.

No bigger than a thimble, but – what a miracle:
To play upon a Stradivarius. How? To whom?
Perhaps I'll jump into the fiery heart of a crater
and ask the laughing Ashmeday: to whom?

To whom was this bird playing on a Stradivarius,
Merciful Nothingness, answer me, to whom?
A bird does not play aimlessly until his wings cease beating,
I want to hear from you a name, or names.

And when I asked the little bird that had the Stradivarius,
he begged for mercy: "please, you mustn't shame me.
For it will crumble into ash and dust, my Stradivarius,
while I am finding out to whom I'm playing."

1983

*

ניטאָ דאָס פֿענצטער און דורך אים דער קאַרשנבוים דער אורח,
געקומען איבערנעכטיקן ביַי מיר פֿון אונטערוועגנס.
ניטאָ דער קאַרשנבוים פֿון שטערן, ס׳האָבן זיי צעגנבֿעט
קאָסמישע גנבֿים.

דער לופֿטן־בויער האָט מיר בלויז געלאָזן פֿאַר אַ זכר
אַ מאָס גן־עדן־לופֿט, וואָס איז אַריַין דורך יענעם פֿענצטער
בריליאַנטיק
און פֿירקאַנטיק.

די מאָס גן־עדן־לופֿט, וואָס איז אַריַין דורך יענעם פֿענצטער
האָט קיינער ניט צעגנבֿעט, ניט צעשאָסן.
אַרומגעראַמט מיט פֿיר דין־דינע שורות
פֿאַרמאָגט אַ היים די זעונג פֿון מיַין לעבן.

און וווּנדער שבוווּנדער: ס׳קומט אַריַין דורך זיי ווי יעמאָלט
צו איבערנעכטיקן ביַי מיר דער קאַרשנבוים דער אורח
און דורך די זעלביקע דין־דינע שורות
קומט אויך אַריַין דער קאַרשנבוים פֿון שטערן.

1983

*

כ׳בין מאַמע־קראַנק. און וואַנדער,
זוך אַ דאָזע
געהיימען סם אין וועלטישע אַפּטייקן,
די וווּנד זאָל ניט פֿאַרגיין,
זאָל ניט פֿאַרגיין,
ביזן לעצטן אָטעם זיך ניט היילן.
ברומען זאָל זי לייביק,
ברומען אייביק,
ניט פֿאַרגיין.
ביז דערמאָנען וועט זיך דער באַשעפֿער
אין דער מאַמען,
אַריַינבלאָזן אַן אָטעם אין איר אויסגעצאַנקט
געביין.

*

The window is not there, nor has the cherry tree, my guest,
come through it from its wanderings to stay the night with me.
The cherry tree of stars is nowhere there, they have been stolen
by cosmic robbers.

The architect of air has merely left me a remembrance,
a little air of Paradise which entered through that window
diamond-bright,
quadrangular.

The air of Paradise which entered through that window –
no one has stolen it, nor shattered it.
Framed by four fine lines,
the vision of my life now owns a home.

And miracle of miracles: there enters as of old
the cherry tree, my guest, to stay the night with me.
And through the same fine lines
there enters too the cherry tree of stars.

1983

*

I am mother-sick. I wander,
seeking a dose
of secret poison in the world's pharmacies,
to stop my wound from disappearing.
May it not disappear,
until I breathe my last, let it not heal.
May it roar like a lion,
roar eternally,
never disappearing.
Till the Creator of the Universe
remembers my mother,
and breathes life into her extinguished
bones.

כ׳בין מאַמע־קראַנק. און שרייב אַליין רעצעפּטן
אין ליד און פּראָזע.
נאָר ניט פֿאַראַן אין וועלטישע אַפּטייקן
איז די דאָזע
געהיימער סם
די וווּנד זאָל ברומען ברעניקער.
ברומען זאָל זי לייביק,
ברומען אייביק,
ווידערשפּעניקער,
די וווּנד זאָל ניט פֿאַרגיין.
ביז דערמאַנען וועט זיך דער באַשעפֿער
אין דער מאַמען,
אַריינבלאָזן אַן אָטעם אין איר אויסגעצאַנקט
געביין.

1983

*

אַקערן די לופֿט. און וואָס פֿאַרזייען?
פֿאַרזייען אָטעם־קערנער. זאָל דער זאַמען
זיך וואַרעמען געדולדיק אין דער לופֿט
אַדורכגעווייקט מיט פֿרילינגזון
און טרערן.

איך אַליין, צי האָלב אַליין,
אָדער גאָר פֿון זיך אַליין אַ שפּליטער,
קומען וועל איך, זאָגט מיר ס׳האַרץ בלחש,
צום אויפֿגאַנג פֿון די אָטעמס.

קומען וועל איך בענטשן
די אומלעבעדיקע מיינע,
וואָס ציִען זיך צום אויפֿגאַנג פֿון די אָטעמס
כּדי צו לעבן.

I am mother-sick. I write my own prescriptions
in poetry and prose.
But in the world's pharmacies the dose
of secret poison
cannot be obtained
to make the wound roar more burningly.
May it roar like a lion,
roar eternally,
and more rebelliously,
may the wound not disappear.
Till the Creator of the Universe
remembers my mother,
and breathes life into her extinguished
bones.

1983

*

Ploughing the air. And sowing what?
Sowing breath grains. May the seed
patiently warm up in the air,
soaked through with spring sunshine
and with tears.

I myself, or half myself,
or even just a splinter of myself,
I will come – whispers my heart –
to see the young emerging breaths.

I will come and bless
all my unliving ones,
who are drawn to the young emerging breaths,
that they may live.

יעמאָלט וועל איך קאָנען זאָגן זיך אַליין אין אויער:
בן־אָדם, אָט איז דער נצחון דײַנער,
דער אײניציקער,
דער ערשטער
און דער לעצטער.

1983

*

פֿאַר מײַן פֿרײַנד רחל קרינסקי־מעלעזין, וואָס האָט מיר
דערמאַנט, אַז כ׳האָב געבעטן אַ כירורג ער זאָל מיר דערלויבן
בײַצוזײַן אין ווילנער געטאָ־שפּיטאָל בײַ אַ מוח־אָפּעראַציע.

דערצײיל, וואָס האָסטו זען געוואַלט בײַם אויפֿשנײַדן אַ שאַרבן
ווען שוין צעשניטן איז געווען די ייִדנשטאָט אויף שטיקער?
– מסתּמא זען דאָס אייביקע וואָס בלײַבט מחוצן שטאַרבן,
אַ נאָמען האָב איך עס געגעבן: פֿינקלענדיקער עיקר.

דער שאַרבן – אָפֿן. ס׳איז דער פֿאַנצער זײַנער ניט קיין דיקער,
אַצינד באַשערט איז מיר צו זען זײַן פֿינקלענדיקן עיקר.
אַזוי האָט קענטיק אויסגעזען די וועלט בײַם בראשית־ברא,
אַזוי האָט ליכט געבוירן ליכט. געבוירן און געבאָרן.

דער שאַרבן – אָפֿן. און איך קוק אַרײַן אין זײַנע תהומען
ווען שוין צעשניטן איז די אַלטע ייִדנשטאָט אויף שטיקער:
דין־אָדערדיקע שריפֿט. איך זע דעם נאָמען־אָן־אַ־נאָמען,
פֿאַרשטעל איך מײַנע אויגן: ס׳איז דער פֿינקלענדיקער עיקר.

פֿאַרלאָשן דער שפּיטאָל. עס נעמען קניִען זײַנע זײַלן.
דער שאַרבן פֿון דער שטאָט איז אָפֿן. כ׳האָב ניט ווו צו אײַלן.
און שיכּור בין איך פֿון דער זעונג, בין משוגע שיכּור:
אַצינד וועט מיך באַשירעמען דער פֿינקלענדיקער עיקר.

1983

Then shall I be able to say in my own ear:
mortal, this is your victory,
the only one,
the first one
and the last.

1983

*

For my friend Rokhl Krinski-Melezin, who reminded
me that I asked a surgeon to allow me to be present
at a brain operation in the Vilna ghetto hospital.

Tell me what you hoped to see when the skull was cut open
when the city of the Jews was already cut to pieces?
Probably the eternal which transcends death itself.
I have given it a name: the glittering essence.

The skull lies open. Its armor is but thin.
And now it's granted me to see its glittering essence.
So must the world have looked "in the beginning,"
so light fathered light. Fathered and gave birth.

The skull lies open. I peer into its caverns
with the ancient city of the Jews already cut to pieces.
Thin-veined script. I see the name-without-a-name.
I hide my eyes: it is the glittering essence.

Extinguished is the hospital. Its pillars start to crumble.
The city's skull lies open. Nowhere for me to go.
But I am intoxicated by the vision, gloriously mad-drunk:
now I shall be protected by the glittering essence.

1983

*

איך לייען טעקסטן וואָס אַ מענטשנהאַנט איז ניט קאַפּאַבל
צו שרײַבן. האַסטיק בליצן זיי פֿאַרבײַ. איך זוך אַ נאָמען.
זיי זענען ענלעכע קױם־קױם צו מעװעס ערבֿ מבול
בשעת דער ים װעט באַלד אַ הײב טאָן אוצרות פֿון די תהומען.

גבֿירן בין איך זיי צו קענען לייענען, די טעקסטן,
כ'מוז לאָקערן אױף זײער גנאָד און גינציקײט באַשטענדיק.
אַרױסגעשיקטע פֿון אַ װײַטן העק, דעם סאַמע העקסטן,
צעזעגן זיי דעם נאָכטגראַניט אַנטפּלעקעריש און בלענדיק.

פֿאַרזאַם איך זיך אַן אױגנבליק, װעט אָפּטאָן זיך מײַן זכיה
צו לײענען די אותיות װאָס דערזען האָט זיי ניט קײנער.
און ס'װעט בײַם אױסלאָז פֿון די טעג ניט קאָנען זיך מײַן וױע
אַן עפֿן טאָן, און בלײַבן טױטע װעלן מײַנע בײַנער.

אין זעלטענע סעקונדעס קאָן איך פֿאַנגען זיי, און צילע
אַרױף די טעקסטן אױף פּאַפּיר, נאָר כ'וױיס ניט אױף אַן אמת
צו װעמען זיי געהערן. און איך בעט בײַ זיי מחילה,
װאָס אױבן שרײַב איך אָן אבֿרהם, כאָטש איך וױיס ניט װעמעס...

1983

*

ס'האָט אָנגעהױבן זיך אַזױ: אַנטקעגן פֿײַלן־בױגן
פֿון זונפֿאַרגאַנג, אַ שװאַרצע קאַץ איז לײַכט פֿאַרבײַיגעשפּרונגען
אַן אַנדער שװאַרצע קאַץ. די פֿאָספֿאָרירנדיקע רוקנס
בײַ בײדע קאַצן־קינדער האָבן באַלד זיך אױפֿגעבערגלט.

אַ מוסקלדיקער װאָלקנשמיד האָט אָנגעהױבן שלאָגן
לאַנג־לאַנגע טשװועקעס אינעם ים. און איך בין יעמאָלט האַסטיק
אַנטרונען אין אַ טורעמל בײַם ים צאַרנדיקן ים־ברעג:
אַ מאָל געװען אַ ליכטמאַגנעט פֿאַר בלאָנקענדיקע שיפֿן.

און אינעװײיניק האָט אַ העגנגבליץ אױף אַ קײַט באַלױכטן
אַ בלאָנדן קאָפּ, אַ שװעבנדיקן שמײיכל אױף אַ פנים:
איך בין דײַן בענקשאַפֿט, האָבן זיך צו מיר דערנענטערט ליפּן,
אַ לױב צו אַ באַגעגעניש נאָך פֿופֿציק יאָר צי מערער.

*

I read texts no human hand is capable of writing.
They flash by hastily. I seek a name.
Closely they resemble gulls before a storm,
just before the sea casts up its treasures from the depths.

I was born to read these texts, and so must keep
a constant watch, and wait upon their favor.
Sent from the most distant, lonely place, they split apart
the granite of the night with their all-revealing gleam.

If I delay an instant, my privilege disappears
of deciphering this alphabet which no one else has glimpsed.
And at the end of days, my eyelids
will not open, nor will my dead bones rise.

In rare and unexpected moments I can catch the texts,
and thread them onto paper, though in truth I do not know
to whom these texts belong. I ask their pardon
for signing them with "Avrom" though I don't know whose they are…

1983

*

It started thus: towards the sunset's longbow
a black cat was springing lightly past
another black cat. Immediately, both cat children
arched their phosphorescent backs.

A muscular cloud-smith then began to hammer
long, long nails into the sea. And hastily I fled
into a tower by the raging sea shore
that once had been a light magnet for wandering ships.

Inside, a hanging bolt of lightning on a chain illuminated
a blond head. A smile was hovering on its face.
Lips drew nearer: "I am your yearning.
Wonderful our meeting after fifty years or more."

כ׳בין צוגעפֿאַלן צום געשטאַלט אין טורעמל: זײַ וויסן,
באַצווייגן בין איך מיט אַ פֿרעמדער הויט, מיט פֿרעמדע יאָרן.
מיר זענען ביידע יונג און אייביק, דו – דרײַ זומערס ייִנגער.

*

און שמייכלענדיקער אַש איז מיר געבליבן אויף די פֿינגער.

1984

*

ווי זענען זיי די ליבלינגען פֿון זומער: ייִנגלעך, מיידלעך,
מיט זיסער זינד וואָס האָט ניט מורא פֿאַר קיין שום גן־עדן?
פֿאַרזיגלט איז דאָס רעטעניש, דער סוד איז אומבאַשײידלעך,
נאָר איך, דער כּישוף־מאַכער, וועל דאָס רעטעניש באַשײידן:

זיי לעבן אין די ווערטער מײַנע אַ באַזונדער לעבעניש,
פֿאַרלוירן ווערט ניט אין די ווערטער ס׳מינדסטע איבערלעבעניש.
אַ שאָק מיט יאָרן האָט אויף זיי קיין דעה און קיין שליטה ניט,
ס׳טוט אָנדערשווו אַחוץ אין זיי מײַן קאָרשנבוים קיין צוויטע ניט.

פֿון שוואַרצן מעל פֿון האַלבנאַכט ווערן אויסגעזיפט מינוטן
ווען מײַנע ווערטער עפֿענען זיך. יעמאָלט בלויז, אָן ווערטער,
שפּאַצירן זיי אַרויס: לבֿנה־גייערס־ליליפּוטן,
און איך דערקען די ייִנגלעך, מיידלעך, פֿון די גרינע ערטער.

דאָס גיבן זיי סימנים: ס׳וועט זיך אונדזער פֿרייד ניט ענדיקן,
הייסבלוטיק לעבן מיר אַ ווערטער־לעבן אַ באַשטענדיקן.
מיר לעבן אין די ווערטער דײַנע אַ באַזונדער לעבעניש,
פֿאַרלוירן ווערט ניט אין די ווערטער ס׳מינדסטע איבערלעבעניש.

1984

I threw myself upon the figure in the tower: "Know that I
am covered over by an alien skin, by alien years.
We are both young, eternal. You – three summers younger."

*

And smiling ash remained upon my fingers.

1984

*

Where are they now, the darlings of the summer: boys and girls,
with their sweet sin that fears not any kind of Eden?
The riddle's sealed, the mystery insoluble,
but I, the magician, now will solve the riddle:

In my words they are living an existence of their own,
and in these words no fragment of experience goes astray.
Three score years have over them no influence or dominion,
in them alone, and nowhere else, blossoms my cherry tree.

From the black flour of midnight, minutes are sifted out
when my words open up. Only then, wordless,
they stroll out: midget moonwalkers.
I recognize the boys, the girls, from the green places.

They give me signs: our joy will have no end,
hot-blooded, we are living an enduring life in words.
In your words we are living a special kind of life,
and in these words no fragment of experience goes astray.

1984

The poem "Murashke-nest" (Anthill), written out by Sutzkever, with a comment, on the flyleaf of a copy of the book *Yidishe gas* in 1987

1988–1995

פֿון ציקל אינעוווייניק

צוווייפֿיסיקע גראָזן, די פֿנימלערע קענטיקע,
דערנענטערן זיך צו מיַין היים די פֿירוווענטיקע.
דערלאַנגען אַ קוש די מזוזה און שאַרן זיך
אַריַין צו מיַין בעט ווו איך מורמל: דערבאַרעם זיך
באַפֿליגלטער וויַיטיק, אַנטפֿלעק דיַין גאָונות
פֿון איַינצייינדלען סם אין געדאַנקען, זכרונות,
אַוווו נאָר אַ ביטערער פֿונק – אים צעבלאָזן.

צי ברענגט איר אַ בשׂורה, צוווייפֿיסיקע גראָזן?

צוווייפֿיסיקע גראָזן, באַשייַידט מיר די רעטעניש:
צי האָט ווער הנאה ווען איַיזערנע קאַמען
צעשינדן דעם גוף מיט נשמה צוזאַמען?
פֿאַר וועמען די פֿרייד פֿון אַזאַ מיַין גערעטעניש?
אַ וויַילע, אַ וויַילע,
מיַין לעצטינקע שאלה:
צי זאָל איך אַצינד מיַין ירושה איַיך לאָזן?

פֿאַרנייגן זיך פֿרום די צוווייפֿיסיקע גראָזן.

1988

פֿון ציקל פּאַריז 1988

א

אַ בלאַט אַראָפּגעשנעלט פֿון צווייַיג מיט ווינטס אַ ליַיכטן פֿינגער
ווי לעבעדיק ער לעבט! נאָר לעבעדיקער ווי בשעת
געצאַפֿעלט האָט ער אויפֿן בוים. איז אַזש געוואָרן ייִנגער
בייַים אָנרירן די ערד, בייַים זשוואַוון קייַקלען זיך אין גאַס.

כ'באַפֿרייַי אַ בליק צו שליסן קאָנטשאַפֿט מיטן בלאַט און לאָקער
מיט גאָר אַן אַנדער בליק אויף בייַידן: שיכור איז דער בלאַט
פֿון ערד און רעגנוויַין און ס'איז די ערד פֿון גוטס דער מקור.
אַזאַ נסיון האָט ער נאָך ביז איצטער ניט געהאַט.

From the cycle **Inside**

Two-legged grasses, whose faces I clearly see,
are walking towards the four walls that are home to me.
They kiss the mezuzah, and shuffle inside
to my bed where I murmur: "take pity, I beg,
o swift-winged pain. Reveal now your genius
for trickling poison into memories and thoughts,
for fanning each bitter spark into a flame.

Do you bring me some message, you two-legged grasses?

Two-legged grasses, just solve me this riddle:
does it give someone pleasure when iron-toothed rakes
are flaying the body as well as the soul?
Who would take pleasure in this kind of harvest?
Just a moment, a moment,
my last little question:
do you think I should leave you my worldly goods now?"

The two-legged grasses piously bow.

1988

From the cycle **Paris 1988**

1.
A leaf plucked from the branch by the wind's light finger,
how full of life it is! Livelier even
than when it trembled on the tree. Rejuvenated
by the earth's touch, by briskly whirling round the street.

I liberate a glance to go and greet the leaf for me,
and wait for both of them with yet another glance: the leaf is drunk
from earth and rain wine. From the earth comes goodness.
This leaf has never known such sweet temptation.

צו אָנרירן די אומבאַקאַנטע ערד, אָ, סאַראַ זכיה!
געלערנט האָב איך פֿון דעם בלאַט אין האַרבסט אַ סך, אַ סך.
און אַז געקומען איז דער בליק אַהיים וואָס אונטער ווי
געבוירן איז אין מיר אַ נייַע שפּראַך.

ב

קאַפּויערדיקע שטאָט. איך בין דיין טייך. און בריק און מויער
קאַפּויערן אין מיר אַריין אַ צירקישן קאַפּויער.
איך זע וואָס בלויז די כוואַליעס מיינע אין זכרון זעען:
איך טרינק נאָך אַלץ אַ גלעזל ווין ביים שרייבן אין קאַפּעען.

פֿון ווענט אַראָפּגעשונדענע, טאַפּעטן-בלומען פֿרישע,
אַ פּאַרל ווי אַ קאָטער מיט אַ קאַץ אין גרינער נישע.
אַ וואָלקן מיט אַ בלאָער באָרד. און ביי די בוקיניסטן
זוכט עמעצער אַ בוך וואָס עקסיסטירט נאָך ניט אומיסטן.

אַ צווייטער שפּרינגט אין מיר אַריין פֿון בריק. וואָס מיינט זיין שפּרינגען?
זיין דינער מאַנטל זעגלט זיך, נאָר בלייבט אין מיינע רינגען.
קאַפּויערדיקע פּאַליציאַנטן פֿייפֿן ווי אַ באַן.
דערווייל ווייס קיינער ניט, אַז יענער מאַן איז פֿאַל צעלאָאַן.

ד

זיין פענדזל – טרוקן. ווי אַ צווייג פֿון אייללבערטבוים, געצונדן
פֿון בליץ. נאָר זעען זע איך ווי ווי דער פענדזל זיינער,
אַדורכגעשלאָגן דורך אַ שטיין אין דר'ערד, נעמט אויפֿגיין, בליען
און האָלטן רעגן-בויגן-וואָרט:
ניט זיין וועט מער קיין מבול.

ער וועט מיר מוחל זיין, אַז כ'וועל ניט קומען
באַוווּנדערן זיין ווערק אין „אַר מאָדערן".
צו זען ווי ס'העַנגט צעשניטן אויף די ווענט
מיין פֿריינדס נשמה,
אַזאַ באַגעגעניש מיט אים
איז ניט פֿאַר מיינע כוחות.

To touch the unknown earth, what a rare privilege!
And from that autumn leaf I learned so much, so much.
When my glance returned to its home behind my eyelids,
within me a new language had been born.

2.

Upside-down city. I am your river. Walls and bridges
topple into me with topsy-turvy circus tricks.
I see what only my waves see in their memory:
myself drinking a glass of wine while writing in cafés.

Torn from their walls, fresh wallpaper-flowers bloom.
A loving couple nestle like two cats in a green nook.
A cloud with a blue beard. Among the bookstalls
someone searches on purpose for a non-existent book.

Someone else jumps off the bridge into my depths. What does it mean?
His thin coat stays afloat, drifts within my rings.
Upside-down policemen blow their whistles like a train.
No one knows it yet: that man is Paul Celan.

4.

His brush: dry. Like an olive branch, set on fire
by lightning. But yet I also see
that, hammered by a stone into the earth, his brush begins to sprout, to blossom
and keep its rainbow promise:
there will never be another Flood.

He will forgive me, if I do not go
and stand before his work in homage in the "Art Moderne".
To see my friend's soul hanging
in fragments on the walls,
to meet with him like that
is more than I can bear.

דער מענטש איז טאָפל מענטש.
און ער איז טאָפל
בלויז יעמאָלט ווען ער איז געזאַלבט
צו זײַן אַן אייניציק-איינער.
איך דאַנק דער אַלמאַכט וואָס האָט צוגעטיילט
אויך מיר אַ טייל פֿון לעבעדיקן טאָפל.

און לאָבן קען ער אויך ווען קיינער לאָכט ניט, ווי דער ייִנגסטער
גן-עדן-וואָסערפֿאַל, און טאָן אַ קלעפל
זײַן פֿרײַנד אין פלייצע:
ברודער-לעב,
מ׳איז אומעטיק – איז דאָ אַ מאָצאַרט,
מ׳איז הונגעריק – איז דאָ אַ סעזאַנס אַן עפל.

צום טאַטנס יאָרצײַט

שניילעכט פֿעלד-אײַן און פֿעלד-אויס ביזן טאָטן,
זונטערארן טריפֿן אין שניי ביזן טאָטן.
זיבעציק יאָר וואָ איך שפאָן צוווישן שניילעכט
אָנקומען זאָל איך צום טאָטן בײַ זײַ צײַיטנס.

ווײַנט עס די שטילקייט אין שניי, צי ס׳באַגלייט מיך
צווישן די שניילעכט זײַן רויטינקע פֿידל?
סאַראַ באַשערטקייט אין שניי ניט צו דערפֿילן:
ס׳נענטערט זיך נענטער, אַלץ נענטער די ווײַטקייט.

זאָל איך דערציילן מײַן טאָטן פֿון וואַנען
כ׳טראָג אויף די הענט מײַנע אָטעמס? צי וועל איך
ווערטער געפֿינען צו ווערקן זײַן שטילקייט,
עפֿענען זאָל ער פֿאַרפֿרוירענע אויגן?

שניילעכט פֿעלד-אײַן און פֿעלד-אויס. ניט פֿאַרזאַמען
זאָל איך אים זאָגן: דײַן זון איז דער זעלבער.
ס׳קאָן דאָך געשען, אַז ניטאָ מער מײַן טאַטע:
אויפֿגעוואַכט לאַנג שוין צו תחית-המתים...

כח תשרי תש״ן

Man is twofold man.
But he is twofold
only when he has been anointed
to be a one-and-only.
I thank the Almighty who has also granted me
a share in this twofold life.

He can laugh even when no one else is laughing,
like the youngest waterfall in Paradise, and can pat
his friend upon the shoulder:
brother mine,
if you are sad – there's Mozart,
if you are hungry – there's an apple of Cézanne's.

My Father's Yortsayt

Snowlight through field after field to my father,
sun tears in the snow, leading on to my father.
For seventy years I have walked through the snowlight
to come to my father in time.

Is it silence that weeps in the snow, or the sound of his rosy-red fiddle
that accompanies me through the snowlight?
Such a destiny I have been granted: to sense in the snow,
how it nears and draws close, ever closer, the distance.

Shall I describe to my father the place
from where I have carried my breath in my arms?
Will I find words to awaken his silence,
so that he opens his long-frozen eyes?

Snowlight through field after field. I must not forget,
I must tell him: Your son has not changed.
It may be my father is no longer there:
that he rose from the dead long ago, to new life.

28 Tishrei 5750 / October 17, 1990

ברויט און זאַלץ

די זון איז אַלעמענס, נאָר מער ווי אַלעמענס
געהערט זי מיר אַליין.

די וואָרצלען פֿון דער פֿינצטערניש
באַדאַרף איך ניט. איך בין
אַ זונקינד.

איך בין אַליין דאָס לעבן,
און שפּורן פֿון אַ זילבערפֿוקס אין שניי
איז מיַין זכּרון.

די האָק וואָס וועט מיר קומען אויסקאָרטשען
זי מ ו ז און וו ע ט מיר בלייבן אונטערטעניק.

איך בין די שטילקייט.
בין איר ברויט און זאַלץ.

כּדאַי געווען

פֿאָר דן מירון

כּדאַי געווען דו זאָלסט געבוירן ווערן. יאָ. כּדאַי.
אַפֿילו אַז דו מוזסט זיך בייגן פֿאַר אַ טראָפּן בליַיי.
אַפֿילו אַז דו ביסט אַ קרבן פֿון אַ מינדסט מיקראָאַבל,
און דו אַליין צו זיך אַליין ביסט מוראדיק אומנאָאַבל;

אַפֿילו אַז דו רופֿסט אַרויס אַ קלאַנג אויף אַ דועל,
אַפֿילו אַז דיַין שׂונא האַלט אין צינדן שוין דיַין שׂוועל.
כּדאַי געווען געבוירן ווערן דו זאָלסט זען דיַין מאַמען,
אַפֿילו אַז די מאַמע וועט זיך לאַנג אויף דר׳ערד ניט זאַמען.

כּדאַי געווען געבוירן ווערן כאָטש אַן איינציק מאָל,
אין קעסלגרוב פֿון אומגעבוירנקייטן אָן אַ צאָל,
אַבי צו זען און לייענען די אייגענע נשמה
און ווי פֿלאַנעטן דרייען זיך אָרום איר אַקס מסתּמא.

Bread and Salt

The sun belongs to everyone, but even more
it is mine alone.

I do not need
the roots of darkness. I am
a sun child.

I am life itself,
my memory
the spoor of a silver fox in snow.

The axe that comes to tear me up by the roots,
It *must* and *shall* submit to my command.

I am silence.
I am its bread and salt.

It Was Worthwhile

For Dan Miron

It was worthwhile being born. Indeed it was worthwhile
Even though you have to bend before a drop of lead.
And though you are the victim of a tiny microbe's might,
and though you treat yourself so badly, day and night.

Even though you challenge every sound to fight a duel,
even though your enemy is burning down your home.
It was worthwhile being born, just to see your mother,
even though she would not linger on this earth for long.

It was worthwhile being born, at least one time,
in that whirlpool of the numberless unborn,
just to see and read the soul that is within you,
and the circling of the planets round its axis.

כדאַי געווען צו לעבן סיַי אַ מאָל און סיַי אַצינד,
אַפֿילו אַז דו האָסט ניט אויסצוקויפֿן דיַינע זינד
גענוג בריליאַנטן, און די נאַכט איז לענגער פֿון דיַין פֿיַיער.
און אפֿשר איז כדאַי צו שטאַרבן? לעבן איז כדאַיער.

יולי–סעפּטעמבער 1995

It was worthwhile to live, both then and now,
even though, to expiate your sins, you don't possess
diamonds enough, and night lasts longer than your fire.
Is it, perhaps, worthwhile to die? To live is more worthwhile.

July–September 1995

1999. 3. 28

"Set sail, my word", courtesy of Tamar Guy, Savyon

1999 – 2000

דער רויטער האָן

דער רויטער האָן בײַ מיר צוקאָפּנס,
וואָס משה־לייב האָט אָנגעמאָלן אויף אַ העמד
און רויזעלע, די האַרציקע אַלמנה פֿון פּאָעט,
געשאָנקען האָט מיר אין ניו־יאָרק
צוריק מיט יאָרן,
האָט פּלוצעם זיך צעקרייט בײַ מיר צוקאָפּנס.

(בײַ רויזעלען אין שטוב, ווו כ׳בין געווען צו גאַסט,
געבלאָזן האָט אַ קעלט, זי האָט געבעטן
איך זאָל בײַם זעצן זיך צום טיש ניט אויסטאָן
מײַן ווינטער־מאַנטל).

דער רויטער האָן וואָס משה־לייב
האָט אָנגעמאָלן אויף אַ העמד,
האָט שטאַרקער זיך צעקרייט בײַ מיר צוקאָפּנס.
און פּלוצעם איז דער רויטער האָן געוואָרן אַ פּאָזשאַרניק.

ווו ברענט בײַ נאַכט? סע ברענט, איך קען זיך ווערן:
די פּוסטקייט אין ניו־יאָרק –
אָן ייִדישע פּאָעטן !

16 יאַנואַר 2000

The Red Rooster

The red rooster at my bedside,
that Moyshe-Leyb once painted on a shirt
and that Royzele, the poet's kind widow
gave me as a present in New York,
years ago,
suddenly started crowing by my bed.

(Royzele's house, where I was a guest,
was cold and draughty, and she asked me
to keep my winter coat on
when we sat down to eat).

The red rooster that Moyshe-Leyb
once painted on a shirt,
crowed more loudly still beside my bed.
And suddenly it turned into a fireman.

Where's the fire to night? I can make a guess:
In New York the emptiness is burning −
empty of Yiddish poets!

January 16, 2000

*

זײ אויפֿגעזעגלט װאָרט מײַנס, אַז דײַן קלאַנג דײַן מינדסטער
זאָל קענען װוּנדער װײַזן און זאָל גליִען אין דער פֿינצטער
און אָניאָגן מײַן צײַט אין אַל די עקן, אַל די העקן,
ס'פֿאַרגאַנגענע זאָל נאָך אַ מאָל זיך לעבעדיק אַנטפֿלעקן.

כ'בין עלטער פֿון גראַניט װאָס װײַנט פֿון צאָרן
אַלמאַי ס'איז אין גראַניטן־האַרץ קיין מלאך ניט געבאָרן.
און ייִנגער פֿון אַ פֿרילינג־בלימל נאָך אַ רעגן בין איך
װען זיך אַליין דערטרונקען אין אַ פֿיצל טױ געפֿין איך.

אַ לױב די גראָזן װאָס איך שרײַב זיי מיט אַ טינט אַ גרינער.
מײַן לשון לעבט. װעט איבערלעבן שװאַרצע ניט־פֿאַרגינער.
איך פֿיל װי אונטערהױטיק װידער מוסקלט זיך מײַן לשון
און ייִדן טוען אָן די װערטער מײַנע װי של־ראָשן.

28 דעצ. 1999

*

Set sail, my word, so that your softest sound
can work wonders, glowing in the dark
and can hunt down my time in all its far-flung hiding places,
so that the past once more reveals itself, alive.

I am older than the granite, weeping in its rage
that in its granite heart no angel has been born.
And younger than a spring flower after rain am I
when I find myself, drowned in a tiny drop of dew.

Praise to the grasses – with green ink I draw them.
My language lives. It will outlive black souls who scorn it.
Under my skin I feel my language rippling its muscles.
And Jews will bind my words upon their brows like *tefillin*.

28 December, 1999

Avrom Sutzkever, drawing

Abbreviations of Titles of Sutzkever's Works

L	לידער	(*Lider*)
V	וואַלדיקס	(*Valdiks*)
YG	ייִדישע גאַס	(*Yidishe gas*)
F	די פֿעסטונג	(*Di festung*)
DV	פֿון דרייַ וועלטן	(*Fun dray veltn*)
VG	ווילנער געטאָ	(*Vilner geto*)
LG	לידער פֿון געטאָ	(*Lider fun geto*)
LY-H	לידער פֿון ים־המות	(*Lider fun yam-hamoves*)
FV	אין פֿײַער־וואָגן	(*In fayer-vogn*)
GK	די גאָלדענע קייט	(*Di goldene keyt*)
OT	אָדע צו דער טויב	(*Ode tsu der toyb*)
MS	אין מידבר סיני	(*In midber Sinay*)
O	אָאַזיס	(*Oazis*)
PVA / B	פּאָעטישע ווערק א / ב	(*Poetishe verk a / b*)
FOM	פֿירקאַנטיקע אותיות און מופֿתים	(*Firkantike oysyes un mofsim*)
TsP	צײַטיקע פּנימער	(*Tsaytike penimer*)
FR	די פֿידלרויז	(*Di fidlroyz*)
LFT	לידער פֿון טאָגבוך	(*Lider fun togbukh*)
KsY	פֿון אַלטע און יונגע כתבֿ־ידן	(*Fun alte un yunge ksav-yadn*)
TsB	צווילינג־ברודער	(*Tsviling-bruder*)
YFR	דער יורש פֿון רעגן	(*Der yoyresh fun regn*)
TsV	צעוואָקלטע ווענט	(*Tsevaklte vent*)

Avrom Sutzkever, self-portrait

Notes on the Poems

The publishing history of the poems up to and including 1972 is taken from Novershtern 1976.

Siberia (p. 56–75)

For the publishing history of this *poeme*, see below, p. 261–264. (The first five poems discussed here – from "In the Hut" to "North Star" – are all part of *Siberia*.)

In the Hut (p. 57)

1. line 10 and passim: Irtysh: The Irtysh River is 4,248 kilometers long. It rises in the Altai Mountains in Xinjiang, China, and flows northwest through Kazakhstan, through Omsk, and finally merges with the Ob River in Western Siberia.

2. eyes of shadows: the Yiddish term used in the original, שאָטן־אַפּלען (*shotn-aplen*) seems to be a variation of the term שוואַרצאַפּלען (*shvartsaplen*, the pupils of the eyes) which is a frequent image in Sutzkever's work; through the tiny pupil of the eye the human being can glimpse the essential reality – it can be seen as the eye of the soul, or the inner eye (cf. Sutzkever 1989). Here and in "My friend Tshanguri", 1, line 4, I have rendered the concept with "eyes of shadows" and "dark eyes" respectively.

3. לוטשינע (*lutshine*): in poor rural homes a glowing piece of kindling wood, or firestick, was often used to give light.

Like a Sledge Jingling with Longing (p. 61)

The last four lines of this poem are difficult to interpret. Their approximate literal meaning is:

"Though the evening-steppe, in whose mirror/snuggling with its nose downwards/crouches the moon, and two wings/beat *or* are reflected."

The Kirghiz (p. 71)

The Kirghiz (or Kyrgyz) are a traditionally nomadic people living mainly in Kyrgyzstan, but also in Afghanistan, Western China, Kazakhstan, Uzbekistan, Tajikistan, Turkey and southwestern Siberia. Their religion is mainly Sunni Muslim. As a child in Siberia, Sutzkever was befriended by a young Kirghiz boy (see the following poem: "My Friend Tshanguri").

My Friend Tshanguri (p. 71)

Line 4: אַפּלען *aplen* = שוואַרצאַפּלען, *shvartsaplen*, literally, the pupils of the eyes. See note on "In the Hut", above.

North Star (p. 75)

Line 8: In the original, Sutzkever has created two verbs from the onomatopoeic sound which represents the resonance of bells in Yiddish: גלין-גלאָן (*glin-glon* like English 'ding-dong'): גלינסטו מיר און גלאָנסט (*glinstu mir un glonst*, literally "you ding and dong to me").

Blond Dawn (p. 77)

Inzikh 5 (1) (June 25, 1936): 2 f; *Literarishe bleter* 13, 39 (646) (September 25, 1936): 620; L 36 f; PVa 28 f.

This, the final version published in PV a, has two amendments: Four lines from the earlier version (after line 17), representing the song of the shepherd, have been omitted: "*Durkh di vayte hiln / rayt der morgn-rayter, / un es tliet, tliet/nokh mayn liber shayter*" (Through the distant veils / rides the morning rider, / and still it glows, it glows, / my dear fire."); line 20: the earlier version reads "*grozn plaplen vegn mir*" (grasses chatter about me).

In the Knapsack of the Wind (p. 79)

Literarishe bleter 12 (42) (October 18, 1935): 673, entitled "*Oyf mayn vander-fayfl*" (On my wander flute); dedication "*A matone F. Levitan*" (A present for F[reydke] Levitan); with the same title in L 63, dated 1935, dedication "Freydken"; PVa 31, entitled "In torbe funem vint", no dedication.

Scream (p. 81)

Haynt (Warsaw) (October 8, 1937): 7; PVA 83 f.

Everything is worthy of my roaming eye (p. 83)

Os 2 (2) (February 1938): 1 f, entitled "*Alts*" (Everything) and with the first line: "*Alts iz verdik far mayn oygn-blikung*" (Everything is worthy of my eyes' gaze); V 5; PVA 93, untitled, with first line: *Alts iz verdik far mayn oygs gevogl*" (Literally: "everything is worthy of my eye's roaming").

Landscape (p. 85)

V 14; PVA 101.

A Bunch of Cherries (p. 85)

Literarishe bleter 14 (34) (August 20, 1937): 544; V 32 f; PVa 118 f.

Anthill (p. 87)

Untervegns (Vilna) 1940: 241; YG 84; PVa 225.

In a copy of *Yidishe gas* which he gave to the present writer in 1987, Sutz-kever transcribed this poem on the title page of the volume, commenting: "*a lid geshribn mit 47 yor tsurik un iz aktuel biz haynt...*" (a poem written 47 years ago which is still relevant today). Though this and the following poem were first published in book form in YG (1948), Sutzkever has placed them in the section of pre-war poems entitled "Epilog tsu Valdiks" (Epilogue to "Of the Forest") in PVa.

Line 8: This line is quite difficult to interpret, since קויל koyl can mean either "coal" or "a bullet".

I. L. Peretz (p. 87)

Emes (Kovno), May 11, 1941: 3; YG 102; PVa 241.

Y[itskhok] L[eybesh] Perets (known in English as I[saac] L[eib] Peretz), 1852–1915, was one of three great Yiddish classical writers, together with Mendele Moykher Sforim, (S. Y. Abramovitsh, 1836–1917), and Sholem Ale-ichem (Sholem Rabinovitsh, 1859–1916). He was the author of dramas and short stories. Many of the latter thematize the dignity of poor and simple Jews, and deal sympathetically with Eastern European Hasidism, including the story "*Oyb nisht nokh hekher...*" ("If not even higher..."). The English translation of this story is entitled "If Not Higher" (The I. L. Peretz Reader, ed. Ruth Wisse, (New York: Schocken Books), 178–181, translated by Marie Syrkin).

Line 7: Here, and in two other poems ווי אַזוי? (*Vi azoy*? "How?"), p. 99 and ווי (*Gezegenish*, "Farewell"), PVa, p. 355, Sutzkever uses this unusual form to designate that which is past and gone, instead of the normal Yiddish פֿאַר-גאַנגענהייט *fargangenhayt*.

I Lie in a Coffin (p. 93)

First published as "Ikh lig in a mite", in F 51; then as "Ikh lig in an orn" in DV 102; PVa 249; LY-H 17. The word מיטה (*mite*) normally denotes the bier on which a body is laid, rather than the coffin itself. Apart from the different word for "coffin", the version in DV and PVa differs from the original only in the 10th line, where the first version has "*ruf ikh dir, shvester*" (I call to you, sister).

This poem is based on a true incident; in *Vilner geto* Sutzkever describes how, fleeing from the Lithuanian *khapunes* (catchers), he came upon some newly-made coffins in the yard of the Jewish Burial Society: איך בין אַרײַנגעקראָכן אין אַן אָרון, צוגעמאַכט איבערן קאָפּ דעם דעק, געלעגן אין דער פֿאַרשטיק-טער לופֿט, און אַזוי ליגנדיק אין אָרון האָב איך אויסגעוועבט מײַן ליד „איך ליג אין אַ מיטה" (I climbed into a coffin, closed the lid over my head, and while I lay there in the stifling atmosphere I composed my poem "Ikh lig in a mite" VG 31.)

Line 10: "I call you, sister": Sutzkever's older sister, Etl, had died at the age of 13. Her memory was a constant inspiration to the poet.

I Long to Say a Prayer (p. 95)
LG 13; YG 25; DV 105; PVa 253; LY-H 21.

To My Child (p. 95)
LG 16 f; YG 16 f; PVa 278 f; LY-H 44 f.

This poem was written about a year after the death of his first-born child in early 1942. In *Vilner geto*, Sutzkever describes how, on his return to the ghetto after having been hidden for some weeks by a Lithuanian peasant woman, he went to see his mother:

איך בין אַוועק צו דער מאַמען. זי האָט מיר אָנגעזאָגט אַ שׂימחה: מײַן פֿרוי האָט געבוירן אין געטאָ־שפּיטאָל אַ קינד. מײַן מאַמע האָט פֿאַרגעסן אָן מורערס געזעץ, אַז קינדער, געבוירן אין געטאָ, מוזן געטויט ווערן. אויף מאָרגן נאָך מײַן קומען איז שוין דאָס קינד ניט געווען: מורערס באַפֿעל איז אויסגעפֿירט געוואָרן.

I went to my mother's. She told me some joyful news: my wife had given birth to a child in the ghetto hospital. My mother had forgotten about Murer's* law, that children born in the ghetto should be killed. The day after my return, the child was already dead; Murer's order had been carried out.

*Franz Murer, known as "the butcher of Vilnius," was an Austrian SS Officer; he set up and was in charge of the ghetto in Vilna.

How? (p. 99)
LG 18; YG 59; PVa 1, 284; LY-H 50.

Line 4: פֿאַרגאַנגענקייט *fargangenkeyt*: See note to "I. L. Peretz", above, p. 211.

Grains of Wheat (p. 101)

Nayvelt (Tel-Aviv) 13 (20) (May 17, 1946): 3; LG 27 f; YG 32 f; PVa 289 f; LY-H 55 f.

For a discussion of this poem, see below, p. 245.

Lines 15–16: Amsterdam, Worms, Livorno, Madrid: these are all cities associated with Jewish culture and scholarship. YIVO: see below p. 236, 244.

Line 17: שײמע sheyme: this word is normally used to denote a detached leaf of a Jewish sacred book. For Sutzkever, the definition of "sacred" would also encompass endangered great secular works of Jewish literature and culture.

Every Hour, Every Day (p. 105)

LG 12; YG 23; DV 103; PVa 302; LY-H 63.

Burnt Pearls (p. 105)

LG 14; YG 43; PVa 323; LY-H 82.

The Lead Plates of Romm's Printing House (p. 107)

Yidishe kultur 7 (2) (February 1945); *Nayvelt* (Tel-Aviv) 12 (17) (April 20, 1945): 5; F 62; DV 131; PVa 335; LY-H 94.

The Romm printing house, founded in 1799, was famous for its 1854 edition of the Babylonian Talmud and for many other fine Hebrew and Yiddish books, both religious and secular. It was one of only two Jewish printing houses permitted by Tsar Nicholas I in the Russian Empire, and was one of the symbols of the rich Jewish culture of Vilna. The printing house closed in 1940. I have so far been unable to discover whether the incident in the poem is imaginary, or whether old lead type from the printing house was in fact used to manufacture bullets.

Line 15: The allusions are to the Babylonian Talmud, and the rich Yiddish literature of Poland.

Line 21: The siege of Jerusalem by the Romans, fiercely opposed by Jewish defenders, led to the fall of the city and the destruction of the Second Temple in 70 CE.

Sing no Sad Songs (p. 109)

F 69; PVa 352; LY-H 111.

Frozen Jews (p. 109)

F 29; DV 122 f; PVa 362 f; LY-H 119 f.

To the Thin Artery in My Head (p. 115)

YG 181 (dated Vilna ghetto, 1943); PVa 550 (dated 1945).

Line 3: "[…] all the seven wisdoms […]": the origin of this phrase is probably Proverbs 9: 1: "Wisdom hath builded her house, she hath hewn out her seven pillars." Various Rabbinic scholars have given interpretations of what the seven wisdoms signify, including the seven books of the Torah (the book of Numbers sometimes being considered as three books), or the seven liberal arts of the medieval curriculum, and many consider the seven branches of the menorah to symbolize the seven pillars of wisdom. Sutzkever appears to be contrasting all the (perishable) wisdoms of the world with the essential, eternal word within himself.

Had I not been here with you (p. 115)

Oyf der vakh (Munich) 2 (50) (November 25, 1948): 13; *Undzers* (Tel-Aviv) 1949, 8; *Heym* 2, August 1950, 39; FV 9; PVв 7.

The first line of the poem originally read װען כ׳װאָלט ניט זיַין מיט אײַך בײַנאַנד (If I had not been together with you [plural]). אײַך was changed to the singular דיר in *In fayer-vogn*… The poem is untitled but introduces the first section of the book which is called שהחײנו (*shekheyonu*), a blessing recited on major holidays or to celebrate a joyous occasion such as the first fruit of a new season.

Line 5: עקדה *akeyde* (Hebrew: 'aqedah, literally 'binding'): the term used of the incident where God commands Abraham to take his son Isaac to a mountain and sacrifice him; Abraham prepares to fulfil God's command, but at the last moment God's angel appears and shows him a ram which is sacrificed in his place (Genesis 22).

Line 10: *fargoyt*: this is an interesting neologism. Sutzkever has created a verb פאַרגױען (*fargoyen*) of which this is the past participle. The word גױ (*goy*) means a gentile, and Sutzkever's term gives the literal sense of "having been turned into a non-Jew"; in other words, if he had not reached the land of Israel he would have been cut off from his deep Jewish roots, and would have died in an alien environment.

The Snow on Mount Hermon (p. 117)

Nayvelt (Tel-Aviv) 16 (12) (February 11, 1949): 4; *Heym* 2 (August 1950): 39; FV 31; DV 157; PVв 30.

Line 1: "What means to me […]?: Sutzkever uses the traditional Rabbinic phrase מאַי קאָ משמע לן (*may ko mashme lon?* what is the significance of…?) with which a discussion on a text of the Torah or Talmud was initiated. Readers of Yiddish literature would also be familiar with its use in a popular poem by Avrom Reyzen (1876–1953), in which a poor yeshiva student asks himself: מאַי קאָ משמע לן דער רעגן? (*may ko mashme lon der regn?* "what is the meaning of the rain?")

Line 11: אל הציפור (*el hatsipor* "To the bird"): a famous poem by the Hebrew poet Khayim Nakhmen Bialik (1873–1934), in which the exiled poet begs a little bird to bring him news from the longed-for land of Zion.

Line 14: עיר ואם (*ir veeym*: "city and mother"). The term occurs in 2 Sam. 20:19, where a wise woman accuses Joab: "Thou seekest to destroy a city and a mother in Israel." The term is widely used for any Jewish community of major cultural or religious importance. The phrase suggests Vilna, but the adjective kindish (of childhood) applied to the snow links the image also to the first phase of the poet's life in Siberia.

Deer at the Red Sea (p. 117)

GK 4, 1949, 55; FV 77; DV 166; PVв 71.

Mirrors of Stone (p. 119)

FV 89; DV 175; PVв 80.

Line 3: "and, perhaps, not die": this may be a reference to God's words to Moses (Exodus 33:20): "And he said, Thou canst not see my face; for there shall no man see me, and live."

From: Commentaries on a Face in the Mirror (p. 119)

GK 5 (1950): 217; FV 110; PVв 98; LY-H 374.

The first of a cycle of 10 short poems – sombre reflections inspired by the events of the recent past.

Line 1: "past Jewish life": the original uses the expression די ייִדישע גאַס (*di yidishe gas*). This literally means "the Jewish street", but it is used to convey the idea of Jewish society, the Jewish world, and here Sutzkever is referring to the now disappeared Jewish world of Eastern Europe.

From: A Letter to the Grasses (p. 119–123)

GK 2 (1949): 178; PVв 155–161.

A cycle of fourteen poems which centre on the nature of art and the experience of the artist.

9. P. 121, line 2: Sambatyen (English: Sambation): this is the legendary river beyond which the Ten Lost Tribes of Israel are said to dwell. It rages and throws up stones for six days of the week, making it impassable, but is calm on the Sabbath, when Jews may not travel.

Line 3: "the yellow plum": In his 1959 lecture in Montreal, Sutzkever alluded to the incident with the yellow plum which inspired this poem cycle (p. 49).

14. P. 123, lines 5 and 8: These lines contain an untranslatable rhyming wordplay: צום ווידערזען (*tsum viderzen*, "goodbye, till we meet again" – literally "till [our] again-seeing") is paired with the neologism צום לידערזען (*tsum liderzen* – literally "till [our] poems/songs-seeing" – דאָס ליד *dos lid* means both song and poem).

Ode to the Dove (p. 127 – 137)

GK 19 (1954): 33–38; OT 7016; PVB 165–174.

II

Who has made these fingers so drunk, that they have created a verse:
"All those who are dying have planted in me their great valor?"
I have retained Sutzekever's punctuation here, though one might expect the question mark to be placed outside the quoted line.

III

Line 7: This line is rather ambiguous: I have interpreted the masculine definite article at the beginning of the line to refer to the sunset, which has masculine gender in Yiddish (דער זונפֿאַרגאַנג, *der zunfargang*). The prefix of the verb דערזינגען (*derzingen*) gives it the sense of singing something to its conclusion, or to perfection.

Line 16: the image in the original line: דו ביסט די מאָס און דער מעסטער (*du bist di mos un der mester*) means '*you* are the measure and the measurer'. I have substituted a different image with a similar meaning.

IV

Line 7: King Saul, in a fit of jealousy, hurled a javelin at David (1. Sam. 28:10).

VII

Lines 4–8: The Italian poet Dante Alighieri (c. 1265–1321) wrote his Divina Commedia (Divine Comedy) between about 1305 and his death. It consists of three sections: Inferno, Purgatorio and Paradiso. The poet's journey through Hell and Purgatory to Paradise can be seen as an allegory (note

Sutzkever's word play!) of the soul's journey towards God. The poem is written in a series of interlocking tercets known as terza rima ('third rhyme'), in which the second line of each tercet rhymes with the first and third lines of the succeeding one.

Line 12: The Spanish Jewish physician, poet and philosopher Judah Halevi (1075–1141) wrote both religious and secular poetry, including a number of poems of yearning for Zion. He travelled to Egypt in 1140, and set out from there to Palestine in 1141. It is not known whether he reached his destination or died in Egypt, though legend has it that he was trampled to death by an Arab horseman in the land of Israel.

X

Line 12: "a cloud violin." The original reads אַ וואָלקן מיט סטרונעס (*a volkn mit strunes*), literally 'a cloud with violin strings.'

In the Beginning (p. 139)

Yidisher kemfer 1071 (1954): 7; OT 29; PVв 184.

The poems "In the beginning," "Elephants at Night. A Hunter's Song," "The Elephants' Graveyard," "Diamond Girl," "Suicide Song of the Hereros" and "To a Tiger" form part of the series of 42 poems entitled "Elephants at Night," first published together in the volume *Ode tsu der toyb*, where the cycle is dated 1950–1954.

Elephants at Night (p. 139)

GK 14 (1952): 72; OT 30 f; PVв 186 f.

The Elephants' Graveyard (p. 141)

GK 12 (1952): 133; OT 32; PVв 188.

Diamond Girl (p. 143)

GK 13, 1952, (1952): 184 (title: "*Dos diment-meydl*"); OT 46; PVв 202.

Suicide Song of the Hereros (p. 145)

GK 14, 1952 (1952): 71; OT 54; PVв 210

Hereros: The Herero people were originally cattle traders who lived in German South West Africa (in the area of modern Namibia). In 1904 they rebelled against German colonial rule. Between 24,000 and 100,000 of them were slaughtered, and many more died in concentration camps, in what is regarded as the first genocide of the 20th century.

insingizi bird: the Zulu name for the southern ground hornbill which lives in grasslands in Southern Africa. In traditional rain rites it is believed to bring rain in times of drought. In reality they are large birds of prey which are now an endangered species.

To a Tiger (p. 145)
GK 12 (1952): 137; OT 72; PVB 226.

Else Lasker-Schüler (p. 147)
GK 28, 1957, 95 f.; MS 26 f; PVB 287 f.

The German-Jewish poet Else Lasker Schüler, (1869–1945), who lived for most of her life in Berlin, was emotionally drawn to the idea of the "land of the Hebrews" (Das Hebräerland, 1937, is the title of the prose work which describes her visits to Palestine in 1934 and 1937). She emigrated to Switzerland in 1933, but finally settled in Jerusalem in 1939, where she lived in poverty in a shabby hotel room until her death in 1945. Her late poem "Mein blaues Klavier" (My blue piano, 1943) depicts her alienation from a lost and destroyed past. In his poem Sutzkever evokes the sensitivity, fantasy and mysticism of Lasker-Schüler's life and work.

Line 4: the Kastel is an ancient Roman and Crusader fortress outside Jerusalem; it played an important role in Israel's War of Independence in 1948. It is now a National Park.

Perets Markish (p. 149)
GK 25 (1956): 10; *Afrikaner yidishe tsaytung* 25 (35) (1956): 25; MS 66b; PVB 323 f.

In the *Afrikaner yidishe tsaytung* the poem was entitled אָפּשייד (Leave-taking), elsewhere פרץ מאַרקיש (Perets Markish).

The Yiddish poet Perets Markish (1895–1952) was born in Ukraine. He was enthusiastic about the Russian Revolution, believing that it would lead to freedom for Jews and the blossoming of Yiddish culture in the Soviet Union. From 1921 until 1926 he lived in Poland, where he was one of the founders of the avant-garde group of Yiddish poets די כאַליאַסטרע (*Di khaliastre*, The gang). After his return to Moscow in 1926 he faced, like most of his fellow Yiddish poets, the difficulties of reconciling independent creativity and individualism with the demands of "socialist realism." He was a leading member of the Jewish Anti-Fascist Committee.

After Sutzkever left Moscow in 1946, Markish remained, and despite having been awarded the Order of Lenin in 1939 and becoming a member of the Communist Party in 1942, he was arrested in 1949 and shot with four other prominent Yiddish writers on August 12, 1952.

Lines 2, 7–8, 13–14: Alexander Pushkin (1799–1837), the great Russian national poet, was also killed by a bullet, in his case as the result of a duel. His statue, which stands in Pushkinskaya Square in the centre of Moscow, was erected in 1880.

Line 17: *a shvartse khupe* (a black wedding canopy): the *khupe* (huppah), the canopy under which the bride and bridegroom stand during the wedding ceremony, is often used to denote the wedding itself. The custom of marrying two impoverished orphans in a cemetery was referred to as a "shvartse khupe," so this motif is closely connected with the idea of death. An interesting variation of this theme, in which the black wedding canopy was used to perform a wedding ceremony between a woman and her dead fiancé is told by Linda Gritz (Gritz 2013).

Line 19: dayn "kupe": Markish's intense and dramatic *poeme Di kupe* (the mound), inspired by the pogroms in Ukraine following the Russian Revolution, was published in 1921.

Line 21: der shney: Sutzkever is alluding to the snow of Siberia, remembered from his childhood, which remained as a seminal image in his poetry. He is prepared to leave it in order to live in a Jewish environment, the land of Israel.

Poetry (p. 151)
Ilustrirte literarishe bleter 7b (1954): 11; MS 75; PVʙ 330.

The Chosen Tree (p. 153)
Letste nayes April 3, 1959: 6; O 24; PVʙ 370.

Line 1: Stradivarius: Antonio Stradivari (1647–1737), born in Cremona, Italy, is considered as the greatest creator of stringed instruments.

Line 10: Music fathered in pain: The original phrase is צער-גידול-מוזיק (*tsar-gidl-muzik*). The only context in which the phrase "tsar-gidl" is normally used is in צער-גידול-בנים (*tsar-gidl-banim*, the trials of bringing up children).

The Kiss (p. 157)
Undzer dor (New York) 5 (September–October 1962): 17; PVʙ 509.

The Third Silence (p. 157)

Almanakh fun di yidishe shrayber in Yisroel (Tel-Aviv) 1967: 91; FOM 135.

This is the penultimate poem of a cycle of five short poems entitled די שערבל-יעגערס (*Di sherbl-yegers*, archaeologists – literally "shard hunters"). The cycle is dated "Eilat, June 1966."

The eye of the soul… (p. 159)

GK 64, 1968, 5; TsP 87.

In the Last Days (p. 159)

TsP 113.

Title and line 12: באַחרית־הימים (*Beakhres-hayomim*, In the last days): This phrase occurs twice in the Tanakh: Genesis 49:1 "And Jacob called unto his sons, and said, Gather yourselves together, that I may tell you that which shall befall you in the last days"; Isaiah 2:2: "And it shall come to pass in the last days, that the mountain of the Lord's house shall be established in the top of the mountains, and shall be exalted above the hills; and all nations shall flow unto it."

The Fiddle Rose (p. 161)

FR 7.

Line 1: the Hebrew term תחית־המים, *tkhies hameysim*, means the resurrection of the dead. Sutzkever has created an adverb from this term by adding the Yiddish suffix *-dik* to it.

The red bricks of your body – you've forgotten how they're built (p. 165)

GK 83, 1974, 175; LₜT 8; KsY 126; TsB 10.

This and the following 17 poems are all taken from Sutzkever's series "*Lider fun togbukh*" ('Poems from my diary' – see p. 278–280). Since they have no titles, the first lines are given here.

Creatures on the seabed, deprived of light and sunshine (p. 165)

GK 83, 1974, 176; LₜT 9; KsY 127; TsB 11.

Line 3: Towers of Babel: Genesis 11:4–9.

Who will remain, what will remain? A breath of wind will stay. (p. 167)

GK 83, 1974, 179; LₜT 16; KsY 134; TsB 18.

Line 6 contains several biblical references: בראשיתדיק (*breyshesdik*): In Yiddish, the book of Genesis is called בראשית (*breyshes*), the first word of the

Hebrew version, which means "in the beginning." The adjective/adverb de-
riving from *breyshes* means "original, primeval". In the same line, אַרויסגראָזן
(*aroysgrozn*) is the verb used in the Yiddish translation of the Tanakh by the
Yiddish poet Yehoash (Solomon Blumgarten, 1870–1927), who translates
Genesis 1:11 as follows:

האָט גאָט געזאָגט: זאָל די ערד אַרויסגראָזן גראָז, קרייטעכץ וואָס גיט אַרויס זאָמען

(*hot got gezogt: zol di erd aroyzgrozn groz, kreytekhts vos git aroys zomen…*).
In the King James version this reads:

"And God said: let the earth bring forth grass, the herb yielding seed…"
The term באַשאַף (*bashaf*, creation) which ends the line also has a Biblical
resonance.

From right-angled book covers, two by two and arm in arm (p. 167)

GK 86, 1975, 140; LFT 30; KsY 146; TsB 32.

Line 13: Havdala spices (Yiddish בשמים, *psomim*): Havdala (Yiddish: *ha-
vdole*) is the religious ceremony marking the end of the Sabbath and the
beginning of the week. A benediction is made over sweet-smelling spices – it
is said that this is so that the soul, which is sad at the passing of the Sabbath,
may be refreshed.

Line 15: פֿאַר ברייטן און פֿאַר לענגען (*far breytn un far lengen*): this phrase
literally means "for breadths and lengths" or "for latitudes and longitudes".
In the context of the poem, Sutzkever seems to be saying that in the little
"inn" (his poetry), there is enough space both for the "dearest people" – representing the whole history of his past experiences – as well as for all sorts of
other wonderful, indefinable things, symbolized by the idea of an angel who
may come to dwell there.

Time's clay has softened. And the dough of sunset after sunset (p. 169)

GK 88 (1975): 5; LFT 35; KsY 150; TsB 36.

Line 4: קאָלטן (*koltn*) usually means a tuft of tangled hair. I have interpreted it here as a thicket.

Line 12: After Cain killed his brother Abel, God condemned him to wander the earth, but put a protective mark on him to prevent anyone killing
him (Genesis 4:15).

An unseen serpent long ago injected (p. 171)

GK 88 (1975): 6; LFT 36; KsY 151; TsB 37.

Line 3: The Dutch Jewish philosopher Baruch Spinoza (1632–1677),
a member of the Portuguese Jewish community of Amsterdam, earned his

living as a lens grinder. His ideas on the Mosaic authorship of the Torah and the nature of the Divine were controversial. A *ḥerem*, an edict expelling him from the Jewish community, was issued against him at the age of 23. Sutzkever wrote four poems about the philosopher dated "Vilna 1937.", "The Hague 1947", "Amsterdam 1947" and "Amsterdam 1947" respectively, which he published together as a cycle entitled שפּינאָזע (Shpinoze) in YG, 188–191, DV, 90–92 and PVA, 593–596.

The fiddler plays, becoming thinner, thinner, thinner (p. 171)

GK 88 (1975): 6; LϜT 37; KsY 152; TsB 38.

From trees, miraculously, we make paper. But I, the opposite: (p. 173)

GK 90 (1976): 227; LϜT 65; KsY 182; TsB 67.

Line 2: The tree of life: God expelled Adam from the Garden of Eden after he had eaten fruit from the forbidden tree of the knowledge of good and evil, "lest he put forth his hand, and take also of the tree of life, and eat, and live for ever: […]" (Genesis 3:22). The Garden of Eden was then protected by Cherubim with a flaming sword "to keep the way of the tree of life." (Genesis 3:24). The central image in Jewish Kabbalah, representing the interlinked ten sephirot,or divine emanations, is also known as the Tree of Life. In Jewish folk tradition, the Torah which God gave to the Israelites is the earthly equivalent of the Tree of Life; the fruit of the tree itself will be eaten by the righteous in the world to come.

From my home town in Lithuania I received a letter (p. 175)

GK 105 (1981): 198; KsY 209; TsB 100.

Line 4: Ponar: See p. 241.

Says a woman to her little boy: "That man at the next table […]" (p. 175)

GK 106 (1981): 176; KsY 232; TsB 121.

Dedication: Yosl Bergner: The son of the Yiddish poet Melekh Ravitsh, the artist Yosl Bergner (1920–2017) was born in Vienna and grew up in Warsaw. The family emigrated to Australia in 1937, and Bergner settled in Israel in 1950. He illustrated Sutzkever's volume *Fun alte un yunge ksav-yadn*.

A bird was playing one evening on a Stradivarius (p. 177)

GK 110–111 (1983): 235; TsB 148.

Line 8: Ashmeday (English: Asmodeus) is traditionally considered to be the king of the demons. He is mentioned in the Book of Tobit and in some

Talmudic legends and Kabbalistic texts. While Ashmeday is a malign, destructive demon in the Book of Tobit, he appears more as a mischievous, humorous character in the Talmudic sources.

The window is not there, nor has the cherry tree, my guest (p. 179)
GK 110 / III, 1983, 241; TsB 160.

I am mother-sick. I wander (p. 179)
GK 112 (1984): 194; TsB 165.

Lines 10–13: cf. Ezekiel 37:1–5: "The hand of the Lord was upon me, and carried me out in the spirit of the Lord, and set me down in the midst of the valley which was full of bones [...] And he said unto me, Son of man, can these bones live? And I answered, O Lord God, thou knowest. Again he said unto me, Prophesy upon these bones, and say unto them, O ye dry bones, hear the word of the Lord. Thus saith the Lord God unto these bones; Behold, I will cause breath to enter into you, and ye shall live [...]"

Ploughing the air. And sowing what? (p. 181)
GK 112 (1984): 195; TsB 166.

Tell me what you hoped to see when the skull was cut open (p. 183)
GK 112 (1984): 195; TsB 167.

Dedication: Rokhl Pupko-Krinski-Melezin (usually known as Rachel Pupko-Krinsky) was a teacher in Vilna, and, like Sutzkever, a member of the "paper brigade" (see p. 244). Her daughter was raised outside the ghetto by their Polish housekeeper. Rokhl escaped into the forests with Shmuel Katsherginski and the Sutzkevers. She and her daughter emigrated to America where she died in 2002.

Line 7: *breyshes boro* is the Ashkenazi pronunciation of the first two words of the Hebrew Bible (בראשית ברא): *breyshes boro* [*eloyhim es hashomaim ve-es hoorets*] (literally: in the beginning created [God the heavens and the earth]).

Line 8: In Yiddish the verb געבוירן (*geboyrn*) means either to beget or to give birth to. The normal past participle is געבוירן (*geboyrn*) but can also be געבאָרן (*geborn*). By using the two forms, it seems as if Sutzkever is combining both the male and female functions in his vision of the birth of light.

Line 11: "the name-without-a-name": it is forbidden to say the Name of God, the tetragrammaton YHWH, and God is often referred to as *Ha-shem* ("the name").

I read texts no human hand is capable of writing (p. 185)

GK 112 (1984): 198; TsB 172.

Line 7: העק, דעם סאמע העקסטן (*hek, dem same hekstn*): the noun דער העק (*der hek*) means a distant, God-forsaken place; in order to emphasise this, Sutzkever creates a superlative adjective from the noun hek: [*fun*] *dem same hekstn* […] ([from] the most distant, lonely [place]).

It started thus: towards the sunset's longbow (p. 185)

GK 113 (1984): 181; TsB 180.

Line 9: Sutzkever's neologism העעגבליץ (*hengblits* – literally "hanging lightning") plays on the word העעגלאָמפ (*henglomp* – a hanging lamp).

Where are they now, the darlings of the summer: boys and girls (p. 187)

GK 113 (1984): 186; TsB 188.

Line 13: לעבעניש (*lebenish*); This is a neologism, composed of the root of the verb לעבן (*lebn*, to live) and the ending ‑עניש (*-enish*) that occurs in other nouns such as איבערלעבעניש (*iberlebenish*, experience) in line 14.

Two-legged grasses, whose faces I clearly see (p. 191)

GK 125 (1988): 9; YfR 23.

The fourth poem of a four-part sequence entitled אינעווייניק (*Ineveynik*, Inside).

Three poems from the five-poem sequence Paris 1988:

1. A leaf plucked from the branch by the wind's light finger (p. 191)

GK 126 (1989): 213; YfR 39.

2. Upside-down city. I am your river. Bridges and walls (p. 193)

GK 126 (1989): 213; YfR 40.

Line 12: The poet Paul Celan (whose original family name was Antschel) was born in Romania to Jewish parents. He and his parents were imprisoned in labour camps during the war, and both his parents perished, which left Celan with a deep sense of guilt. He continued to write poetry in German, despite settling in France in 1948 and becoming a French citizen in 1955. He took his own life in Paris in 1970 by jumping from the Pont Mirabeau into the Seine.

4. His brush: dry. Like an olive branch, set on fire (p. 193)

GK 127 (1989): 213; YfR 42.

The poem explores Sutzkever's relationship with the artist Marc Chagall, who died on March 28, 1985.

Line 7: אַר מאָדערן (*ar modern*): the Musée d'Art Moderne in Paris, situated in the Centre Pompidou since 1977.

My Father's Yortsayt (p. 195)

GK 130 (1990): 5; YfR 59.

Title: *yortsayt*: the anniversary of someone's death, according to the Jewish calendar. Each year, on this date, near relatives light a candle (*yortsayt-likht*) which burns for 24 hours and say Kaddish, the prayer for the dead. Sutzkever's father died on this date in 1920, in Siberia (see, p. 235, 65).

Bread and Salt (p. 197)

GK 141 (1995): 5; TsV 80.

It Was Worthwhile (p. 197)

GK 141 (1995): 9; TsV 90.

Dedication: Dan Miron (born 1934): Israeli literary critic and author of books on Hebrew and Yiddish literature. Professor emeritus of the Hebrew University of Jerusalem and currently Professor of Hebrew at Columbia University, New York. In 1993 Miron received the Israel Prize for Hebrew literature.

This poem is often cited as Sutzkever's last published poem. It does appear to be the poet's farewell, and no more poetry was published until 2000 when The red rooster appeared in the new Yiddish journal טאָפּלפּונקט (*Toplpunkt*).

The Red Rooster (p. 203)

Toplpunkt 1 (2000): 5.

This is indeed the last poem Sutzkever published in his lifetime.

Line 2: Moyshe-Leyb: The Yiddish poet Moyshe-Leyb Halpern (1886–1932) was born in Galicia, worked as a commercial artist in Vienna for nine years, and emigrated to New York in 1908. He married Royzele Baron in 1919. He scraped a living from journalism, and published two books of powerful, highly original poetry, in which the poet often featured in different personas, including the self-mocking character "Moyshe-Leyb". He was also a talented artist. Though he became an extremely popular poet, the family always struggled to make ends meet. Halpern died on August 31st, 1932, and two further collections of poetry were published by his widow in 1934.

Set sail, my word, so that your softest sound (p. 205)

This poem, in Sutzkever's handwriting, was found in early 2015 among the possessions of the late Shalom Rosenfeld (1914–2008), an influential Israeli journalist and former editor-in-chief of the newspaper *Maariv*. The poem appears in print here for the first time, and we are most grateful to Shalom Rosenfeld's daughter, Tamar Guy, for permission to publish the poem and the photo of Sutzkever's manuscript.

Line 12: *tefillin.* This is the Hebrew and Yiddish word for phylacteries, small boxes containing Biblical text, which are bound on the forehead and left arm during morning prayers. Sutzkever uses the plural form of the word *shel-rosh*, which means the phylactery for the forehead. I have used the general word *tefillin*, because, unlike *shel-rosh*, it is often used in an English context.

Here, in Sutzkever's last metapoetic poem, the poet daringly uses the image of the *tefillin* to suggest an equivalence between his poetic words and the holy language of Jewish prayer. The poem expresses his serene conviction that his poetry will endure throughout future generations.

Avrom Sutzkever, c. 1990

Left: Avrom Sutzkever, Vilna 1927

Right, left to right: Sutzkever, his mother, his brother Moyshe, Vilna 1928

Left, left to right: Shmerke Katsherginski and Avrom Sutzkever, c. 1934

Right: Sutzkever as a partisan

Above, left to right: Shmerke Katsherginski, Avrom Sutzkever, B. Zuckerman, Chaim Grade

Below, back row, left to right: Y. M. Neuman, Simkha Lev, Avrom-Iser Yoskovitsh, Zalman Aran; front row, left to right: H. Leyvik, Kadye Molodowsky, Avrom Sutzkever, Tel Aviv, June 1950

Left: Sutzkever with Marc Chagall, Paris, 1955

Right: Sutzkever with Czesław Miłosz, 1979

Freydke and Avrom Sutzkever, 1969

Heather Valencia

Avrom Sutzkever's Life and Work

און ס׳וועט זײַן בײַם אויסלאָז פֿון די טעג,	And thus it shall be in the last days,
דעמאָלט וועט געשען: דער בן־אָדם	then it will come to pass: a mortal
וועט ניט מער דערנענטערן צו זײַן הונגעריק מויל	will bring to his hungry mouth
ניט קיין ברויט, ניט קיין רינדפֿלייש,	neither bread nor meat,
ניט קיין פֿײַג, ניט קיין האָניק;	neither fig nor honey;
פֿאַרזוכן וועט ער בלויז אַ וואָרט אָדער צוויי	he will simply try a word or two
און וועָרן געזעטיקט.	and will be satisfied.

These lines could be a motto for Avrom Sutzkever's whole life.[1] They form the epigraph of his book פֿון אַלטע און יונגע כתבֿ־ידן (From Old and Young Man-uscripts), published in 1982. To Sutzkever the word was the true reality, and the word as nourishment is a key motif throughout his work.

Sutzkever is generally considered to be the greatest modern Yiddish poet, and is increasingly being recognized as one of the foremost poets of the twen-tieth century. His oeuvre encompasses lyrical poetry and longer epic poems, short prose narratives, autobiographical writing and literary criticism. He raised the Yiddish language to a new level of literary expression, and enriched it through a host of creative neologisms. His poetry fuses the modern with the classical: his subject matter, as well as his strikingly original expression and imagery are very much of the twentieth century, but he combines these with impeccably regular meter and rhyme, and traditional verse forms.

Sutzkever's long life spans almost the whole of the twentieth century, and his work reflects the fate of the Jewish people in that most catastrophic and transformative era. He himself narrowly escaped the fate of millions of Jews and other persecuted people, and his survival led him to describe himself in a later poem as a פֿעניקס־מענטש (feniks-mentsh, phoenix man, p. 175). The interdependence of his biography and his literary work was aptly described by the German critic Jost Blum:

1   A definitive biography of Sutzkever has not yet been written. The main sources I have used for the biographical information are Astur 1963, Cammy 2007, Fishman 1996, Harshav 1991, No-vershtern 1983b, Katsherginski 1953 and 1955. Where I have quoted information given by Sutzkever either in written essays, interviews, or personal conversations held with me, this has been stated in the text or in a footnote.

Sutzkevers Werk folgt eng den Linien seines eigenen äußeren und inneren Erlebens; es ist in hohem Maße autobiographisch, ohne sich je im Autobiographischen zu erschöpfen oder zu verlieren: Vielleicht wurden gerade deshalb große Teile seines Werkes zu einer unvergleichlichen dichterischen Chronik dieser grausam verfolgten Generation.[2]

Sutzkever's work closely follows the lines of his own outer and inner experience; it is highly autobiographical, without ever becoming totally confined to or defined by the autobiographical. For this reason, perhaps, a large proportion of his work is an incomparable poetic chronicle of this cruelly persecuted generation.

Sutzkever's life

Childhood and youth in Siberia and Vilna

Smorgon (now Smarhon), where Avrom Sutzkever was born on July 15, 1913, is an industrial city to the south east of Vilna (now Vilnius). At that time, like Vilna itself, it belonged to the Russian Empire, but now the city is in Belarus. In the late nineteenth century the majority of its population were Jews, and Smorgon was the birthplace of another famous Yiddish writer, Moyshe Kulbak (1896–1937), who was a legendary figure in Vilna when Sutzkever was growing up there, though he had moved to Berlin in 1920.

Sutzkever was the youngest of three children and came from an illustrious family on his mother's side: his maternal grandfather, Shabse Feinberg, was the rabbi of Michalishok (a town about sixteen kilometers to the north-east of Vilna) and the author of a well-known religious commentary.[3] Sutzkever's father, Herts,who owned a small leather factory, had studied at a yeshiva, a Talmudic academy, and was also a scholar of Jewish religious law. Throughout the poet's life, his grandfather and his father were significant figures in his life and work.

Sutzkever did not become acquainted with his birthplace as a child, because in 1915, during fighting between the Russians and Germans for control of Lithuania, the Jews of the area, suspected by the Russians of spying for the Germans, were ordered to leave. The Sutzkever family fled eastwards and, thanks to the help of a merchant they met during their journey, they settled in Omsk, Siberia.

---

2   Blum 1992: 138.
3   *Afikey maginim*, see p. 23–25.

Life there was full of hardship. During the Russian Civil War the family suffered from cold, poverty, hunger and illness; Sutzkever himself caught typhoid fever which was rampant in the region. His father, who had a weak heart, struggled to make ends meet through tutoring, but died in Siberia at the age of thirty. These early childhood experiences were later transformed in Sutzkever's magnificent long poem סיביר (*Sibir*, Siberia), and were, in his own eyes, seminal for his development as a human being and a poet.[4]

In 1920, when the Civil War ended, Reyne Sutzkever and her three children returned to Lithuania, now an independent sovereign state. They settled in Vilna, which, together with the surrounding region, was under Polish rule from 1922 until 1939. Vilna became the second significant place in Sutzkever's life and creative work. Here too the child soon experienced loss and death: his brother Moyshe left home to study in France, then emigrated to Israel as a pioneer. In 1925 his beloved elder sister Etl, an unusually gifted child who wrote poetry in Russian, died of meningitis at the age of thirteen. Sutzkever has related that on hearing of her death he wrote in the sand the word אייביק (*eybik*, eternal).[5] He and his mother lived in two rooms on the second floor of an old house in Snipishok (Šnipiškės), a working class district of Vilna, helped financially by her elder brother in America.

The importance of Vilna for Sutzkever's emergence and development as a poet was immense. The city itself had legendary status among Jews from Eastern Europe and beyond, a significance signaled by its symbolic designation as ירושלים ד'ליטע (*Yerusholayim de-lite*, the Jerusalem of Lithuania).[6] And indeed, over the centuries, Vilna was a great centre of religious and, later, secular Jewish culture. Many famous rabbis and scholars flourished in the city. The most illustrious of them was the Gaon (Yiddish *goen*, genius) of Vilna, Rabbi Elyahu ben Shlomo Zalmen (1720–1797). Regarded as a great authority on religious questions, he opposed what he saw as the emotional, mystical excesses of he Hassidic movement, and through his teaching and writings he established Vilna as a famous centre of Jewish learning and research.

The dissemination of his learning was facilitated by the founding of the Romm printing house in 1789. After the second partition of Poland in 1795, Lithuania became part of the Russian Empire, and from 1836 onwards, only two Jewish publishers were permitted to exist there, one being the Romm

---

4   P. 57–75 and 261–264.
5   Harshav 1991: 12.
6   On the history of Jewish Vilna, cf. Frakes 2011: 1–15; Briedis 2012: 193–218. Alfred Döblin writes vividly of his impressions of prewar Jewish life in Vilna (Döblin 1987: 115–153), especially its Yiddish teachers' seminar (ibid.: 139–146).

printing house, which flourished until the Second World War.[7] It published a wide variety of texts in Hebrew and, to a lesser extent, Yiddish, including translations of works of world literature. Its most famous achievement is an edition of the Talmud, published between 1880–1886.

As well as the religious learning which characterized *Yerusholayim de-lite*, Vilna became a leading centre of the new Jewish secular movements of the second half of the nineteenth century. In 1897 the אַלגעמיינער אַרבעטער־בונד אין ליטע, פּוילן און רוסלאַנד (*Algemeyner yidisher arbeter-bund in Lite, Poyln un Rusland*, General Jewish Labour Bund in Lithuania, Poland and Russia), commonly known as the Bund, was founded in Vilna. The Bund's ideals were grounded in the idea of Yiddish as the medium of Jewish secular culture in the Diaspora, by which an educated, Yiddish-speaking working class would grow in Eastern Europe. By the first quarter of the twentieth century Vilna had various Yiddish-language educational and cultural institutions, including a גימנאַזיע (*gimnazye*, high school), a technical college, theatre, youth clubs, libraries and five Yiddish newspapers. The Vilna Yiddish לערער־סעמינאַר (*lerer-seminar*, teachers' college), where Moyshe Kulbak had been a tutor, promoted radical secular ideas among the young teachers who would go on to staff the Yiddish-language schools of Poland and Russia. It co-existed with Hebrew- and Polish-language teachers' colleges, and with religious institutions teaching traditional texts in Yiddish: the Vilna of the early twentieth century was a melting pot of traditional religious and modern secular Jewish culture.

In 1925 the ייִדישער װיסנשאַפֿטלעכער אינסטיטוט (*Yidisher visnshaftlekher institut*, Jewish Research Institute), known under the acronym YIVO, was founded in Berlin by Elias Tsherikover, Nokhem Shtif and other Eastern European Jewish intellectuals who were resident there. Their aim was to study, preserve and promote Yiddish culture. The philological section, under the leadership of Max Weinreich and Zelig Kalmanovitsh was established in Vilna, and from 1926 onward, the headquarters of the institute moved there.[8] This organization was to play a very important role in Sutzkever's life before, during and after the war years.

In his earlier youth, however, Sutzkever had little direct knowledge of secular Yiddish culture. He was educated in a Polish-language Jewish high school,[9] where strong emphasis was placed on Polish literature and culture,

---

7   See Sutzkever's poem די בלייַענע פּלאַטן פֿון ראָמס דרוקעריַי (*Di blayene platn fun Roms drukeray*, The Lead Plates of Romm's Printing House), p. 107. For more information on the history of the Romm press, see Notes on the Poems, and also Gries 2008.
8   Other branches were established in centers with a significant Yiddish-speaking population, such as Warsaw and New York, and during the Second World War the New York center became the headquarters of the institute.
9   Cf. p. 27.

and Sutzkever gained wide knowledge of Polish poetry. He particularly revered the modernist poet Cyprian Norvid and published a long poem about him in his first poetry collection, לידער (*Lider*, Poems), 1937.[10]

Like many Yiddish writers, Sutzkever's literary beginning was in a language other than Yiddish.[11] Initially he wrote poems in Hebrew, and in an interview recorded as late as 2001, he said: ווען איך האָב אָנגעהױבן שרײַבן העברעיִש, האָב איך נאָך ניט געװוּסט, אַז ס׳איז פֿאַראַן אַ ייִדישע פּאָעזיע (When I began writing in Hebrew, I didn't yet know that Yiddish poetry existed).[12] This situation was remedied partly through the intervention of two friends made during his teenage years. Leyzer Volf (real name: Mekler) was three years older than Sutzkever, and was already writing poems in Yiddish. He was an eccentric personality, who had taken the name of a Sholem Aleichem character as his nom de plume, and became well-known for his parodies, grotesque poems and extravagant gestures (such as writing 1,001 poems in one month!). In the same late interview Sutzkever acknowledges the importance of Leyzer Volf's influence: ער האָט מיר געלייִענט זײַנע לידער, און איך האָב דערשפּירט, אַז דאָס איז אַן עניין װאָס האָט אַ גרױסע שײַכות צו מיר (He read me his poems, and I sensed that this was something which had great relevance for me).[13]

The second person to contribute to Sutzkever's developing awareness and love of Yiddish poetry was Freydke Levitan who was three years younger than him and whom he met when he was about fifteen. Freydke, whom Sutzkever married in 1939, was educated in a Yiddish-language high school, and had a thorough knowledge of Yiddish literature. At the age of fourteen she began working in the bibliography section of YIVO, where Sutzkever got to know Max Weinreich, who also encouraged his study of Yiddish classical and modern literature. Sutzkever read for hours every day in Vilna's Strashun Library and attended lectures on literary theory by the Polish literary historian Professor Manfred Kridl at the University of Vilna.

In 1930 Sutzkever joined the Jewish scout organization בין (*Bin*, the Bee), of which Leyzer Volf was a member, as was Miki Tshernikhov, with whom

10 Sutzkever 1937: 45–52. It has recently been convincingly argued that Norvid and other Polish poets exerted an influence on his poetic consciousness that lasted throughout his creative life (cf. Adamczyk-Garbowska 2011; Cammy and Figlerowicz 2007).

11 In this context, Benjamin Harshav comments that most Yiddish poets "had a basic Hebrew religious education; some continued in general schools in other languages; eventually, all of them made up their private university by reading books in a number of languages, including Yiddish. Quite often, the first poetry they read was not in Yiddish. Many Yiddish poets even began by writing poetry in other languages – [H.] Leyvik in Hebrew; M. L. Halpern in German; Dovid Edelshtat and A. Leyeles in Russian; Malka Heifets-Tussman in English – before they turned to Yiddish verse" (Harshav 1990: 143).

12 Sutzkever 2001: 6.

13 Ibid.

Sutzkever also formed a productive friendship.[14] Two important characteristics of the ideology of *Bin* for Sutzkever's development were its enthusiasm for nature, and for Yiddish language and culture. Tshernikhov, writing in 1963 as Mikhoel Astur, pinpoints both of these as having exerted a deep and lasting influence on the poet:

אַז סוצקע- [...] עס קען ניט זײַן קיין ספֿק
װערס איינגעבאָרענע פֿעיקייט צו זען, צו
פֿילן, צו פֿאַרשטיין און איבערצוגעבן די
נאַטור איז סטימולירט געװאָרן און איז
אויסגעװאַקסן אַ דאַנק די בינישע עקסקור-
סיעס און לאַגערן. ניט װיייניקער װיכטיק
איז געװען די השפּעה פֿון ,בין' אויף סוצ-
קעװערס באַציונג צו יידיש. ער איז געװען
מסתּמא דער איינציקער מיטגליד פֿון דער
אָרגאַניזאַציע, װאָס האָט זיך קיין מאָל ניט
געלערנט אין קיין יידיש־װעלטלעכער שול.
,בין' האָט ניט געהאַט קיין שום שטעלונג
אין געזעלשאַפֿטלעכע פּראָבלעמען, אָבער
איין זאַך איז בײַ איר געװען קלאָר און קאָנ-
סעקװענט: [...] אַ גװאַלדיקע ליבשאַפֿט צו
דער יידישער שפּראַך און דער גאַנצער יידי-
שער קולטור־שאַפֿונג. דאָס האָט זי באַװיזן
איינצוגעבן סוצקעװערן װי ס'באַדאַרף צו
זײַן.

There can be no doubt [...] that Sutzkever's native ability to see, to feel, to understand and convey the essence of nature was stimulated and developed through the excursions and camps of *Bin*. No less important was the influence of *Bin* on Sutzkever's relationship with Yiddish. He was probably the only member of the organization who had not been educated in a secular Yiddish school. *Bin* took no position on social problems, but one thing was clear and consistent in [the organization]: [...] a deep love of the Yiddish language and all its cultural creativity. And this it managed very successfully to inculcate into Sutzkever.[15]

Sutzkever and Tshernikhov only remained in the organization for about two years, but their friendship continued, and particularly important was the time Sutzkever spent at the *dacha* of Miki's family in the countryside near Vilna in the summer of 1932. In the evenings the parents and the two young men read Pushkin:

אַזוי האָבן מיר איבערגעלייענט גאַנץ ,יעװגע-
ני אָנעגין" און אַ ריי לירישע לידער. סוצקע-
װער האָט זיך צוגעהערט מיט געשפּאַנטן
אינטערעס און אַרײַנגעזאַפּט אין זיך דעם
ריטעם און דעם גײַסט פֿון פּושקינס פּאָעזיע.

So we read the whole of *Eugene One-gin* and a variety of lyrical poems. Sutzkever listened with eager interest, soaking up the rhythm and the spirit of Pushkin's poetry.[16]

---

14   Miki Tshernikhov (1916–2004) had a very cultured family background: his parents were a historian and a prominent Vilna lawyer. He survived Soviet labour camps and later became Professor Michael Czernichow Astour, Professor of Yiddish and Russian Literature at Brandeis University and Professor of History (Classical Cultures and Ancient Near East) at Southern Illinois University (Edwardsville).

15   Astur 1963: 24.

16   Ibid.: 29.

Before he left to study in Paris in 1934, Tshernikhov had acquainted Sutzkever with a spectrum of writers from different literary traditions: the Russian Symbolists, German and French poetry, and Edgar Allan Poe – all of whom, in Tshernikhov's opinion had פֿאַרברייטערט סוצקעוּוערס האָריזאָנט און אין אייניקע פֿאַלן דירעקט אָדער אומדירעקט אינספּירירט זײַנע לידער (broadened Sutzkever's horizon and in some cases directly or indirectly inspired his poems).[17]

Leyzer Volf was a member of the group of poets known as יונג ווילנע (*Yung Vilne*, Young Vilna) which included, among others, Chaim Grade and Shmerke Katsherginski. These were radical leftist young poets who took their craft very seriously and had clear ideas about the role and nature of poetry. Again, Astour has summed up their credo succinctly:

[די דיכטער פֿון „יונג ווילנע"] האָבן אַלץ געזוכט דעם פּשט, דעם נימשל, די טענ־ דענץ, דעם נוצן, וואָס אַזאַ מין ליד קען ברענגען דער זאַך פֿון דער פּראָלעטאַרישער רעוואָלוציע. „קונסט לשם קונסט?" פֿון דעם האָט מען דעמאָלט אין „יונג־ווילנע" ווייניק געהאַלטן.	[The poets of Young Vilna] constantly searched for meaning, a moral, a [political] tendency, for the contribution a poem can make to the cause of proletarian revolution. "Art for art's sake?" The poets of Young Vilna at that time didn't think much of that idea.[18]

Sutzkever's early poetry with its pantheistic nature imagery, grotesque elements and individualism was therefore foreign to their way of thinking – the times they were living were לויטער שטאָל און ניט קרישטאָל (made purely of steel, not of crystal),[19] as Katsherginski gently rebuked his friend – and Sutzkever was refused entry to the group at his first application in 1931. Not until 1934 did he become a member, but even then he remained to a certain extent an outsider, because, despite the darkening political mood in Poland, he maintained his aesthetic approach to poetry. It is true, however, that Sutzkever's political consciousness was growing, and even before the outbreak of war, he was beginning to allow the circumstances of the time to invade his inner poetic world.[20] It is far from fanciful to suggest that his contact with the poets of Young Vilna may well have contributed to the development of his conception of the nature of poetry.

17   Ibid.: 34.
18   Ibid. 28 f.
19   Katsherginski 1953: 59.
20   For example, מאָרגנקינד (*Morgnkind*, Morning child), 1939. In: Sutzkever 1963 (I): 221 f; מלחמה (*Milkhome*, War), 1939. Ibid.: 223.

If the poets of Young Vilna were somewhat skeptical of Sutzkever's work, it appealed strongly to the leaders of the modernist אינזיכיסטן (*Inzikhistn*, Introspectivists) in New York, Arn Glants-Leyeles and Yankev Glatsteyn. From 1935, poems of his appeared in their journal אינזיך (*Inzikh*, Within the self) and he began to become well-known to an international audience. Sutzkever's friendship with Glants-Leyeles lasted until the latter's death in 1966. Sutzkever also spent some time in Warsaw, the main centre of Yiddish literature in Eastern Europe, where he became acquainted not only with the Yiddish writers and intellectuals there, including Itsik Manger, Y. Y. Trunk, Noyekh Prilutski and Arn Tseytlin, but also with poets writing in Polish, like Julian Tuvim. Several of Sutzkever's poems, including אויף מיין וואַנדער-פֿיַיפֿל (*Oyf mayn vander-fayfl*, On my wander flute) later retitled אין טאָרבע פֿונעם ווינט (*In torbe funem vint*, In the knapsack of the wind)[21] were published in the prestigious Warsaw journal ליטעראַרישע בלעטער (*Literarishe bleter*, Literary Pages).

His growing fame also led to the publication of his first collection of poetry, partly through the intervention of the Austrian Jewish writer Joseph Roth, whom Sutzkever met just before leaving for Warsaw in 1937.[22] Roth, (whom Sutzkever suspected of being inebriated at the time, as was frequently the case!) asked him to recite one of his poems, and Roth was so impressed with it[23] that he praised him to the members of the ליטעראַטן-פֿאַראיין (*Literatn-fareyn*, Literary Association) in Warsaw, as Sutzkever relates in a later letter to Glants-Leyeles:

[...] און שטעלט אייַך פֿאָר, אַז ווען איך בין דאָרט געקומען אויף איבער מאָרגן, האָבן מיר אַלע רעדאַקטאָרן און פּראָמינענטן אָפּ־ געגעבן אַ גרוס טאַקע פֿון אים, ראָט. ער האָט אַלעמען דערציילט וועגן די וווּנדערלעכע ליד [sic] וואָס איך האָב אים געלייענט. ער האָט אַפֿילו ציטירט אויף אויסנווייניק עט־ לעכע סטראָפֿן... דער באָדן איז, אַלזאָ, שוין געוואָרן צוגעגרייט.	Just imagine, when I arrived two days later, all the editors and prominent people gave me greetings from him, Roth. He had told everyone about the wonderful poem that I had read to him. He even quoted whole stanzas by heart... Therefore the ground had already been prepared for me.[24]

21 See above, p. 79.
22 In his book *Juden auf Wanderschaft* (Jews on their Travels), written in 1927 when Roth was travelling in France Russia, Poland and Albania as a correspondent for the liberal newspaper Frankfurter Zeitung, he expressed great admiration for the Jews of Eastern Europe and their culture. Roth 1985, 11–39.
23 The poem was באַשאַפֿונג (*Bashafung*, Creation), Sutzkever 1937: 27.
24 Letter to Arn Glants-Leyeles, 26 May 1937. Quoted in Noverstern 1983 b: 110.

Shortly afterwards, the volume of his early poetry, entitled לידער (*Lider*, Poems) was published by the Jewish PEN Club in Warsaw. The collection comprised lyrical poems written between 1934 and 1937, and the first version of a long poem, or *poeme*,[25] about Siberia, entitled שטערן אין שניי (*Shtern in shney*, Star in the Snow).[26]

The war years: in the Vilna ghetto and the Narocz forest
In September 1939 the Soviet Army occupied Polish-ruled Vilna and returned it to Lithuania as its capital. There followed a short period of political independence, but at the beginning of August 1940, the Soviet Union occupied the whole country, and Lithuania became a Soviet Republic. During the short period of independence, Sutzkever managed to publish his second volume of poetry, וואַלדיקס (*Valdiks*, Of the Forest), in 1940. Most of the poems of this collection, written between 1937 and 1939, contrast markedly with the darkening mood and political upheavals of the time when they were written, though there are, as already suggested,[27] intimations of unease and change in some of the later poems of the collection.

Indeed Sutzkever was aware that the political situation was not without danger for him: his close links to the *Inzikhistn* in America and his own individualistic poetry were bound to render him suspect to the Soviet authorities, and he attempted to acquire a visa to travel to Palestine, for himself and his wife. It was too late, however, for on July 22, 1941 the German army marched into Lithuania, and the years of Nazi terror had begun.

During the first six months of the occupation, thousands of Jews from Vilna were massacred in Ponary (Yiddish: פּאָנאַר, Ponar), a wooded area about seven kilometers from Vilna, popular before the war as a holiday resort. In his prose memoir, ווילנער געטאָ (*Vilner geto*, Vilna Ghetto), Sutzkever described its beauty:

די געגנט איז באַרימט מיט איר שיינער	The area is famous for its beautiful
לאַנדשאַפֿט. זי איז באַזונגען דורך אַדאַם	landscape. Adam Mickiewicz [the
מיצקעוויטשן. נאַפּאָלעאָן האָט זיך אין	Polish poet] praised it in song. When
ווילנע געהאַט אויסגעדריקט, אַז ער וואָלט	he was in Vilna Napoleon declared
אויף די הענט אַריבערגעטראָגן פּאָנאַר קיין	that he would have liked to carry

---

25   The Yiddish word פּאָעמע (*poeme*) designates a long, narrative poem or epic, in contrast to ליד (*lid*), which means either song, or shorter lyrical poem.
26   This poem was revised by Sutzkever over a number of years. See below, p. 262.
27   Cf. fn. 20.

פֿראַנקרייך. [...] ווען די טויט־פֿאַבריק איז

שוין געווען פֿאַרטיק, [איז] דאָס וואָרט „פּאָ־

נאַר" [...] געוואָרן אַ שרעק און אַ קללה.[28]

Ponary over to France. [...] When the death factory was ready, [...] the word "Ponary" [...] became a horror and a curse.[28]

The victims were shot and buried in pits. At the beginning of September, the remaining Jewish population was driven into two ghettos, divided by a "non-ghetto" area.[29] The men were particularly at risk of being arrested by the SS or the Lithuanian כאַפּונעס (*khapunes*, snatchers), which meant either forced labour, the infamous Lukishki prison, or death. Sutzkever and many others hid in various מאַלינעס (*malines*, hiding places). He describes the consequences of the נאַכט פֿון געלע שייַנען (*nakht fun gele shaynen*, night of the yellow [work] passes), October 28, 1941, when it was announced that all who had yellow passes were to assemble to be sent to work in some unspecified place – it was widely believed that those without passes would either be murdered or sent to the prison. Sutzkever, who had no pass, fled from the ghetto, evaded several guards en route and knocked at a random door in a neighboring village. The elderly inhabitant, Janova Bartoshevitsh and her family welcomed him and hid him for about three months – Janova, at great risk to herself, regularly went to the ghetto, taking food for Sutzkever's wife and mother, and carrying letters between him and his wife.[30]

When he returned to the ghetto at the beginning of 1942, he discovered that his wife had just given birth to a son in the ghetto hospital, but the child had immediately been killed in accordance with a new edict that no child was to be born in the ghetto.[31] Shortly afterwards, his mother was captured and shot.

Almost immediately afterwards, Sutzkever began participating in an important cultural development in the ghetto. In *Vilna ghetto*, he describes how it began:

28   Sutzkever 1947: 35. It is estimated that by 1944 around 70,000 Jews, 5,000 Soviet prisoners, 1,000 other "Soviet activists," 1,500–2,000 Poles, and 40 Romany people had been murdered and buried in Ponary. See איך האָב אַ בריוו דערהאַלטן פֿון מייַן היימשטאָט אין דער ליטע (I have received a letter from my home in Lithuania), p. 175.

29   The smaller ghetto was liquidated in October 1942, and most of its residents were shot in Ponary. On the history of the Vilna ghetto, cf. Schroeter 2008; Kruk 2002.

30   Sutzkever describes this period in *Vilner geto*, Sutzkever 1947: 63–72. He never forgot Janova and wrote three poems about her: Sutzkever 1963 (I): 287; Sutzkever 1963 (II): 303; Sutzkever 1986: 83.

31   Cf. צום קינד (*Tsum kind*, To my child), p. 95.

אין אַ טאָג אַרום נאָכן דערשיסן מײַן מאַמען
איז געקומען מיך מנחם־אָבֿל זײַן דער יונגער
רעזשיסער וויסקינד. ער האָט מיך פֿאַרבעטן
אויף אַ צונויפֿקום מיט ייִדישע אַקטיאָרן. עס
איז דאָ אַ געדאַנק צו שאַפֿן אַ טעאַטער.
איך האָב אים אָנגעקוקט פֿאַרוווּנדערט:
– אַ טעאַטער אין געטאָ?

> The day after my mother was shot, the young theater director Viskind came to express his condolences. He invited me to a meeting with Yiddish actors. They were thinking of starting a theatre.
> I looked at him in amazement:
> – A theatre in the ghetto?[32]

The enterprise did initially arouse controversy, but the productions, exhibitions, concerts and other events which Sutzkever and others organized became a true enrichment of the lives of ghetto inhabitants, helping to restore their dignity and self-esteem. The young Yitskhok Rudashevski describes in his diary the delight of the public in an exhibition and reading evening in honor of the poet Yehoash, which Sutzkever organized:[33]

קוקנדיק אויף דער אויסשטעלונג, אויף
אונדזער אַרבעט, ווערט דאָס האַרץ אָנגע־
קוואָלן מיט באַגײַסטערונג, מען פֿאַרגעסט
טאַקע, אַז מען איז אין אַ פֿינצטערן געטאָ.
[...] ס'איז געווען טאַקע יום־טובֿ, אַ דע־
מאָנסטראַציע פֿון ייִדישער ליטעראַטור און
קולטור.

> Looking at the exhibition, at our work, your heart swells with enthusiasm. You really forget that you're in a dark ghetto. [...] It was a real celebration, a demonstration of Yiddish literature and culture.[34]

Not only was Sutzkever involved in organizing literary events, but throughout the years in the ghetto, in cramped hiding places, and later, in extremely precarious circumstances in the Narocz forest with the partisans, he constantly wrote, meticulously dating each poem and indicating where it was written – a practice which he had not consistently followed previously. It indicates that for Sutzkever, these poems were a record of the catastrophic time. He concealed the poems or gave them to trustworthy acquaintances outside the ghetto for safekeeping.

In fact, Sutzkever's official work in the ghetto, ordered by the Germans, for the so-called Rosenberg-Stab (Rosenberg task force) helped to facilitate the concealment of his poems and other documents. The "Einsatzstab Reichsleiter Rosenberg" (Reichsleiter Rosenberg task force) had been set up to

32 Sutzkever 1947: 105.
33 Yitskhok Rudashevski (1927–1943) kept a diary from June 1941 until April 1943. He was shot in Ponary in October 1943.
34 Quoted in Novershtern 1983: 140. On the morale-building importance of cultural events in the Nazi ghettos, cf. Tory 1990: 136, 432–433; Gilbert 2005; Gilbert n.d.

collect and assess valuable cultural documents and Judaica from the occupied regions of Europe, some of which would be sent to Germany, to the Institut zur Erforschung der Judenfrage (Institute for Research into the Jewish Question) in Frankfurt.[35] One of the senior members of the institute, Dr Johannes Pohl, was a scholar of Judaism who had studied Judaica at the Hebrew University of Jerusalem, and was the author of a book on the Talmud. He oversaw the project, the aim of which was defined in the Nazi press in Germany as "Judenforschung ohne Juden" (research on Jews without Jews).[36]

Vilna had several very important sources of materials, including the 40,000 volumes of the Strashun library, and the holdings of YIVO, which held treasures collected in the important ethnographic expeditions of the 1920s and 30s. Sutzkever and about 40 other intellectuals were forced to work in the YIVO building outside the ghetto, sorting the materials which had been transported there – 70% were to be disposed of as trash and the rest packed up to be sent to Germany.

Sutzkever and his colleagues employed all sorts of ruses to prevent their destruction – it is related, for example, that one of the Lithuanian guards aspired to a higher education, so two scholars in the work group taught him Latin, German and mathematics in the lunch break, while Sutzkever and others took the opportunity to run up to the attic and hide books and manuscripts there.[37] (Unfortunately all this cache was lost as the YIVO building was reduced to rubble, but much other material was saved.)

In the evenings the group smuggled materials into the ghetto under their clothes – the Jewish ghetto police did not bother much about this, giving the group the slightly sarcastic title of "the paper brigade." Sutzkever actually obtained official permission from the German overseer to take bundles of 'rubbish' papers into the ghetto to light people's ovens. In this way he saved, among other treasures, letters of Tolstoy, Gorky, Bialik, rare books from the fifteenth and sixteenth century, manuscripts of Sholem Aleichem and the only extant handwritten document by the Gaon of Vilna.[38] Several hiding places were found in the ghetto, including a large cellar, which remained intact until the end of the war. The work of the "paper brigade" also enabled weapons to be smuggled into the ghetto – they were delivered to the YIVO

35   Alfred Rosenberg (1893–1946), the Reich Minister for the Occupied Eastern Territories, was one of the foremost theorists of Nazi ideology.
36   "Zum erstenmal in der Geschichte: Judenforschung ohne Juden" (For the first time in history: Research on Jews without Jews). Title of an article in the *Illustierter Beobachter*, 30.04.1942. Quoted in Rupnow 2005: 190.
37   Fishman 1996: 10.
38   Sutzkever 1947: 116.

building and brought into the ghetto by Sutzkever and his colleagues, though the planned uprising in the Vilna ghetto did not in the end take place. This enterprise was of course extremely risky – one day the barrel of a machine gun was lying exposed on a table when some German officials made a surprise visit to the YIVO building – a Chagall painting was hastily laid over it, and when one of the visitors was about to lift up the painting to examine it, another worker created a diversion by running over to show the German a rare 17th century book, and the weapon was swiftly removed.[39]

Sutzkever depicted his work in the Rosenberg task force, both directly, in *Vilna Ghetto*,[40] and symbolically, in קערנדלעך ווייץ (*Kerndlekh veyts*, Grains of Wheat, p. 101), a poem dated March 10, 1943. Here the poet evokes his efforts to save the the precious manuscripts:

ווי ביים באַשיצן אַן עופֿל –	As if protecting a baby –,
איך לויף מיטן יידישן וואָרט,	I run with the Yiddish word,
נישטער אין איטלעכן הייפֿל,	digging in every courtyard,
דער גייַסט זאָל ניט ווערן דערמאָרדעט.	that the soul may not be destroyed.

The poet buries, or *plants* the manuscripts, the latter term bringing to his mind a legend: grains of wheat buried in a Pharaoh's tomb were sown thousands of years later, producing a crop of grain:

ניַין טויזנט יאָר שוין פֿאַרגאַנגען!	Nine thousand years had passed,
נאָר ווען מ'האָט די קערנער פֿאַרזייט, –	but when the grains were sown, –
האָבן אין זוניקע זאַנגען	sunny ears of wheat
צעבליט זיך אַ בייט נאָך אַ בייט.	blossomed, row upon row.

The poem ends with the expression of the poet's faith in the survival and renewed vigor of the word and of the Jewish people:

אפֿשר אויך וועלן די ווערטער	Perhaps these words will also
דערוואָרטן זיך ווען אויך דעם ליכט –	live to see the light –
וועלן אין שעה אין באַשערטער	and in the destined hour,
צעבליִען זיך אויך אומגעריכט?	will blossom again, shining bright?

און ווי דער אוראַלטער קערן	And like the ancient grain
וואָס האָט זיך פֿאַרוואַנדלט אין זאַנג, –	transformed into wheat once more,
וועלן די ווערטער אויך נערן,	these words will also nourish
וועלן די ווערטער געהערן	these words will also belong
דעם פֿאָלק, אין זיַין אייביקן גאַנג.	to the people, for evermore.

39 Fishman 1996: 9 f.
40 Sutzkever 1947: 112–117.

It seems particularly significant that the first explicit use of this trope of the word as nourishment should occur at a time when physical nourishment was a desperate issue.

Between May and September 1943, morale in the ghetto deteriorated, reaching a low point in July, after the death of Yitskhok Vitnberg (Wittenberg), the leader of the פֿאַראײניקטע פּאַרטיזאַנער אָרגאַניזאַציע (*Fareynikte partizaner organizatsye*, FPO, United Partisan Organization), the resistance organization in the ghetto.[41] By August it was becoming clear that the liquidation of the ghetto was imminent, and many younger people left to join the Jewish partisans in the Narocz forest. Avrom and Freydke Sutzkever, Shmerke Katsherginski and other members of the FPO escaped on September 12, and after walking one hundred kilometers through swamps and mined terrain, they reached the Jewish partisan unit נקמה (*Nekome*, Vengeance) in the area round the Narocz Lake. The ghetto was liquidated between 23 and 25 September, and the remaining population sent to death camps or killed in Ponary.

Even among the partisans, life was difficult for Jews. They encountered antisemitism among the non-Jewish partisan units, and shortly after the Sutzkevers' arrival, the Russian brigade commander, Markov, ordered the Jewish unit to disarm and disband.[42] This left them totally exposed to German attack, as an extant letter from Sutzkever and Katsherginski to Markov testifies:

אַלע אָטריאַדן זענען אַוועקגעגאַנגען און מיר זענען געבליבן אָן פֿאַרבינדונג, אָן עסן – הפֿקר אויף גאָטס באָראָט. [...] אַלע אונד־ זערע האָפֿענונגען זענען דערפֿאַר געוועגדט צו אײַך [...], און מיר דערוואַרטן פֿון אײַך אַן ענטפֿער און הילף גאָר אין גיכן. מיר זענען פֿאַרלאָזענע און הונגעריקע און דאָך האָבן מיר ניט פֿאַרלוירן דעם שטאַרקן ווילן צו קעמפֿן און ראַנגלען זיך, ביזן לעצטן צווײשן אונדז, פֿאַר דעם הײליקן ציל.	All the units have left and we remain here without contacts or food – abandoned and forsaken. [...] Therefore our only hope lies with you [...] and we await your answer and help urgently. Even though we are abandoned and hungry, we have not lost our strong will to fight and struggle until the last man and woman, for the holy goal.[43]

41   The Gestapo threatened to kill thousands in the ghetto if Wittenberg could not be arrested, and many of the ghetto population demanded that the FPO deliver Wittenberg to the Gestapo. Wittenberg gave himself up, and was found dead in his cell the next day, reputedly having committed suicide (cf. Gilbert 1986: 593). On the history of the FPO in Vilna, cf. Dawidowicz 1979: 392–394; Reznik n.d.
42   On the widespread antisemitism among non-Jewish partisans, cf. Dawidowicz 1979: 389. For the complex relations between non-Jewish partisans and Jews, see Zimmerman 2015.
43   Quoted in Novershtern 1983: 146.

It is not known whether Markov answered this letter directly, but later the situation improved somewhat for the Jewish partisans. Katsherginski remained in the forest, fighting with the partisans, until the liberation in July 1944, but for the Sutzkevers, an extraordinary turn of events took them to safety in Moscow.

Before he fled from the ghetto, Sutzkever had managed to have a manuscript of his long poem כל-נדרי (*Kol-Nidre*)[44] sent to the Yiddish writers of the Jewish Anti-Fascist Committee in Moscow for safe keeping. This *poeme*, written in February 1943, is based on a true incident: on Yom Kippur 1941 the Germans murdered 4,000 Jews from Vilna in Ponar. In Sutzkever's *poeme* a father recognizes among the doomed Jews his wounded son whom he had not seen since the latter had joined the Red Army. The father kills his own son in order to spare him any further suffering at the hands of the Nazis. This tragic poem made a deep impression at a public reading in Moscow, and the Jewish Anti-Fascist Committee, headed by Ilya Ehrenburg, the prolific Soviet writer and journalist, and the famous Yiddish actor Shloyme Mikhoels, decided to rescue Sutzkever and his wife. An important role in implementing this plan was also played by Justas Paleckis, whom the Russians had appointed President of the Lithuanian Soviet Socialist Republic in 1940, and who lived in Moscow at this time. He had met Sutzkever in Vilna and thought highly of his work.

On March 12, 1944 a small plane from Moscow attempted to land on a frozen river in order to pick up Avrom and Freydke Sutzkever, who had reached this meeting point after a long journey on foot through mined territory. This plane was shot down by German snipers. According to Sutzkever the resulting fire caused the deaths of eleven people hiding in a barn.[45] A second plane managed to land two hours later, and, after a perilous journey the couple arrived in Moscow.

1944–1947: Sutzkever in Moscow, Vilna, Nuremberg, Łódź and Paris

As soon as Sutzkever arrived in Moscow he spoke publicly, under the aegis of the Jewish Anti-Fascist Committee, about the fate of the Jews in Vilna and the courageous efforts of the Jewish partisans. An article about him in Pravda, written by Ilya Ehrenburg,[46] aroused great interest among the Jews in the

---

44　Kol-Nidre is the name of a prayer said at the religious service of the same name on the eve of Yom Kippur (the Day of Atonement), the most important and solemn of the Jewish religious festivals. For an analysis of Sutzkever's poem, cf. Pollin-Galay 2016: 12–18.

45　Sutzkever 2001: 8.

46　Ilya Ehrenburg, "The victory of the human being," *Pravda*, April 29, 1944, quoted in Novershtern 1983: 149.

Soviet Union, and Sutzkever became a public figure, working with the Jewish Anti-Fascist Committee to disseminate information about the catastrophe in Lithuania and Poland. He was one of a group compiling evidence of Nazi atrocities for a projected Black Book under the editorship of Vassily Grossman, which in the end was never published in the Soviet Union.[47]

On 13th July 1944, Vilna was liberated by the Red Army, and Sutzkever returned to the city, where together with Katsherginski and Aba Kovner, the former commander of the ghetto partisans, he searched for the hidden documents and works of art. The task was immense, and their initial plan was to attempt to establish a Jewish Museum. Rescued materials were brought to the apartment Sutzkever shared with Katsherginski, which became "the Jewish address in the city; the place where Jewish soldiers, partisans and survivors gathered, where the short-lived Jewish school was founded, and where all letters addressed to surviving Jews in Vilna were forwarded."[48] Later the museum was moved into a building which had contained the ghetto library but also the prison, so that "[t]he staff of the Jewish Museum worked in the prison cells where Jewish inmates had been tortured by the Gestapo."[49] Fishman describes the fate of the Jewish materials: some were destroyed by the Lithuanian authorities, some were smuggled out by Sutzkever and Katsherginski and sent by a roundabout route to YIVO in New York, and a substantial amount of material was hidden in Vilna and did not reach YIVO until 1995 and 1996.[50]

To see the destroyed city, where only a few hundred of the originally 60,000-strong Jewish population remained, was a tragic and traumatic experience for Sutzkever. He wrote to Ilya Ehrenburg:

שוין צוויי וואָכן ווי איך פֿלאַטער צווישן די געסלער. כ׳האָב אויפֿגעגראָבן קולטור-אוצרות און געווען אויף פּאָנאַר. כ׳האָב דאָרט קיינעם ניט געפֿונען. בלויז אַש. [...] כ׳האָב אָנגעשאָטן אַ זעקל אַש (קען זיַין ס׳איז מיַין קינד, אָדער מיַין מאַמע) און האַלט עס לעבן זיך.	I've been wandering round the streets for two weeks now. I've dug up cultural treasures, and I've been to Ponary. I found no one there. Only ash. [...] I filled a little bag with the ash (it could be my child, or my mother) and I keep it with me.[51]

47 For a history of the *Black Book*, see Lustiger 2003: 157–169. For more detailed discussion of the variety of Sutzkever's "testimony and cultural rescue work" during the years 1944–1946, cf. Schwarz 2005. Hannah Pollin-Galay (2016) illuminates Sutzkever's role as a witness in the Soviet Union, 1944–1946, focussing especially on the differences between Sutzkever's testimony and other Soviet testimonies, and discussing the epistolary exchanges between Sutzkever and Jewish refugees in the Soviet Union.
48 Fishman 1996: 11.
49 Ibid.
50 Ibid.: 11–15.
51 Quoted in Novershtern 1983: 155.

It became clear that there was very little likelihood of renewing Jewish life in Lithuania: the communist authorities frustrated their efforts to set up a Jewish museum, a Yiddish newspaper and schools for Jewish children. Sutzkever remained in Vilna for three months, then returned to Moscow, where he wrote his prose account of the war years, ווילנער געטאָ (*Vilner geto*, Vilna Ghetto). In this work he describes his life in the ghetto and in the woods with the partisans. As well as giving factual details, he vividly evokes his own experiences and emotions, and those of others, so that the reader has a real sense of the suffering and courage of the victims of Nazi persecution. The work also reveals the origin of various poems from this period, which gives insight into his creative process.

On February 27, 1946, Sutzkever appeared as a witness at the Nuremberg Trials of the Major War Criminals.[52] He had been nominated by Ilya Ehrenburg and the Yiddish actor and theatre director Shloyme Mikhoels. This responsibility affected Sutzkever deeply, as he testified in his report of the experience:[53]

That great responsibility filled all the cells of my consciousness. For the two nights before my appearance I was unable to close my eyes at all. I kept seeing before me my mother running naked over a snow-covered field, – and the warm blood from her pierced heart began to trickle across my room and surrounded me like a ring.[54]

He had wanted to give his testimony in Yiddish, but had to speak in Russian, a language in which he was not totally fluent:

Without doubt, divine Providence put the Russian language into my mouth. I didn't expect that I would be able to express my feelings and thoughts in that language.

52 Part of Sutzkever's testimony can be seen at http://www.youtube.com/watch?v=rY4GnquFCmE (accessed September 22, 2014).
53 Avrom Sutskever, מײַן עדות־זאָגן פֿאַרן נירנבערגער טריבונאַל (*Mayn eydes-zogn farn Nirnberger tribunal*, My witness statement before the Nuremberg Tribunal), in *Di goldene keyt* 54 (1966): 5–16. Reprinted with small alterations in Sutzkever 1993: 150–166. The following quotations are taken from the later version of the essay.
54 Sutzkever 1993: 162.

מיר איז נאָך שווער אָפּצוווועגן מײַנע גע־
פֿילן. וואָסער פֿון זיי איז שטאַרקער, דאָס
געפֿיל פֿון טרויער, צי דאָס געפֿיל פֿון נקמה?
מיר דאַכט, אַז שטאַרקער פֿאַר ביידע, איז
דאָס אויפֿלויכטנדיקע, מעכטיקע געפֿיל, אַז
אונדזער פֿאָלק לעבט, האָט איבערגעלעבט
זײַנע תּלינים – און קיין שום פֿינצטערער
כּוח איז אונדז ניט ביכולת צו פֿאַרטיליקן.

I still find it difficult to weigh up
my feelings. Which is stronger, the
feeling of grief or the feeling of vengeance? I think that stronger than
both of them is the mighty feeling
that is beginning to glow inside me,
that our people lives, that it has survived its executioners – and that no
dark force is able to annihilate us.[55]

During his two years in Moscow, Sutzkever had become closely acquainted
with the great personalities of Soviet Yiddish culture – among them the poets
Perets Markish and Dovid Hofshteyn, the prose writer Dovid Bergelson and
the actor and theatre director Shloyme Mikhoels – as well as Boris Pasternak
and other Russian writers. The situation was precarious for writers in the
Soviet Union, and for Jewish writers in particular. On the surface Yiddish
cultural life was flourishing at this period; Jews were able to publish their
work, to found newspapers and organize cultural events, but the political
atmosphere in Stalin's Russia was extremely volatile, and in their writing they
had to be constantly on guard against being guilty of "Jewish nationalism"
or "bourgeois individualism."[56] Sutzkever had already sailed very near the
wind by failing to mention Stalin's name in his first public appearance in
Moscow, and by openly expressing the desire for a renewal of Jewish life in
Eastern Europe. Moreover, his close relationship to the modernist poets in
New York, and the individualism of his poetry were absolutely at odds with
the official political line. It became increasingly clear to him and Freydke that
their future lay elsewhere, and when the repatriation agreements between
Poland and the Soviet Union came into force, the Sutzkevers, as citizens of
Vilna when it was under Polish rule, moved to Łódź in 1946, and eventually
managed to set sail for the land of Israel in 1947. The intervening months
were a time of wandering for Sutzkever, as can be clearly seen from the places
where the poems of that period were written: as well as poems written in
Berlin, Nuremberg, Fürth, and Landsberg – Sutzkever appears to have spent

55   Ibid.: 161 f.
56   All the above-mentioned intellectuals died in Stalin's purges: Mikhoels was assassinated in
1948 in a fake road accident, and Markish, Hofshteyn and Bergelson were among 13 members of
the Jewish Anti-Fascist Committee shot on August 12, 1952. See Sutzkever's poems about Pasternak (Sutzkever 1986: 74), Mikhoels (Sutzkever 1986: 104) and Markish, above, p. 149. For further
information about Jewish life and Yiddish culture in Stalins's Russia, cf. Estraikh 2004; Lustiger
2003; Sherman 2012.

almost two months in Germany after his appearance in Nuremberg – there
are poems inscribed Warsaw, Łódź, Paris, The Hague, Amsterdam, Lucerne,
and finally "[on the] ship Patria, September 1947."[57]

During this period two important works came to fruition. The epic *poeme*
געהיימשטאָט (*Geheymshtot*, Secret City)[58] was written between 1945 and 1947,
and published in Tel Aviv in 1948. It consists of a prologue, forty-two narrative sections of varying length, each containing between two and ten stanzas
of ten lines, and an epilogue. The consistent rhyme and meter demonstrates
Sutzkever's virtuosity. The poem tells the story, based on a real encounter
Sutzkever had, of a group of Jews who survived the Holocaust in the underground sewer system of Vilna. The composition of the group changes: someone leaves or dies, someone new joins them, or a baby is born, but the group
always remains as a little community of ten, a figure which is very important
in Jewish tradition: a מנין (*minyen*) or group of ten men is necessary for prayer
in a synagogue. In "Secret City" both the ten-line stanzaic form and the constant group of ten symbolize therefore the survival of the Jewish people.

In the other longer poem of this period, צו פּוילן (*Tsu poyln*, To Poland),[59]
1946, Sutzkever bids farewell to his homeland in Eastern Europe. As in
Geheymshtot and elsewhere, Sutzkever imposes strict poetic form on material
which is intensely emotional and wide-ranging; the whole poem is written
in rhyming couplets, with pure and often extremely inventive rhymes. The
poet addresses the land of Poland, contemplating the centuries of Jewish life
there, and the troubled but often fruitful co-existence of Jews and Poles. He
comes to the sad conclusion that he must leave. The two important literary
allusions in the poem symbolize the non-Jewish and Jewish sides of Polish intellectual life respectively: the phrase *Smutno mi, Boże!* (I am sad, Lord!), the
refrain of the Polish poet Juliusz Słowacki's (1809–1849) "Hymn" is repeated
throughout Sutzkever's poem like the tolling of a bell, expressing his own
deep sadness. Sutzkever also quotes the last lines of the play די גאָלדענע קייט
(*Di goldene keyt*, The golden chain) by I. L. Peretz, one of the first great Polish
Yiddish writers. At the end of "To Poland" the first-person narrator visits
Peretz's mausoleum in the Jewish cemetery in Warsaw for a final leave-taking. Instead of bidding the revered writer farewell, however, the narrator lifts
Peretz's tomb onto his shoulders and carries it away with him to his future
life, the last lines of Peretz's famous play ringing in his ears:

---

57   Sutzkever 1963 (I): 578–606.
58   Ibid.: 443–537.
59   Ibid.: 567–577. Cf. Cammy and Figlerowicz 2007: 444–446; Adamczyk-Garbowska 2011:
100–102.

[...] און איך, וואָס אַהער בין געקומען כדי צו
געזעגענען זיך – נעם אַרויף אויף מײַן פלייצע
דעם אוהל און וואַנדער אַוועק מיט זײַן ניגון
וואָס גאָר די פֿאַרגאַנגעניש טוט ער צעוויגן
און וועט מיר אַ וועג אין די מאָרגנס פֿאַראַקערן:
– „אָט אַזוי גייען מיר,
די נשמות – פֿלאַקערן!"

[...] and I, who had come here
to bid him farewell – take onto my shoulders
his tomb and wander away with his melody
which sets the past swaying
and will plough me a path into the future:
    "And so we go on,
    Our souls – blazing!" [60]

To Sutzkever the symbolic significance of Peretz's unbroken "golden chain" of Jewish existence was very important, and in 1949, when he succeeded in establishing a Yiddish literary journal in Israel, he named it די גאָלדענע קייט. פֿערטליאָרשריפֿט פֿאָר ליטעראַטור און געזעלשאַפֿטלעכע פּראָבלעמען (*Di golde-ne keyt. Fertlyorshrift far literatur un gezelshaftlekhe problemen*, The Golden Chain. Quarterly journal for literature and social problems).

With the help of Golda Meir, the future prime minister of Israel, whom he had met at the Zionist Congress in Basle, Sutzkever obtained British 'certificates' for himself and his wife and daughter Reyne (Rina),[61] and after a dangerous sea voyage they arrived in Palestine in September 1947, just months before the official founding of the State of Israel. They settled in Tel Aviv, where their second daughter, Mire (Mira) was born.

Israel: Sutzkever's third and final homeland

Sutzkever's relationship to Zionism is not altogether clear. In the pre-war period in Vilna he was not involved in Zionist activities, and indeed when the question of emigration became acute, a letter which Freydke wrote him from Moscow suggests that both Palestine and America were being considered as possible choices. His decisive meeting with Golda Meir shows that he did attend the Zionist Congress in Basle in 1947, and her intervention may well have been decisive. In his early years in Israel he worked to create, through his poetry and his life, a deep and strong affinity to the land and the new state of Israel.[62]

He arrived in the old-new homeland with the metaphorical tomb of Peretz on his shoulders; his sense of responsibility for keeping the memory, culture and language of the Jews of Eastern Europe alive was very strong. The question of Yiddish was a fraught and, for the immigrants from Eastern Europe, sorrowful issue, as the authorities attempted to suppress Yiddish,

60   Sutzkever 1963 (I): 577.
61   Rina Sutzkever later became a well-known Israeli artist.
62   For a wide-ranging and nuanced discussion of the Zionist element in Sutzkever's early Israeli poetry, see Cammy 2004: 240–265.

widely seen as symbolic of oppressed Jewish life in the Diaspora, in order that Hebrew should grow and flourish as the language of the strong young Jewish state.[63]

The deeply problematic nature of all these issues of identity for Yiddish-speaking Holocaust survivors in the early years of the Israeli state are exemplified in the ambitious work that Sutzkever wrote between 1958 and 1960: the long epic poem גייסטיקע ערד (*Gaystike erd*, Spiritual Soil), a fascinating if flawed work which, in three long sections and an epilogue, depicts a group of survivors, including the narrator, traveling to Israel, the narrator's experiences in the early years of the state, the 1948 Israeli War of Independence and, in a patriotic and rhetorical climax, a symbolic commemoration of the Warsaw ghetto uprising on the fortress of Masada. The *poeme*, in the words of a recent commentator, Gali Drucker Bar-Am, is "an attempt to establish an identity mythology for Yiddish-speaking Jews in post-Holocaust Israel" which "expresses Sutzkever's challenge to the inventory of mythological images that cradled the established Israeli collective identity."[64] Drucker Bar-Am demonstrates convincingly that the dissonance between the nuanced early sections and the rhetorical espousal of conventional Zionist ideology and imagery in the epilogue epitomizes the complex dilemmas in Sutzkever's consciousness.

Sutzkever, however, was determined to fight for the language and culture of Yiddish. In the early poems he wrote in Israel he combines a mystical sense of belonging to the land with the conviction that only through acknowledging the Jewish past, which still lived within him, and integrating it with the new reality, would it be possible to forge a new identity in this country – not just for him, but for all its citizens.[65]

An essential component of this past was of course the Yiddish language, and it was truly remarkable that Sutzkever managed to realize his ambition to found a literary journal in Yiddish. He recounted how on the very first evening he spent in Tel Aviv, having experienced a bomb exploding in a café, he was asked what he intended to do in Israel:

---

63   Cf. Aptroot and Gruschka 2010: 164; Katz, 2004: 310–323.
64   Drucker Bar-Am 2016: 157 f.
65   See for example the poems ווען כ׳וואָלט ניט זײַן מיט דיר ביַינאַנד (*Ven kh'volt nit zayn mit dir banand*, Had I not been here with you), p. 115, and דער שניי אויפֿן חרמון (*Der shney oyfn Khermon*, The Snow on Mount Hermon), p. 117.

האָב איך געענטפֿערט אַז איך האָב דאָ אין בדעה   I answered that I intended to found
צו גרינדן און רעדאַקטירן אַ גרויסן ייִדישן   and edit a great Yiddish journal, and
זשורנאַל און קיין שום באָמבעס וועלן מיך   no bombs were going to frighten me
ניט אָפּשרעקן...   off...[66]

Despite all the political and economic difficulties, the first issue of *Di goldene keyt* appeared in the winter of 1949, with the financial support of the
Histadrut trade union organization. There was indeed some criticism of the
title,[67] because it was obviously inspired by Peretz's play and therefore looked
back to the East European Diaspora, but for Sutzkever – as for Peretz – this
concept embodied the continuity and constant renewal of the Jewish people.

The journal was published from 1949 until 1995; there were between two
and four issues each year, mostly containing about 150 – 200 pages. It was the
most important post war publication in Yiddish, giving a platform to Yiddish
writers scattered around the world, as well as encouraging Yiddish creativity
in Israel. There were also many translations of works from other cultures,
literary analyses, and important collections of letters by well-known writers.
Sutzkever himself contributed many articles on literary and cultural topics,
and his strict editorial eye ensured that the standard of accuracy and linguistic level were consistently high.

Sutzkever remained extraordinarily creative throughout his long life.[68] He
published eighteen further volumes of poetry,[69] several volumes containing
poetry and prose, and four volumes of short narrative prose. Much of his
work was printed in *Di goldene keyt* before it was collected and published in
book form.

From the beginning he was at the centre of the small, but gradually growing Yiddish literary movement in Israel. He was a founder member of the
group of young writers established in 1951, called יונג ישׂראל (*Yung Yisroel,
Young Israel*), which also included the prose writers Jossel Birstein and Avrom Karpinovitsh, the poet and prose writer Tsvi Ayznman, and the poet,
prosaist and artist Mendl Man, who became secretary of *Di goldene keyt*.
Sutzkever was in close contact with leading Yiddish writers from America
and elsewhere – H. Leyvik, Meylekh Ravitsh, Arn Tseytlin, Rokhl Korn, Itsik
Manger, Dovid Pinski, Sholem Ash, Yankev Glatshteyn, Arn Glants-Leye-

---

66 Sutzkever 1973: 6.
67 See Novershtern 1983: 179.
68 Sutzkever's last published poem is dated 2000: דער רויטער האָן (*The red rooster*), p. 203.
69 For a more detailed analysis of Sutzkever's poetry, see p. 258 – 287.

les, and others, many of whom visited Israel. Among all these contacts and friends in the literary and artistic world, two personalities are particularly important: Marc Chagall[70] and Mordkhe Litvine.

Sutzkever and Chagall had met at a YIVO Congress in Vilna in 1935, but their friendship really began about 1949, when Chagall responded positively to Sutzkever's request that he write something for *Di goldene keyt*. Chagall, whose mother tongue was Yiddish, had already published essays and poems in several Yiddish journals including the famous *Literarishe bleter*,[71] and from the first issue of Sutzkever's journal, he was an occasional contributor. He illustrated two of Sutzkever's books: *Siberia* (1955) and די פֿידלרויז (*Di fidl-royz*, The Fiddle Rose, 1974). From 1950 onwards, Sutzkever visited Chagall at least once a year in Paris, or the south of France, and he wrote at length of his friendship with the artist, reproducing conversations they had, and publishing letters from Chagall to him.[72] Their writings reveal that the two artists had a mutual deep affection and admiration for each other. For Sutzkever, Chagall and his art represented a link to his own childhood in Eastern Europe:

פֿאַר מיר פּערזענלעך איז שאַגאַל, דער מענטש און דער קינסטלער, אַן אומ־ פֿאַרגלײַכלעכע אינספּיראַציע. אַ ווידער־ אויפֿשפּיל פֿון אַ פֿאַרקלונגענער קינדהייט. ס׳האָט זיך געדאַכט, אַז אָט די קינדהייט איז שוין „גראָ געוואָרן". ערשט מיט אַ מאָל – זע און הער: זי אייביקט גאָר אַ יונג, אַ פֿרישע, אַ לויטערע.	For me personally, Chagall, the human being and the artist, is an incomparable inspiration. A resurgence of a vanished childhood. This childhood seemed to have "become grey." But suddenly – see and hear: it is eternally alive: young, fresh and pure.[73]

There was a close affinity between the two artists with respect to their view of reality and of art. Central to the consciousness of both was the rejection of any, in their eyes, artificial boundaries between the world of outer reality and that of the imagination. The artist creates a world which is, in its essence, more real than so-called concrete reality. Thus Sutzkever wrote of Chagall's painting:

70 Further literature about the relationship of Marc Chagall with Sutzkever and other Yiddish writers includes Harshav 2003 and Koller 2012.

71 ליטעראַרישע בלעטער, the leading Yiddish literary journal of its time, appeared in Warsaw from April 1924 until June 1939. It was founded by Melekh Ravitsh, Perets Markish, I. J. Singer and Nakhman Mayzel, and the latter became its main editor.

72 Sutzkever 1951, 1973, 1982 b, 1985 and 1993: 235–274.

73 Sutzkever 1951: 5.

איז דען אַ קלעזמער אױף אַ דאַך אומרעאַ־
לער פֿון סתם אַזױ אַ קלעזמער? איז דען
ס׳פֿידעלע אונטער דער מאַרדע פֿון אַ פֿערד
ניט נאַטירלערָ? דװוקא אין דעם [...] קאָמ־
פּאַנירן אױבנאױפֿיק־סתירותדיקע עלעמענ־
טן, אין דעם אױסקערן די יצירה אױף דער
אַנדער זײַט, אין דעם פֿאַרקנסן מוזיק און
ליניע – דװוקא אין דערינען אַנטפּלעקט זיך
די טיפֿערע רעאַליטעט.

Is a klezmer on a roof any less real
than any other klezmer? Is the fiddle
under the chin of a horse not natural? It's in that very [...] combining
of apparently contrary elements, in
turning Creation inside out, in wedding together music and line – it is
in this way that the deeper reality reveals itself.[74]

Chagall expressed the same idea in an essay on art and the artist:

איך בין קעגן די טערמינען „פֿאַנטאַזיע‟ און
„סימבאָליזם‟. אונדזער גאַנצע אינעװױניק־
סטע װעלט איז װירקלעכקײט – אפֿשר מער
װירקלעכער װי די װעלט, װאָס מיר זעען.

I am against the terms "fantasy" and
"symbolism". Our whole inner world
is reality – perhaps more real than the
world we see.[75]

A similar fusing of fantasy and 'reality' is the essence of Sutzkever's poetry
and prose. And just as Sutzkever saw Chagall's art as the wedding together of
music and line – the visual and the aural –, so Chagall saw Sutzkever's poetry
not just from the point of view of its sense or sound, but as an image, a form.
In a letter of 1949 he wrote to Sutzkever: איר זײַט מיר נאָענט. אײַערע לידער זײַנען
בילדער (I feel close to you. Your poems are pictures)[76] and in a speech in Paris
in 1950, he declared:

סוצקעװווער איז מיר ליב און טײַער װי אַ ברו־
דער. און דערהויפֿט איז ער מיר ליב װי דער
ייִדישער פּאָעט, װעמענס װואָרט ־ ליניע
און װואָרט ־ פֿאָרעם עס דערגייען צו די
שענסטע ייִדישע נשמה־שפּיצן.

Sutzkever is as dear to me as a brother.
And he is especially dear to me as the
Yiddish poet whose words have a *line*
and *form* which reach the most beautiful pinnacles of the Jewish soul.[77]

Both Sutzkever and Chagall represent the fusion of the traditional and the
modern; in Chagall's case, there is on the one hand the traditional Eastern
European Jewish world with its figures, landscapes and symbols, and on the
other, the liberating influence of European modernism. Sutzkever's oeuvre

74   Ibid.
75   Chagall 1950: 37.
76   Sutzkever 1973: 31.
77   Chagall 1953: 64. My emphasis.

is also, both thematically and formally, a creative combination of traditional and modernist elements. The affinity between the two artists can be seen in the work they composed for or about each other.[78]

Sutzkever's friendship with Mordkhe Litvine (1906–1993) was also a thread that constantly drew him back to France. Like Sutzkever, Litvine came from Lithuania, and was a literary critic and translator of French, Russian and German poetry into Yiddish.[79] He survived the war in France as an active member of the Resistance. Sutzkever met him in Paris in 1946, and they remained friends until Litvine's death. Litvine's translations of Baudelaire, Mallarmé, Valéry and other French poets, as well as his essays on literary topics appeared regularly in *Di goldene keyt*. As a schoolboy in Vilna and in the 1930s in Warsaw, Sutzkever had read French poetry in Polish translation, and without doubt his friendship with Litvine enhanced his knowledge of French and other European poetry and strengthened his ties with France. Litvine was a deeply perceptive commentator on Sutzkever's work.

Sutzkever travelled widely; he was a powerful speaker and dramatic reader of his own poetry, and was greatly in demand in the various Jewish communities throughout the world. He appeared in the USA, Canada, Argentina, Africa, and several European countries, always creating a lasting impression with his heartfelt talks and readings, delivered in his resonant voice. Particularly productive was his African sojourn in 1950; invited by the Jewish community of Johannesburg, he spent several months traveling round Southern Africa, which gave rise to his cycle of African poems העלפֿאַנדן בײַ נאַכט (*Helfandn bay nakht*, Elephants at Night).[80]

He was awarded many literary prizes: in 1969 he received the Itsik Manger Prize for Yiddish literature, and in 1983, in honor of his 70th birthday, there was an exhibition of his life and work in the National and University Library in Jerusalem. In 1985 he was awarded the prestigious Israel Prize for literature, and in 1983 he was given the freedom of the city of Tel Aviv. After the death of his wife in 2002, Sutzkever's health gradually deteriorated, and he died in a nursing home in Tel Aviv on January 10, 2010. On April 28, 2011,

---

78 See Sutzkever's poems שאַגאַלישער גאָרטן (*Shagalisher gortn*, Chagallian Garden), Sutzkever 1963 (II): 357; שאַגאַלישע ווערטער (*Shagalishe verter*, Chagallian words), Sutzkever 1968: 139; זײַן פּענדזל – טרוקן. ווי אַ צווײַג פֿון אײלבערטבוים, געזונדן (*Zayn pendzl – trukn. Vi a tsvayg fun eylbertboym, getsundn*, His brush: dry. Like an olive branch, set on fire), p. 193. Chagall's illustrations for Sutzkever's *poeme Siberia* reveal his understanding of the work, cf. below p. 264; Valencia 1994: 181–195; Amminger 2015.

79 Litvine published two volumes of translations (Litvine 1968–1986). A third volume appeared posthumously (Litvine 2003).

80 Sutzkever 1955: 19–72. See 139–147 and 274 f.

in a ceremony attended by the Vilnius City mayor, the Chairman of the Lithuanian Jewish Community, and Sutzkever's two daughters and granddaughter, a memorial plaque was placed on the wall of the house in Vilna where Sutzkever had lived with his beloved mother.

The poetry of Avrom Sutzkever

Early work

Sutzkever's biography is significant because the evolution of his oeuvre is closely bound up with the events of his life, and with the three places which were his actual and spiritual homes: the Siberia of his early childhood, Vilna and its surrounding countryside, and the land of Israel. These symbolic places pervade his poetry; the ice and snow of Siberia and the fiery heat of Israel are frequent motifs in a network of key images which change and develop throughout his work.

Sutzkever's early work shows clear Romantic influence, which is evident in the first four poems (after *Siberia*) in this volume.[81] Nature is experienced with ecstatic intensity, as in בלאָנדער באַגינען (*Blonder baginen*, Blond Dawn),[82] a subjective poetic landscape full of anthropomorphic nature images. This poem can be seen as emblematic because it contains many of the key images and ideas which are developed throughout Sutzkever's oeuvre; it is therefore worthwhile considering it in some detail.

The poem evokes the individual's experience of the gradual approach of daybreak. The איך (*ikh*, I) stands in the midst of nature and in the first half of the poem addresses a דו (*du*, you) whom he urges to watch and listen: קוק זיך אײַן אין דעם געבורט פֿון וועלטן! (Look and see the birth of worlds!).

The plural form "worlds" takes the idea beyond the visible world to encompass the whole universe, raising the poet's experience onto a mystical plane. With the *du*, the poet is addressing himself, as becomes clear in the second half of the poem when the *du* becomes the *ikh* who does not merely watch but participates in the wonder of nature. Through the use of the *du*, however, the reader is drawn in to share the poet's vision. This dual function of *du* as addressee is a permanent feature of Sutzkever's poetry.

---

81   p. 77–83.
82   p. 77. By giving the whole group of poems from the volume *Poems* (1937) this title when they were republished in the *Poetic Works* (1963), Sutzkever showed the significance he ascribed to the poem; the titles of cycles or groups of poems, and the first and last poems of groups, are never without thematic significance in Sutzkever's work.

All the attributes of nature in the first part of the poem are anthropomorphic images: the morning star watches, the branches of the birch trees are like fingers; the elements of the natural world babble, kiss each other, laugh, speak, weep. The elements singled out in this early poem as the vehicles of the poet's experience of the dawn – grasses, roots, trees and ears of corn – recur throughout his work, and their symbolic significance is heralded in this early poem by the anthropomorphic qualities with which he invests them.
The lines:

[...] ביימער זענען שטומע וויאָלאָנטששעלן.	[...] Trees are mute violoncellos.
און די טויזנט שטילקייטן באַזונדער	And each of the thousand silences
ריידן אויף דער בלאָנדער שפראָך	speaks the blond language
פֿון זאַנגען.	of the ears of corn.

express a paradoxical relationship which is seminal in Sutzkever's work: the interplay between concepts of שטומקייט (shtumkayt, muteness) and שטילקייט (shtilkayt, calm or silence). The trees are cellos, which are mute, whereas the silences speak.[83] Shtumkayt and shtilkayt become key concepts in Sutzkever's metapoetic poetry, the former denoting the state of being before the "birth" of the poetic word, and the latter the essence of the poetic, which lies beyond words.[84] The mute tree cellos, anticipating the dawn, have not yet found their melody.

Ears of corn and grasses are two further motifs which later become infused with metapoetic significance.[85] The zangen here are still under the earth – they have the potential for growth, and their essence is already perceptible to the senses of the poet:

[...] עס שמעקט	[...] you can smell
פֿון זיי מיט בלאָנדן יום-טוב.	their blond, festive joy.[86]

At the end of the first part of the poem the inner contemplation of the forces of nature is interrupted by another human being – the shepherd whose song resounds through the valley – and in the second part contemplation gives way to action: the ikh "stride[s] out barefoot on the dawning paths." All

83 The multiplicity of plural forms in this poem is worth noting (including the normally singular concept of שטילקייט). This creates a feeling of the extraordinary abundance of nature.
84 Cf. my further discussion of this aspect, p. 286f.
85 Cf. p. 119–123, 175 and 191.
86 The Yiddish term יום-טוב (yontev) specifically denotes a Jewish holiday or festival; in many poems Sutzkever uses the term to convey the feelings of joy or celebration which the yontev brings.

the imagery of the first half of the poem is intensified, and there is positive interaction between the human being and sentient nature: גראָזן טראַכטן וועגן מיר (Grasses are thinking *of me*);[87] "A little breeze drapes itself around my neck." The contemplative verbs of the first part ("watches," "look and see") are replaced by verbs of action: "stride out," "fly," "drapes itself." The *ikh* has taken a central role in nature – it is not without significance that when Sutzkever revised the poem for its publication in the פּאָעטישע ווערק (*Poetishe verk*), he removed the rather superfluous song of the shepherd, and the word *ikh* appears almost exactly at the central point of the poem.[88]

The last three stanzas depict the harmony between *ikh* and nature through quasi-religious imagery. Like the shepherd, the wanderer is a familiar figure in European Romanticism,[89] and here the mysterious wanderer gives spiritual nourishment (the unspecified 'faith') in return for physical nourishment ("my last piece of bread"). This is the earliest occurrence of the linking of physical and spiritual nourishment which is a central motif in Sutzkever's work, as seen in the lines from 1978 at the beginning of this essay.

In the poem "Blond Dawn" the human being is in harmony with nature, but separate from it, and nature is drawn to him; the unity between the *ikh* and the natural world is taken even further in the opening poem of Sutzkever's second book, *Of the forest*. Here the *ikh* sees himself mirrored within nature:

כ׳זע מיין לייב אין ווייס פֿון דער בעריאָזע,	I see my body in the whiteness of the birch,
כ׳פֿיל מיין בלוט אין בליִונג פֿון אַ רויז [...]	feel my blood throb in the blossoming rose [...][90]

and everything in nature is a reflection of the divine:

און אין אַלץ אַנטפּלעקט זיך מיין געביטער	And in everything my Master is revealed –
טיף און גרויס.	deep and great.[91]

---

87   My emphasis. It is interesting that in the earlier version of the poem (Sutzkever 1937: 36), Sutzkever repeated the verb פּלאַפּלען (*plaplen*, to babble) at this point: די גראָזן פּלאַפּלען וועגן מיר (*di grozn plaplen vegn mir*, the grasses are babbling about me). The change, giving the grasses the power of thought heralds the later importance of the motif as a metapoetic image.
88   Sutzkever 1963 (I): 28.
89   Cf. אין טאָרבע פֿונעם ווינט (*In torbe funem vint*, In the knapsack of the wind), p. 79.
90   אַלץ איז ווערדיק פֿאַר מיין אויגס געוואָגל... (*Alts iz verdik far mayn oygs gevogl*, All is Worthy of My Roaming Eye...), p. 83.
91   For a discussion of Sutzkever's concept of the divine, see p. 284–286.

It is significant, however, that in contrast to the prevalent impulse in Romantic poetry towards fusion of the self with the natural world, with Sutzkever there is always a drawing back to the separate and sovereign *self*, as in an early poem געשרייַ (*Geshrey*, Scream, p. 81). In this poem the speaker stridently demands, and is on the point of achieving his own metamorphosis into nature; at the last moment however, he recoils from the imminent fulfillment of his desire to flow into the universe, and, screaming, he demands the return to his flesh-and-blood self:

באַשאַף מיך אויף דאָס נײַ	Create me now anew
מיט אויגן, האַרץ און צייין,	with eyes and heart and teeth,
פֿאַרוואַנדל מיך צוריק	transform me once again
פֿון אַלץ אין מיר אַליין.	from *all* into my self.

The self-irony here is worthy of Heine: there is deliberate bathos in his demand for the return of his physical attributes. At the same time, the poem is a victory for the idea of the self; nature remains subservient to the *ikh* who indeed stamps his identity on nature through the power of his word, as in the final lines of the poem beginning "All is worthy of my roaming eye":

אַלץ, וואָס ווערט פֿון מיר דערפֿילט, איז מייַניק.	Everything I feel belongs to me entirely.
ווו נאָר ס׳גרייכט מייַן וואָרט, בין איך פֿאַראַן.	Wherever my word reaches, there I stand.
ווי אַ קוואַל אין מידבר שלאָגט דער תענוג	My pleasure gushes like a desert spring,
און ער לאָקט מייַן לעבנס-קאַראוואַן.	drawing with it my life's thread.
און אין אַלץ, אין אַלץ איז דאָ דער סימן	And in everything I see the imprint
פֿון מייַן שפּאַן.⁹²	of my tread.[92]

Siberia

The creative relationship between the poetic *ikh* and nature also inspires the *poeme* סיביר (*Sibir*, Siberia, p. 57–75), which plays a central role in Sutzkever's oeuvre. In conversation with his friend Shmerke Katsherginski, Sutzkever described how his early childhood in Siberia shaped his poetic consciousness:

יעדער מענטש, און בפֿרט אַ שרייַבער, האָט	Every human being, but especially
זיך אין זייַן לעבן און שאַפֿן זייַן בענקשאַפֿט,	a writer, has in his life and work his
זייַן אילוזיע. מייַן אילוזיע איז סיביר. איך	yearning, his fantasy. My fantasy is
האַלט [...] אַז דאָרט בין איך שוין אויך גע-	Siberia. I consider [...] that there I
וואָרן אַ שרייַבער, כאָטש קיין לידער האָב	became a writer, even though I had

92 See p. 83.

אֵיך נאָך ניט געשריבן דאַן, אָבער אין מײַנע   not written any poems at that time,
דעמאָלטיקע איבערלעבונגען בין אֵיך גע־   but in the experiences I had then, I
וואָרן אַ פֿאָלשטענדיקער דיכטער.   became a true poet.[93]

Here and throughout his life and work, the term "poet" signifies for Sutz-kever the person who is full of poetic sensitivity, for whom poetry is the essence of life. He stated the importance of the Siberian experience even more directly in another interview, when he said: מײַנע איבערלעבונגען אין סיביר זײַנען דער מקור פֿון מײַנע שאַפֿונגען (My experiences in Siberia are the source of my created works).[94]

The genesis of the *poeme* spans the period from 1936 to 1952. In 1936 Sutz-kever published eight poems about Siberia in the journal *In zikh* and in the newspaper ווילנער טאָג (*Vilner tog*, Vilna Day). This series, comprising seventeen poems of unequal length, appeared as שטערן אין שניי. סיבירער פּאָעמע (*Shtern in shney. Sibirer poeme*, Star in the snow. Siberian *poeme*) in his first volume of poems, לידער (*Lider*).[95] In a later essay on his relationship with Chagall, Sutzkever describes the further development of the work:

נאָך דעם ווי ס'איז שוין אַרויס מײַן בוך   After my book *Valdiks* (Vilna 1940)
וואַלדיקס, ווילנע 1940, האָב אֵיך זיך   had already appeared, I returned to
אומגעקערט צו דער פּאָעמע, זי געשליפֿן,   the *poeme*, polished it, shortened
געקירצט און צוגעשריבן אַנדערע סטראָ־   it and added other stanzas and po-
פֿעס און לידער. אויך אין ווילנער געטאָ   ems. Even in the Vilna ghetto I still
האָב אֵיך אויף דער פּאָעמע נאָך געאַרבעט.   worked on the *poeme*. A girl from the
אַ מיידל פֿון דאָרטיקן „יוגנטקלוב" האָט   local youth club made some copies,
איבערגעשריבן עטלעכע קאָפּיעס, אפֿשר   so that one of them might, perhaps,
וועט זיך איינע ראַטעווען. און ס'איז געשען   be saved. And a miracle happened:
אַ נס: מײַן קינדשאַפֿט איז ניט פֿאַרברע־   my childhood was not burnt. After
נט געוואָרן. כ'האָב זי נאָך דער באַפֿרײַונג   the liberation I dug it up from the
אויסגעגראָבן פֿון דער ערד און זי געבראַכט   earth and brought it to the land of
אין ארץ־ישראל.   Israel.[96]

The revised *poeme*, entitled *Sibir*, was published in Israel, first in Hebrew translation (1952), then in Yiddish (1953), and in 1955 an English version by Joseph Sonntag appeared. All three are elegant large-format editions, with eight illustrations by Chagall.[97]

93 Katsherginski 1955, quoted in Novershtern 1983: 114.
94 Pat 1960: 159.
95 Sutzkever 1937: 75–98.
96 Sutzkever 1973: 10.
97 For a discussion of Chagall's *Sibir* illustrations, see Amminger 2015 and Koller 2012.

The earlier work has been transformed.[98] Both versions conjure up a lost childhood, but "Star in the Snow" is a poem of memory, consisting of a loose cycle of poems that nostalgically recall landscapes, episodes and people from that early period of the poet's life. "Siberia", in contrast, is the evocation of a magic landscape of the imagination; it is carefully structured in order to depict the process whereby the *ikh* became a "true poet." It is an inner journey, and the architecture and movement of the *poeme* mirror the awakening poetic consciousness of the child. The *poeme* presents a sweeping movement outward and upward; from the protective environment of the childhood home, the child goes out into the natural world, becomes symbolically independent of his father, experiences the approach of spring, then the untamed life of the Kirghiz people and finally, he depicts himself soaring over landscapes and walking with the North Star, his mentor. This development within the child is mirrored in the transformation of the natural world: the river Irtysh, freed of ice, flows freely and the silent frozen world gives way to the living, moving, colorful rebirth of spring.

This passage from frozen to rushing river reflects an anecdote which Sutzkever recalled to Yankev Pat; once, during his Siberian childhood, he saw a little boat frozen in the river. The next morning he was amazed to hear

[...] אַ געווודער אויפֿן טײַך. דאָס אײַז האָט זיך געבראָכן, זיך געלאָזט. דאָס שיפֿל איז אַוועק מיטן וואַסער.[...] איך זע אין דעם בילד די פֿאַרקערפּערונג פֿון מײַן גורל.	[...] a noise on the river. The ice had broken up, had melted. The little boat had floated away on the water. [...] I see in that image the embodiment of my destiny.[99]

The only human beings who appear in the final version of "Siberia" are figures who play a seminal role in the poet's inner journey: the Kirghiz, who embody the Dionysian ecstasy of music and dance, his friend, the young Kirghiz boy Tshanguri, and above all, the poet's father with his violin music. Two significant turning points in the work are the poems דערקענטעניש (*Der-kentenish*, Realization), and צום טאַטן (*Tsum tatn*, To my father). In the first of these, the child, running to a hilltop ahead of his father, discovers that the world does not end behind the hut on the hill, as his father had told him:

טאַטינקע! עס ציט די וועלט זיך ווײַטער,	Dear little father! Look, the world goes on,
און קיין סוף – ניטאָ, ניטאָ, ניטאָ.	And has no end – no end, no end at all.

98 For a detailed comparison of the two works see Valencia 1991: 128–175 and Valencia 1994: 181–195.
99 Pat 1960, quoted in Novershtern 1983: 100.

This experience represents the moment when the child gains independence from the father, who is, symbolically, a tiny dot below him, whereas the *ikh* is transformed into אַ לאַווינע/ וועמען ליכט און וווּנדער האָט געבוירן (an avalanche / created by a miracle of light).

In "To my father" (situated exactly in the middle of the *poeme*), the father's burial is described. The son, drawn to his beloved father, is on the point of jumping into the coffin:

נאָר מײַן טויב איז דעמאָלט גראָד פֿאַרפֿלויגן,	But suddenly just then my dove flew up,
אָוונטזון געקרוינט מיט ווײַסן גאָלד,	Crowning the evening sun with her white gold,
און אַרויף צום לעבן מיך געצווייגן...	And drew me upwards with her, into life…

Chagall's representation of this scene perfectly captures its symbolic nature: the father descending into the earth, the boy rising up, following his dove-muse, but both figures are joined together like a playing-card figure, signifying that the father will always remain part of the poet. The key images of the *poeme* "Siberia", snow and ice, the father and his violin, the dove and the North Star recur throughout Sutzkever's poetry in ever evolving forms and contexts.

It is extraordinary that even in the Vilna ghetto, Sutzkever not only produced the rich body of poetry which has as its central theme the events of that dreadful time, but worked simultaneously on the revisions to his Siberian *poeme*. Even in circumstances of unimaginable horror he was able – indeed perhaps it was an inner necessity – to conjure up images of the enchanted landscape of his childhood Siberia. The central importance which he himself accords the work can be seen in the fact that he printed "Siberia" as the first work in his two-volume *Poetic Works*, even though apart from this the poems and poem cycles are in chronological order. And although this is the second version of the *poeme*, which he worked on in the early 1940s, he gave it the date of 1936, perhaps because this seminal work originated in the period before the Holocaust.

Poetry of the war years
Yankev Glatshteyn wrote of the war period in Sutzkever's work:

ער איז דער איינציקער ייִדישער דיכטער,	He is the only Yiddish poet to come
וואָס איז צוריקגעקומען פֿון יאָמערטאָל	back from the vale of tears with po-
מיט לידער. אַנדערע האָבן געשריבן אויסגע־	ems. Some wrote screams of pain,
שרייען, אַנדערע האָבן געזאָגט קינות, אָבער	others recited lamentations, but

סוצקעווער האָט געהאַט אַ מיסיע, אַ פֿאַר־
שאָלטענע מיסיע, צו שפּילן אױף זײַן פֿאַרכּי־
שופֿטער פֿלײט די לידער פֿון גרעסטן חורבן
פֿון אונדזער צײַט. [...] איבער סוצקעווערס
לידער פֿלאַטערט אַ גרױזאַמע באַשערטקײט.
[...] ס׳איז געווען אַ סאַדיסטישער אײַנפֿאַל
אױסצוקלײַבן דעם קנעכט פֿון פֿערפֿעקציע
און אים באַפֿעלן צו געבן פֿאָרם צום בלו־
טיקסטן כאָאָס פֿון אַלע צײַטן.

Sutzkever had a mission, an accursed
mission, to play on his enchanted
flute the songs of the greatest disaster
of our time. [...] Over Sutzkever's
poems there hovers a cruel destiny.
[...] It was a sadistic idea to choo-
se the servant of perfection and to
command him to give a form to the
bloodiest chaos of all times.[100]

Glatshteyn's remarks pinpoint two seminal aspects of Sutzkever's literary development during this period. First, by his own admission, Sutzkever had in
his youth little sense of social interaction in his poetry. In 1962, in a short
article which he called טאָגבוך־נאָטיצן (*Togbukh-notitsn*, Notes From My Diary), he wrote of those early years:

דעמאָלט האָב איך מער געװאָלט דער־
גרײכן בײמער און שנײען אײדער מענטשן.
איך האָב אױסגעקליבן פֿאַר מײַנע לײענער
שטערן און גראָזן.

At that time I wanted to reach trees
and snows rather than human beings.
I chose for my readers stars and grasses.[101]

Now he increasingly developed a sense of vocation, as a witness to his own
and future generations. Secondly, he felt a compulsion to reconcile beauty and
horror, to give form to chaos, and to ask himself what role his poetry could
play in a situation where mere survival was everyone's priority. He himself
answered this question in the prologue to his great epic poem "Secret City",[102]
where the narrator realizes that it was his destiny to be אַ גרױזיק־שטילער
לאָקערדיקער עדות/פֿון פּײַן, װאָס מוז פֿאַרװאַנדלען זיך אין שײַן (an eerily, silently
hovering witness / of agony that must be transformed into shining light).

Indeed, as Glatshteyn indicated, rather than leading to a creative crisis,
the experiences of the war years deepened Sutzkever's poetry: the aestheticism
and formal beauty of his work is enriched by a social and political dimension.
This, and his belief in the quasi-mystical protective power of his word became
the essence of his survival. In 1968 he wrote of these years:

װען די זון גופֿא איז, דאַכט זיך, פֿאַרװאַנדלט
געװאָרן אין אַש, האָב איך געגלײבט באמו־
נה־שלמה: כּל־זמן דאָס ליד פֿאַרלאָזט מיך

When the sun itself had, it seemed,
been turned into ash, I believed with
absolute faith: as long as the poem

100 Glatshteyn 1947: 57 f.
101 Sutzkever 1962: 166.
102 See above, p. 251.

ניט, וועט מיך דאָס בלייַ ניט פֿאַרטיליקן;
כּל-זמן איך וועל אין טויט-אַרומרינגלונג
לעבן דיכטעריש, וועלן אויסגעלייזט ווערן
און אַ תּיקון באַקומען מייַנע יסורים.

does not forsake me, the lead [bullet] will not destroy me; as long as, surrounded by death, I live poetically, all my torments will be healed and turned to good.[103]

In the war years, therefore, Sutzkever perceived his poetry as a kind of talisman. It is also an act of resistance, both in the sense of an individual spiritual process and, as Novershtern puts it:

דאָס ווערק וואָס האָט אין זינען אַ ברייטערן
עולם, ווּ די רעטאָרישע נאָטע האָט גע־
דאַרפֿט וועקן און רופֿן צום ווידערשטאַנד.

The work which had a wider public in mind, where the rhetorical note was intended to awaken and call to resistance.[104]

Most of the poems are based on real events which affected Sutzkever or other well known Vilna personalities. Sutzkever uses various poetic forms: there are longer narrative *poemes* like דאָס קבֿר-קינד (*Dos keyver-kind*, The Grave Child) [105] or "Kol-Nidre" [106], shorter lyrical poems and longer ones with several sections of varying rhythms like מייַן מאַמע (*Mayn mame*, My Mother),[107] above all, the regular, strictly rhymed form of the ballad plays an important role. In the apparently simple form of the ballad, dark subject matter is conveyed in regular meter and rhyme; the powerful emotions are held in check by the strict form. This is exemplified in די לערערין מירע (*Di lererin Mire*, Mire the teacher) which describes the fate of the well-known Vilna schoolteacher Mire Bernstein and her pupils, and אַ וואָגן שיך (*A vogn shikh*, A wagonload of shoes), which is based on a real experience of Sutzkever's.[108] The shoes of the murdered Jews are being sent to Germany, and in the absence of their owners, the shoes speak out:

---

103 Sutzkever 1968: foreword (no page number). In a very concrete way his poetic word was his salvation, for it was the reading of his poem כּל-נדרי (Kol nidre) in Moscow which directly led to the sending of the plane to rescue him and his wife.

104 Novershtern 1983: 133. One such poem is "The Lead Plates of Romm's Printing House", p. 107.

105 Sutzkever 1963 (I): 395.

106 Ibid.: 404.

107 Ibid.: 265.

108 Ibid.: 307 and 275 respectively. With regard to the latter poem, Sutzkever writes in *Vilner geto*: איך האָב געזען אַ מאָל אין געטאָ אַ וואָגן שיך. איך האָב דערקענט צווישן זיי דער מאַמעס אַ טופֿל (Once I saw in the ghetto a wagonload of shoes. Among them I recognized a slipper belonging to my mother.) Sutzkever 1947, 88.

עס קלאָפֿן די אָפּצאַסן:
ווּהין, ווּהין, ווּהין?
פֿון אַלטע ווילנער גאַסן
מע טרײַבט אונדז קיין בערלין.

The heels clatter:
where to, where to, where to?
From the old streets of Vilna
they're driving us to Berlin.

The powerful effect of the ballad is achieved through the contrast between the dancing rhythm and naïve narrative style on the one hand, and the stark, shocking subject matter on the other.

The underlying theme of all the poetry of this time is the poet's relationship to his word, as Sutzkever later declared:

אין די געטאָיאָרן איז מײַן דיכטערישע אינ־
ספּירֿאַציע געווען [...] דאָס גערֿאַנגל פֿונעם
וואָרט, ווי דער עסענץ פֿון לעבן, מיט זײַן
פּאָטענציעלן אומברענגער.

In the ghetto years my poetic inspiration was [...] the struggle of the word, the essence of life, with its potential murderer.[109]

It is remarkable that in the middle of the most life-threatening situations he was able to summon up the mental discipline and poetic imagination not only to write polished, carefully structured poems but also to reflect on the nature and justification of his activity, as in the powerful poem, פֿאַרברענטע פּערל (*Farbrente perl*, Burnt Pearls, p. 105).

This tightly structured poem consists of one single complex sentence, containing three powerful similes for the poet's word(s): broken hands, teeth which tear at human flesh, and a burnt string of pearls in an extinguished pyre. The change from the plural "words" to the singular "word" is significant; one may surmise that the ווערטער (*verter*, words) represent the poems which he is writing at this time. The rage and despair of the poet are not caused by the fact that his words are helpless like the disembodied hands, or have been changed by the circumstances into savage beasts, but that his essential *word*, his poetic inspiration – his alternative (and more real) world, the addressee of the poem – has been damaged like the burned pearl necklace of an anonymous victim. The kernel of the poem is his rage at the threatened destruction of his word, his "alternative world." Through the three similes, however, Sutzkever creates a double texture: the broken hands, the flesh-eating teeth and the victim with her burnt pearls, all remain in the mind of the reader as images of the savagery of the Holocaust; the pearl necklace and its former wearer, now annihilated, come into the foreground as a terrible real-

---

109 Sutzkever 1962: 166.

ity, so that the poem is simultaneously a lament for the poetic word and the human victim – fused in one vivid image. As in the ballad "A wagonload of shoes," the effect is obtained through an image of absence: in the ballad the victims are evoked through their empty shoes, and here the string of pearls is all that remains of the murdered woman. This is a poem of great economy and eloquence.

In some poems the act of writing itself enables Sutzkever to create a new reality out of the traumatic circumstances. In *Vilna Ghetto* Sutzkever describes how, desperately trying to elude the snatchers, who were out in force, he saw some newly made coffins in the courtyard of the burial society:

איך בין אַרייַנגעקראָכן אין אַן אָרון, צוגע־ מאַכט איבערן קאָפּ דעם דעק, געלעגן אין דער פֿאַרשטיקטער לופֿט, און אַזוי ליגנדיק אין אָרון האָב איך אויסגעוועבט מייַן ליד „איך ליג אין אַ מיטה".	I climbed into a coffin, closed the lid over my head, and while I lay there in the stifling atmosphere I composed my poem "I lie in a coffin." [110]

By the act of composing the poem, Sutzkever transforms the gruesome circumstances into a different poetic reality. Through the power of his word he turns the coffin – the epitome of immobility (clothes made of wood) – into an image of freedom and movement (the boat on the waves, the rocking of the cradle); death, symbolized by the coffin, becomes new life. The double image of boat and cradle also has a strong resonance of the saving of Moses from Pharaoh, one of the archetypal motifs of Jewish survival. Thus the coffin has become its opposite: the embodiment of freedom, life and the survival of the Jewish people.

In the light of this transformation the poet feels the presence of his dead sister who had always been a source of inspiration to him. Her appearance as his muse leads to his acceptance of his present situation and to his triumphant assertion at the end of the poem

[...] איצט אין אַן אָרון, ווי אין הילצערנע קליידער, זינגט אַלץ נאָך מייַן וואָרט.	[...] now, in a coffin, as in clothes made of wood, still my word sings.

The poem itself has become the vehicle of inner resistance.

---

110   Sutzkever 1947, 33. מיטה (*mite*): see Notes to the Poems, p. 211.

For Sutzkever, even the most tragic personal experience could be transfigured through poetry. One year after the murder of his newborn child, Sutzkever wrote the poem צום קינד (*Tsum kind*, To my child, p. 95) which begins, shockingly, with the father's grief-stricken urge to swallow the dead child:

צי פֿון הונגער,	Whether from hunger,
צי פֿון גרױסער ליבשאַפֿט, –	or my great love for you
נאָר אָן עדות איז דערבײַ דײַן מאַמע:	– only your mother can bear witness to it –
איך האָב געװאָלט דיך אײַנשלינגען, מײַן קינד,	I wanted to devour you, my child,
בײַם פֿילן װי דײַן גופֿל קילט זיך אָפּ	when I felt your little body cooling down
אין מײַנע פֿינגער [...]	between my fingers [...]

After this outburst of despair the poet begins to wrestle with his painful emotions, and in the course of the poem he succeeds in transcending his own personal anguish, and is able to see the child as part of the great chain of life, stretching through the generations; finally he is able to take leave of the child and relinquish him to the snow:

נאָר איך בין ניט װערט צו זײַן דײַן קבֿר.	I am not worthy, though, to be your tomb,
װעל איך דיך אָװעקשענקען	so I will part with you
דעם רופֿנדיקן שנײַ,	and give you to the calling snow,
דעם שנײַ – מײַן ערשטן יום־טובֿ,	to the snow – my first delight –
און װעסט זינקען	and you will sink
װי אַ שפֿליטער זוננפֿאַרגאַנג	like a splinter of the sunset
אין זײַנע שטילע טיפֿן	into its still depths
און אָפּגעבן אַ גרוס פֿון מיר	and greet for me
די אײַנגעפֿרירטע גרעזלער – – –	the frozen blades of grass...

The Siberian snow, with new life beneath it, symbolizes for Sutzkever the realm of the poetic; by burying him there, the father gives the child immortality through poetry, which can overcome death.[III]

Among the works which address his fellow Jews, either directly or implicitly, and which thematize physical resistance, the poem "The Lead Plates of Romm's Printing House" focuses on the holiness of the act of resistance. Here the poet describes how he and other resistance fighters melted down the lead type from the famous printing house, to make bullets. This was the type used to print the Babylonian Talmud, or Yiddish literature from Poland: אַ שורה פֿון בבֿל, אַ שורה פֿון פֿױלן (One line from Babylon, one line from Poland). In Jewish tradition the written word is sacred, and may not be destroyed; the

---

III   For a detailed interpretation of this poem, cf. Roskies 1983.

melting of the lead type, from which the eternal words emerge, is therefore a powerful trope. But for Sutzkever the words are not destroyed – they live on in the bullets which embody the will to resist and survive. The lead plates with their letters embody the spirit and history of the Jewish people, and as the plates are melted into bullets, that inspiration becomes the weapon of resistance, protecting the Jewish people against the enemy. In this imagery we see the concretization of the idea of the word as protection and resistance.

Thus the war years changed Sutzkever's poetic vision. The aesthetic aspect and the primacy of the poetic word as the deepest reality were still at the center of his poetic consciousness, but new insights and dimensions entered his work as a result of the catastrophe of the Holocaust. Whereas in the poetry of his youth the only obligation he recognized had been to himself at the center of his enchanted poetic reality, from the war years on he clearly saw himself as part of a community and as a link in the "golden chain" of Jewish survival.

In 1946, however, Sutzkever wrote to Yankev Glatshteyn:

אין געטאָ האָב איך נאָך געגלייבט אין וואָרט און האָב געקניט פאַר אים און געזונגען [ער ברענגט זיין ליד „צום דינעם אָדערל אין קאָפ"]. איצט, אין מיין ,באַפֿרייַטקייט' וואָלט איך שוין אַזוי ניט קענען שרייַבן. [...] איצט קען איך שוין ניט ווערן אָנגעצונדן. איך סמאָליע זיך ווי אַ נאַסע טוך, אַ פֿאַר־ ראַטענער פֿון אַלע געטער.	In the ghetto I still believed in the word and knelt before it and sang. [He quotes his poem "Tsum dinem oderl in kop"]. Now, in my 'free-dom', I would not be able to write like that. [...] Now I cannot become ignited. I smolder like a wet rag, be-trayed by all the gods.[112]

The poetry of the three years between Sutzkever's arrival in Moscow and his departure for Israel reflects the gulf described here between the poetic convic-tion of the years in the ghetto, and the inner desolation which accompanied the 'liberation'; much of it deals with guilt, disintegration of identity, and his struggle to reconstruct a sense of his role as a poet. In some of the poems this emotional state is conveyed by images of nature which are usually the vehicles of Sutzkever's positive metapoetic theme, being reversed and given negative connotations. One example of this is the symbol of ice in the poem פֿאַרפֿרוירענע ייִדן (Farfroyrene yidn, Frozen Jews, p. 109). In the poeme "Si-beria", ice had been an integral part of the magic landscape of Siberia: the patterns on the window pane, the glittering crystals covering the river. This was ice which melted and allowed new life to begin; and there is the beautiful image of his father, though dead, sparkling under the ice. The ice covering the frozen Jews, however, is an image of imprisonment and rigidity – their limbs and spirit can never be free, and the poet's mind, when he visualizes them, is covered by "a layer of marble" which freezes his movements into immobility. This contrasts strikingly, too, with the ghetto poem I lie in a coffin, where the poet's will transforms the rigidity of the "clothes made of wood" into spiritual freedom and creativity.

"Frozen Jews" does, however, signify, as Novershtern has noted, a new stage in Sutzkever's poetic treatment of the Holocaust; it is דער ערשטער אויסדרוק פֿון דעם מרחק צווישן היינט און אַ מאָל (the first expression of the distance between the present and the past).[113] It marks the beginning of the transition from immediacy to memory, from poetry where the starting point is a specific event or individual, or the emotions and perceptions of the poet about his own situation, – to poems which memorialize the murdered Jewish people as a collective. The gradual transformation of the Holocaust theme is a process which continues throughout Sutzkever's work, both poetry and prose.

The Fiery Chariot

The first volume of poetry which Sutzkever published in Israel, אין פֿייער־וואָגן (In fayer-vogn, In the Fiery Chariot) 1952, is a dialogue with the future and with the past; with the land itself, which promises new life for the survivors, and with the traumas they have recently suffered. The land of Israel itself encompasses both past and future: the ancient history of the Jewish people and the plan to build a new state and nation, a dual identity which Sutzkever exploits in the imagery of the densely woven introductory poem to the collection (p. 115). The poem has no title, but opens the first section of the book, which is significantly entitled שהחיינו (Shekheyonu), the name of the prayer recited to welcome each major holiday and other joyous occasions. The use of this term indicates an important developing trend in Sutzkever's imagery. Whereas, in his early poetry, specifically Jewish imagery was almost completely absent, it began to feature more strongly in the poetry of the war years, as the poet's feeling of identification with his people and its history intensified.[114] The use of biblical and religious motifs developed very markedly in the early Israel poems – signalled, indeed by the title of the 1952 volume In the Fiery Chariot – as Sutzkever sought to establish his identity in the land of his ancestors.

---

113   Novershtern 1983: 153 f.
114   Cf. "The Lead Plates of Romm's Printing House," p. 107.

This introductory poem, with the first line: ווען כ׳וואָלט ניט זייַן מיט דיר
בייַנאַנד (*Ven kh'volt nit zayn mit dir banand*, Had I not been here with you)
is interesting for many reasons.[115] Like "Burnt pearls", the poem is, as Ruth
Wisse points out, constructed as one sentence, which presents alternatives:
it expresses not only his present happy situation, but also what might have
been his fate. The speaker addresses the land itself, which is both the mother
giving birth, and the child itself (the land is אין חבֿלי־לידה, *in khevle-leyde*,
in labor), but the speaker also says that he is being born "together with the
land"). In this double "birth" metaphor he signifies the land's long history
as a mother of the Jewish people; but that ancient land is now giving birth to
a new land, a rebirth of itself. In the same way the *ikh* is being (re)born, but
simultaneously belongs to the generations of Jews who peopled the ancient
land, וווּ יעדער שטיינדל איז מייַן זיידע (where every stone is my grandfather).

The central pivot of the poem is the Biblical image of the *akeyde*, the
binding of Isaac in preparation for the sacrifice of his life demanded by God.
Sutzkever here identifies himself with Isaac, having been saved from death
like his great ancestor. After this image, the second half of the sentence depicts what would have been his fate had this not happened; it would have
been a death both physical and spiritual. Bread and water would not have
kept him alive, and the untranslatable neologism פֿאַרגויט (which I have rendered as "a stranger") suggests the spiritual death which would have accompanied the physical one.[116]

The rhymes in this poem display Sutzkever's virtuosity, and they also
have thematic significance. The two Hebrew terms *khevle-leyde* and *akeyde* are
rhymed with Yiddish terms of Germanic and Slavic origin, *vey do* and *zeyde*;
this creates a symbolic fusion of the two parts of the speaker's identity – his
roots both in the diaspora and in the ancient land of Israel.

The poems of *In the Fiery Chariot* attempt to reconcile the past – both
the poet's childhood and youth in Siberia and Vilna, and the catastrophe of
the Holocaust – with his present situation: the fledgling Jewish state and the
complex issue of establishing a meaningful identity as a Yiddish poet there.
While celebrating the landscape and history of Israel, he feels it to be a moral
and existential imperative, not merely to memorialize the past, but to keep it
alive as an essential part of the new life. In the five-line introduction to the

115 For a detailed analysis of the poem, see Wisse 2002.
116 With the last line Sutzkever draws on a long tradition of poetry expressing longing for Zion,
like the poems of Yehuda Halevi (1075–1141) or Khayem Nakhmen Bialik's אל הציפור (*'El ha-
zippor*, To the bird, 1891). See also Sutzkever's poem "The Snow on Mount Hermon", p. 117.

cycle קאָמענטאַרן צו אַ פנים אין שפּיגל (*Komentarn tsu a ponem in shpigl*, Commentaries on a Face in the Mirror, p. 119), he gives powerful voice to this ethical duty.

Sutzkever ends *In the Fiery Chariot* with a cycle of short poems which muse on the various facets of poetry and the poet's relationship to his word, אַ בריוו צו די גראָזן (*A briv tsu di grozn*, A Letter to the Grasses, p. 119–123). Significantly, the point of departure is the essential link between the poetic impulse and pain: by deliberately cutting his finger with a piece of glass, the poet rejoices to discover that he feels the pain – and, by implication, is no longer numb. This joyful revelation enables him to greet the grasses, a key image of poetic inspiration,[117] once again. This return to a clear metapoetic theme foreshadows the major *poeme* אָדע צו דער טויב (*Ode tsu der toyb*, Ode to the Dove, p. 127–137), written in 1954, which forms one section of the book of the same name, that appeared in 1955.

Ode to the Dove

The book entitled *Ode to the Dove* consists of three sections: first, the eponymous *poeme*, second, "Elephants at Night", – the poem cycle inspired by Sutzkever's travels in southern Africa – and third, Sutzkever's first collection of prose, גרינער אַקוואַריום (*Griner akvarium*, Green Aquarium.)[118] Together these works represent a turning point in Sutzkever's oeuvre. The poeme "Ode to the Dove" is a חשבון־הנפֿש (*kheshbm-hanefesh*), a 'spiritual stocktaking'; in it the poetic *ikh* looks back on his past and seeks to justify his poetic vocation, asking himself whether he can still pursue his calling after the Holocaust. It takes the form of a dialogue with his muse, the dove, which was born during his early childhood in Siberia, from the feather of an angel's wing. The dove accompanies the poetic *ikh* through his nightmare memories of the war years, which are depicted in surreal images; she finally dispels his anguished doubts about the possibility of creating art after the Holocaust. In the joyful last stanza she appears on his shoulder in the land of Israel, giving him the assurance that he may continue his poetic task:

– טײַבעלע, ביסטו די זעלבע, די פֿליגל ניט גראָ, איז דאָס מעגלעך?
זאָל איך דאָ בויען מײַן טעמפּל, ווי איך האָב געבויט אים טאָג־טעגלעך?
זאָל איך מײַן צוריבערדיק לעמפּל צעגרינען אויף ס׳נײַ און צעבלויען?
– בויען און בויען דעם טעמפּל, מיט זוניקן שכל אים בויען!

117 See below p. 283 f.
118 It is not possible to discuss Sutzkever's large corpus of prose writing here. For a closer analysis see Wisse 1975, Wisse 1989, Valencia 2013.

"Little dove, are you still as you were, and your wings are not grey,

                                         can that be?

Shall I build my temple here, as I built it day after day?

Shall I make my magic lamp shine green again, and blue?"

"Keep building and building your temple, with sunlit reason you'll build

                                          it anew!

Sutzkever's ode is his most classical work, marrying the form to the idea. Its ten sections, each consisting of four four-line rhymed stanzas, achieve a slow, stately rhythm through the regular classical meter: dactylic hexameters with a caesura in each line, a metrical form associated with Greek and Latin verse. This formal harmony is echoed in the conclusion of the poem, when the dark forces of destruction give way to an Apollonian concept of poetic creativity; the temple, which had been burnt out, can be rebuilt in the new land, מיט זוניקן שכל (with sunlit reason).[119]

In stark contrast to this, the underlying tone of "Elephants at Night", a cycle of 42 poems, is wild and pagan. Sutzkever described his African experience as בראשותדיק (*breyshesdik*, primordial),[120] and this cycle marks a new dimension in his work. It is significant that, although Sutzkever was based in the city of Johannesburg, modern, urban Africa is completely absent from the work, apart from one poem about the diamond mines of Kimberley.[121] Rather he creates a timeless, mythical world, where human beings, gods, and the untamed elements of nature are locked in an eternal struggle. The gods are either cruel pranksters, indifferent to the fates of their creatures, or are themselves powerless against the forces which threaten their creation. The boundaries between magic and reality, history and myth are erased; humans and animals are driven by the same passions and at the mercy of the same natural forces.

This world is peopled by legendary kings, magicians, pygmies, hunters and wild animals. On the surface at least, no Jewish motif can be perceived, and the *ikh*, – usually at the centre of Sutzkever's poetry – appears very rarely, and then usually in a fictitious role – for example as a leper, a dying girl or a young widow.

---

119 Cf. The poem ברויט און זאַלץ (Bread and Salt, p. 197) from 1996, where Sutzkever, at the end of his long creative life again defines himself in terms of the sunny, Apollonian principle: די וואָרצלעןֿ פֿון דער פֿינצטערניש/באַדאַרף איך ניט. איך בין/אַ זונקינד (I do not need/the roots of darkness. I am/a sun child).

120 In a conversation with the present writer, 1987.

121 דימענט־מיידל (*Diment-meydl*, Diamond Girl), p. 143.

In the relationship between human being and nature there is a constant tension between fear of the elemental forces of nature and the opposite impulse – to succumb and be absorbed into this primeval sphere, as in the last poem of the cycle, צו אַ טיגער (*Tsu a tiger*, To a Tiger, p. 145). This is one of the few poems of the cycle where the poetic *ikh* appears, and, as in the early poem געשריי (*Geschrey*, "Scream", p. 81), he is tempted to let himself be dissolved in that primeval universe, here by being devoured by the tiger. At the last moment, however, as in "Scream", he draws back:

צו שפּעט. איך בין פֿון דיר דערווײַטערט	Too late. I went away from you
צען טויזנט מײַל.	ten thousand miles.
צוריק צום וואָרט דעם אויסטערליש ניט־זאַטן.	Back to the word that's weirdly never satisfied.

In "Elephants at Night," the elephant is the noble creature which lives in complete harmony with nature, as in בית־עולם פֿון העלפֿאַנדן (*Besoylem fun helfandn*, The Elephants' Graveyard, p. 141) where the wise elephants, when they sense that their time of death has come, proceed in dignity to their destined graveyard. At the end of the poem, only man destroys the harmony between the creatures and nature.

The title poem narrates a legend which may be Sutzkever's own invention, though it does have striking similarities to folklore of other countries.[122] In bringing together two such different creatures, the gentle girl and the massive elephant, he unites two basic elements of the cycle: the elephant is the first ancestor of the human being, as another poem of the cycle, אין אָנהייב (*In onheyb*, In the Beginning, p. 139) relates. The swimming maidens who "cleave the water with their breasts" are an image full of sensuality. Sutzkever's elephant/girl image unites therefore the erotic impulse with the Creation myth, and the union of the hunter with the girl attains a quasi-sacred significance.

During the terrible war years, nature and the the sensual realm were pushed to the background in Sutzkever's creative work. In "Elephants at Night" he regains the inner freedom to return to the nature theme and explore the sensual realm, inspired by the overwhelming landscape and myths of Africa. It is true, however, as the critic Yitskhok Niborski has remarked, that his relationship to nature in his mature poetry is radically different from the joyful immediacy of his approach to the natural world in his early period:

---

122 For example, the Scottish / Irish / Faroese legend of the Selkies: the seals who shed their skin and become men and women. If a man steals the skin of a Selkie woman, she must marry him and cannot return to the sea.

אָנשטאָט דער דבֿקותדיקער פֿרייד אין
אָנבליק פֿון דער נאַטורפּראַכט, קומט
באַטראַכטונג און, אָפֿט מאָל, אַריַינקלער
אינעם ענין טויט.[123]

Instead of ecstatic joy at seeing the
splendor of nature, there is reflection
and often contemplation of the theme of death.[123]

The three elements of the book *Ode to the Dove* – the *kheshbm hanefesh* of the
ode, the 'primordial' experiences of the African environment, and the poet's
discovery of prose writing as a new medium by which to transform aspects of
his past experience into art – together play a seminal role in the inner freeing
of the poet for a new phase in his poetic creativity.

Later poetry

One illuminating analysis of the development of Sutzkever's oeuvre was made
by his close friend, the translator and literary critic Mordkhe Litvine, who
considered that the stages in Sutzkever's poetry are characterized by

די געענדערטע שיַיכותן [...] צווישן
איַינדרוק און אויסדרוק: דעם שטראָם
פֿון וועלט צום דיכטערישן איך און דעם
שטראָם פֿונעם איך צו דער וועלט [...]

The changed relationships [...] between impression and expression: the
flowing from the world to the poetic
self, and the flowing from the self to
the world.[124]

Sutzkever's first period – the solipsistic nature poetry of the 1930s, the traumatic but formative experiences of the war years, the encounter with Israel
and Africa – was, according to Litvine's analysis, dominated by איַינדרוק (*ayn-
druk*, impression): the poet absorbed the world into himself and his poetry
evokes the impression the world has made on him. After the *poeme* "Ode to
the Dove,"

[...] הייבט זיך אָן אָן איבערגאַנג צו אַ
צווייטן פּעריאָד. אין אים וועגט אַלץ שווע־
רער דאָס פּראָיעצירן פֿונעם אינעווייניקסטן
נשמה־בילד אויף דער וועלט [...] אַלץ
שטאַרקער דאָמינירט דער דראַנג צו געפֿי־
נען די לעצטגילטיקע גליַיכעניש פֿאַר דער
אייגענער טוונג, פֿאַרן באַדינג בכלל פֿון דיכ־
טער [...]

[...] a transition to a second period
begins, in which the projection of
the image within the soul onto the
world becomes ever more important.
[...] The urge to find the ultimate
metaphor for his own creation, for
the very essence of the poet's being,
dominates [his work] more and more
[...][125]

123 Niborski 2013: 17.
124 Litvine 1983: 125.
125 Ibid.: 125.

From the mid-1950s on, the search for an "ultimate metaphor" becomes one of the central themes of his work. The boundaries between the outer world and the inner poetic landscape disappear; both are equally real for the poet. Poetry itself becomes the theme; he endeavors with increasing intensity, but often with humor, to fathom and express the nature of the poet's craft and of poetry itself. He also, as Niborski notes, explores his own artistic credo by writing of other artists and creators such as Rembrandt, Chagall, Else Lasker-Schüler or Stradivarius.[126]

The Holocaust remains ever-present in Sutzkever's work, but the gradual transformation in his representation of it, the transition from immediacy to memory, continues.[127] In some post war collections, poems dealing overtly with the topic of the Holocaust are grouped in specific sections: in the book *In the Fiery Chariot* they are entitled די קארש פֿון דערמאָנונג (*Di karsh fun dermonung*, The Cherry of Remembrance), and אַקאָרדן פֿון שטאָלצן וואַלד (*Akordn fun shtoltsn vald*, Chords from the Proud Forest),[128] and in a collection published in 1968 there is a section called זכר לגעטאָ (*Zeykher legeto*, In memory of the ghetto).[129] The first and last of these titles signal the passing of the Holocaust into memory, and indeed *zeykher legeto* is a conscious allusion to such phrases as זכר ליציאת־מצרים (*zeykher litsias-Mitsraim*, in memory of the Exodus from Egypt) or זכר לחורבן (*zeykher lekhurbm*, in memory of the destruction [of the Temple]), – both injunctions to Jews to remember their history. Later, there is no such separation of these poems, so that the past is integrated with his creative life in the present. In his "Notes From My Diary" of 1962, Sutzkever wrote:

דעם טויטס קעניקרייַך איז שוין אַצינד אַ לעגענדע. טויטע לעבן דאָרטן אויף דער אַנ־ דער זייַט פֿון לעבן. איך שיק צו זיי דיכטע־ רישע סיגנאַלן, ווי צו וועזנס אויף אַן אַנדער פּלאַנעט. איך זוך זוך בשותּפֿותדיקע ווערטער, מיר זאָלן זיך פֿאַרשטיין און ליב האָבן.	Death's kingdom has already become a legend. The dead live there on the other side of life. I send them poetic signals, as to beings on another planet. I seek words that we have in common, so that we can understand and love each other.[130]

In this remarkable statement it is no longer a question of merely memorializing the dead; for Sutzkever, they are alive and he wants to communicate with them. Rather than returning to the world of the dead, the poet calls them

126 Niborski 2013: 17. Cf. "Else Lasker-Schüler", p. 147, "The Chosen Tree", p. 153, "Paris 1988", 4, p. 193.

127 For a more detailed discussion of this topic, cf. Valencia 2004.

128 Sutzkever 1952: 107–156, 157–172.

129 Sutzkever 1968b: 53–71.

130 Sutzkever 1962: 166.

into the present, through the power of his poetic word. This impulse towards integration of the dead into the world of the living, and the poetic image of resurrection, permeate many poems from the fifties and sixties,[131] even resonating in poems whose theme is not explicitly a Holocaust one.

A striking image of resurrection is in the poem "The Fiddle Rose" (p. 161). Here, two key Sutzkeverian images – the fiddle and the rose – combine to form a strange new being, which seems to suggest poetry, eternally reborn and existing for itself with "no need of a fiddler," nor of praise. However, the fiddle rose, and therefore poetry itself, must encompass all the past experiences of grief and death, and the mixture of pain and sweetness represented by the oxymoronic bee "whose honey is bitter/though sweet is its succulent, blossomy sting."[132]

"The Fiddle Rose" reveals a new mood of serene assurance and calm acceptance, and in this it is a precursor of the great poetic work of his maturity, the monumental לידער פֿון טאָגבוך (*Lider fun togbukh*, Poems From My Diary), which Litvine saw as the pinnacle of Sutzkever's late period.[133] This is a series of 166 poems which Sutzkever wrote over more than a decade, 1974–1985. Individual poems were published gradually in *Di goldene keyt*, and the first series, to 1977, were published as *Lider fun togbukh* in 1977. The poems written between 1974 and 1981 formed the final section of the book פֿון אַלטע און יונגע כתבֿ־ידן (*Fun alte un yunge ksav-yadn*, From Old and Young Manuscripts), 1982. Finally the complete collection of the "Poems From My Diary", together with two other poem cycles, צוויילינג־ברודער (*Tsviling-bruder*, Twin brother) and אין ערגעצדיקער נאַכט פֿון שוואַרצן האָניק (*In ergetsdiker nakht fun shvartsn honik*, In Some Night of Wild Honey), comprised the volume entitled *Twin Brother*.

The poems are presented chronologically, like diary entries. As in a diary, the texts comment on occurrences in the poet's life, and people he has known (for example Chagall, Pasternak, Shloyme Mikhoels) and they trace his reflections on life and death, on poetry, and on his own immortality as a poet. There is a strong sense of time passing: the collection opens with a typical Sutzkeverian oxymoron: ס׳דערנענטעררט זיך די ווײַט (distance nears). The concept of די ווײַט (*di vayt*, distance) suggests, as Ruth Wisse has com-

---

131 Cf. רויכן פֿון ייִדישע קינדער (*Roykhn fun yidishe kinder*, Smoke of Jewish Children), Sutzkever 1963 (II): 320–322, and צווײַג מיט לעצטע קאַרשן (*Tsvayg mit letste karshn*, Branch With Last Cherries), Sutzkever 1970: 90.
132 The evolution of this image is discussed in greater detail below, p. 281–283.
133 Litvine 1983: 123.

mented, both the past and the future: "A man advanced in years feels the past crowding in on him, but the provocative oxymoron also points forward, to the approach of endlessness, perhaps eternal life."[134]

Like a diary, the poems reflect ever-changing moods: humor, fear, sadness, exultation. But the fragmentary nature of the diary concept is counterbalanced by the structure of the whole series: as so often with Sutzkever, a multiplicity of themes and images is held together by classical strictness of form. The majority of the poems consist of four rhymed four-line stanzas with a regular meter, usually iambic heptameters. The "Poems From My Diary" display his virtuosity in rhyme and meter to its highest degree.

Reflecting the fusion of past, present and future which underlies this work, there are no separate sections of 'Holocaust poems.' Sutzkever achieves his desire to "transform death into life" (p. 171). The dead live again; he even creates from his poetic words a little inn in the forest for them (p. 167). Sometimes he depicts them – in contrast to earlier poems like "Frozen Jews" – with playful humor. In די ליים פֿון צײַט איז װײך געװאָרן... (*Time's clay has softened...* p. 169) they appear to be a group of ebullient senior citizens:

די מתים זענען לאַנג שוין אויפֿגעשטאַנען! זענען האַסטיק
אַנטרונען דאָ פֿון יענער־װעלט, פֿון הױקערדיקער משׂא
און מאַכן יאָגאַ, שפּילן שאַך און זענען פֿרײַ און גאַסטיק,
באַלעגערן די אָפּערע און פּיקן אויס איר קאַסע.

The dead have long since risen! Hastily
they fled from the Other World, their humpbacked burden;
they're doing yoga, playing chess – they're sociable and free;
they besiege the opera and plunder all the tickets.

The trauma of their past has dimmed with the passing of time; Sutzkever evokes this almost comically, through an image of the frailty of old age: צו װאַקלדיק און שװאַך די צײן מע זאָל אַזױנס צעקײַען (Too wobbly and weak their teeth to chew on such a mouthful). They enjoy the delights of this world rather than probing into the issues of guilt and punishment.

This poem is, however, tantalizingly ambiguous. Should it be read as a celebration of the poet's serene reconciliation with the past, which enables him to write with loving humor of his טײַערסטע געשטאַלטן (*tayerste geshtaltn,* dearest figures p. 167)? Underneath the gentle irony, however, it seems as if

134 Wisse 1990: 30.

the poet, like the owl in the first stanza, is wailing over the fading of people's memories, over the trivialization of life, as if the tragedy had never happened. It seems as if only the mysterious blind seer of the final stanza still remembers the chasm, the depths, the victims, with painful intensity.[135]

The "Poems From My Diary" are Sutzkever's most mature expression of his metapoetic theme. He has complete faith in his own poetic calling. He sees himself as a כישוף־מאַכער (*kishef-makher*, magician) who can reveal secrets (p. 187), as the one who can decipher texts which no human hand has written (p. 185); he looks into the future and feels confident of his own immortality:

אַיך טונק אין זון מײַן זיגלרינג און שטעל אים אין דער פֿינצטער
צו היטן די פֿאַרוואַנדלונגען. מײַן קומענדיקער יורש,
דער קאָסמישער פּאָעט, זאָל קאָנען זוכן און געפֿינען,
און מײַן געבײַין זאָל שמײיכלען.

> I dip in sun my signet ring and place it in the darkness
> To guard the transformations. So that my future heir,
> The cosmic poet, shall seek and find them,
> And my bones shall smile.[136]

But even when addressing this, his most essential theme, he can delight in some typically Sutzkeverian self-irony; when a woman at a neighboring table in a Tel Aviv café points out the famous poet to her son, calling him a legend, Sutzkever, the "phoenix man," suddenly feels a strong urge to bite his own writing hand, in order to "taste his legend" (p. 175).

This monumental series of poems gives a powerful picture of the personality and thought of the mature poet who looks back over his life with yearning and sadness for its passing, but also with sovereign calm and acceptance. "Ode to the Dove" was Sutzkever's emotional and spiritual accounting of the first part of his life as a poet; the "Poems From My Diary" are a summing-up of his whole creative life. The work can indeed be seen as the pinnacle of his poetic oeuvre, though until the late 1990s he continued to produce poetry of great sensitivity and beauty.[137]

---

135 Elsewhere in the "Poems From My Diary", for example in the poem about the blade of grass from Ponary (p. 175), the tone is more unambiguously elegiac.

136 P. 173.

137 Cf. p. 191–205.

Sutzkever's web of imagery

Sutzkever's poetic vision erases the barriers between matter and spirit, reality and imagination; all aspects of the universe – stars, minerals, plants and many different creatures – are imbued with sentient life. Consonant with this idea of the equivalence of all aspects of consciousness, the different senses combine, as in the frequent oxymorons (bitter honey, a sweet sting, p. 161), and often the unity of all entities is conveyed by the interchangeability of attributes and actions, as when lips kneel (p. 121) or bones smile (p. 173). There is a constant movement of change and renewal in his universe, as in the early poem אויף אַ באַרג (Oyf a barg, On a mountain):

אַלצדינג איז פֿאַרוואַנדלעניש, באַנײַונג.	Everything is change, renewal.
אַ סעקונד – און אַנדערש זעען אויס	A second, and the mountains change their form
די געבערג. די אַלטקייט ווערט אויף ס׳נײַ יונג.	
קליין ווערט גרויס.	The old becomes young again
	Small becomes huge.[138]

Reflecting this fluidity, images of metamorphosis abound within his poetry; often, in imagery reminiscent of Ovid, the real being is hidden by a strange disguise – the girl in the elephant skin (p. 139) or the *ikh* as a snowman "in a cloak of skin" (p. 75).

The idea of change and renewal is reflected too in the propensity of his key images to develop, transform themselves and combine with others to form new expressions of his evolving vision. This process can be illustrated very clearly from one example: the evolution of the motif of the fiddle.

In the poem "Siberia", his father's fiddle music is one of the earliest inspirations of the child:

[...] אַ שאָטן נעמט אַראָפּ	[...] A shadow takes
ס׳פֿידעלע פֿון וואַנט. און דין־דין־דינע	The fiddle from the wall. And soft-soft
שנייענקלאַנגען פֿאַלן אויף מיַין קאָפּ.	snow sounds fall upon my head.

The image of the fiddle returns in a poem written in the war years, דער געטאָ־פֿידלער (Der geto-fidler, The Ghetto Fiddler).[139] Here the victory of art over death is symbolized by a musician venturing outside the ghetto wall to

---

138 Sutzkever 1963 (I): 130.
139 Sutzkever 1945: 23. This poem was written in 1943, during the period when Sutzkever was revising his Siberian *poeme*.

dig up his buried fiddle, and bring it into the ghetto, where the beauty of its music resurrects the dead. In the the Siberian *poeme*, a real fiddle is the starting point, and the symbolic reverberations arise from emotional associations with the father, his childhood, the snow, the delight of the music. In the second poem the fiddle is still a real musical instrument, but its symbolic significance has intensified, and it has become invested with magic power. The next stage of the image is the esoteric "fiddle rose," reification of the essence of poetry. The fiddle carries all the resonance of its earlier appearances in Sutzkever's verse: his father's fiddle music, and also his death, and the resurrecting power of the fiddle in the ghetto. Roses, a symbol of beauty, are also associated in Sutzkever's oeuvre with pain and death: in an earlier work they symbolized the wounds of his mother, but also her eternal existence in his consciousness.[140] All these associations are present in the mysterious "fiddle rose" which rises alone from "her black earthen tomb." [141]

The fusion of rose and fiddle in this image of poetry signifies the fusion of past and present through the power of the poetic word, and also suggests, through the associations of the rose image, the pain which is an indissoluble part of the poetic process. The fiddle has here taken a new identity, divorced from any 'real' fiddle – the image stands alone, an absolute metaphor, a development which characterizes the poetry of Sutzkever's later years.

The metaphorical significance of the fiddle image means that other related concepts like the סטרונע (*strune*, violin string), in images like אַ װאָלקן מיט סטרונעס (*a volkn mit strunes*, a cloud with violin strings, p. 136), or in the neologism סטרוניק (*strunik*, like a violin string, p. 87) as well as the פֿידלענע פּנימער לאַנגע (*fidlene penemer lange*, long violin faces) of the deer at the Red Sea (p. 117), take on the particular symbolic resonance of the 'parent image.'

The fiddle image finds an unusual variation in one of the "Poems From My Diary": אַ פֿויגל האָט געשפּילט אין אָװנט אויף אַ סטראַדיװואַריוס (*A foygl hot geshpilt in ovnt oyf a stradivarius*, A bird was playing one evening on a Stradivarius, p. 177). This poem is an almost playful statement about the fragility of artistic inspiration, and its destruction if the artist becomes self-conscious. It stands on its own as a delightful fantasy, but gains extra resonance when the previous evolution of the violin imagery is taken into account. The little bird's Stradivarius contains within it the father's violin, the magic fiddle of the ghetto fiddler, the mystery of the fiddle rose, and the imagery of the

---

140 This is the poem cycle דרײַ רויזן (*Dray royzn*, Three Roses), of which one part was published as מײַן מאַמע (*Mayn mame*, My Mother) in Sutzkever 195 3b: 108–112, and another part: פֿון דער פּאָעמע „דרײַ רויזן" (*Fun der poeme "Dray royzn"*, From the poem "Three Roses") in Sutzkever 1979: 12–19. Both parts were written in 1942.

141 See p. 161.

powerful poem אויסדערוועוילטער בוים (*Oysderveylter boym*, The Chosen Tree, p. 153) from 1959, about the transformation of the dying Stradivarius into his own "last fiddle."

The development of the fiddle motif illustrates therefore Sutzkever's tendency to imbue objects which have emotional significance for him with a very particular meaning, built up gradually over the years, so that individual images like the fiddle, grasses, and the bee become many-layered concepts embodying a 'meaning' which may be very far from normal associations of the term. They can often be understood intuitively from the context of the poem, but their full breadth and depth can only be appreciated by peeling away the layers of their evolution.

There are indeed many other images that acquire specifically Sutzkeverian coloring in his work, constantly returning, in the words of Mordkhe Litvine, in

בסדר נײַע אָריגינעלע קריסטאַליזאַציעס און	constantly new, original crystalliza-
אָרגאַנישע פֿאַרבינדונגען	tions and organic connections.[142]

These images fall into several groups. There are the two poles of snow and fire. Because the poet felt his poetic identity to have been completely bound up with Siberia, snow is associated with the birth of the poetic word. Fire is also a motif from his early poetry: the fire of the Kirghiz nomads accompanies the ecstasy of music and dance. This creative fire is transformed into the hellish flames of the Nazi murderers – in, for example "Burnt Pearls" (p. 105) – but reaches its creative apotheosis in the poems written in Israel. The fusion of snow and fire denotes reconciliation between past and present, as in the oxymoron which ends דער שניי אויפֿן חרמון "The Snow on Mount Hermon", p. 117): אָנעם שניי קאַלט וועט זיַין אין דער פֿלאַמיקער מדינה (Without that snow it will be cold in this hot fiery land).

Two other significant groups of nature images are, on the one hand, growing things: grasses, corn, the cherry, the plum and the tree, which is often closely connected to the symbol of the Tree of Life (p. 173). On the other hand, already important in his earliest poetry, but increasing in significance in his Israeli period, is the realm of rocks and minerals: for example, granite cliffs, pearls, and buried treasure. Through all these images of nature Sutzkever pursues his vision of פֿאַרוואַנדלעניש, באַניַיונג (*farvandlenish, banayung*, transformation, renewal). Common to them all is the idea of the hidden

142 Litvine 1983: 54.

mystery of regrowth: the roots of the tree, from which it is nourished, lie buried under the earth; inside the plum there is the 'shining kernel' which creates new fruit; the grasses grow from under the snow; the seeds of corn, buried for thousands of years, can germinate and sprout. All these interrelated images can be seen as imagery of the kernel or the essence. In fact one significant phrase which Sutzkever uses in several poems is דער פֿינקלענדיקער עיקר (*der finklendiker iker*, the glittering essence, p. 165, 177, 183), which conveys the absolute mystery at the heart of the individual human being,[143] unknowable except in a rare moment of revelation.

A further source of key nature imagery is the realm of living creatures; these include, among many others, the lion, the tiger, the elephant, the deer, the eagle, and, most important, the dove, which, from the time of the second version of the Siberian *poeme*, is established as a symbol of the poet's muse. Characteristically, Sutzkever does not use animals in the manner of the fable writer, taking traditional qualities (the lion for courage, the fox for cunning etc.), but invests them with different symbolic colorings which are entirely his own. Few of the other animals share the clear symbolic identity of the dove, but one other type of creature becomes firmly established as a permanent metaphor, alluding to the poetic word: the very tiny creatures, like the ant (p. 87), and the bee (p. 161).[144]

The Jewish poet?

A further strand of Sutzkever's imagery derives from the Tanakh (Hebrew Bible), and from Jewish history, folklore and mysticism. As we have seen, his early poetry is almost devoid of specific Jewish references, but Jewish imagery plays a significant role in the poetry of his early period in Israel. Motifs from Jewish culture, already imbued with their own historical and symbolic significance, are pre-formed and more static than Sutzkever's other imagery. By weaving these archetypal Jewish images into his own personal poetic quest, however, he invests this with a universal Jewish dimension.

The important role which Jewish imagery plays in his work raises the complex question which is inseparable from any consideration of a Jewish writer: whether it is possible to define wherein the inherent 'Jewishness' of that writer lies. Even in Sutzkever's early poems, allusions to the divine and

---

143 In "A Letter to the Grasses" (p. 121) Sutzkever uses the "shining kernel" of the plum to evoke his own 'glittering essence'.

144 The bee is established very early as a metapoetic image. In 1935 Sutzkever wrote: אָט בין איך דאָ, אַן אויפֿגעבליטער אין מײַן גאַנצער גרײס,/פֿאַרשטאָכן מיט געזאַנגען ווי מיט פֿײַערדיקע בינען (*Ot bin ikh dokh, an oyfgebliter in mayn gantser greys, / farshtokhn mit gezangen vi mit fayerdike binen,* Here I am, blossoming and fully grown/ stung by poems as if by fiery bees. Sutzkever 1963 (I): 23.

frequent use of words for the Creator, which persist throughout his work, would seem to point to a fundamentally religious experience of the world. However, Sutzkever's use of Jewish images and religious concepts is very far from any orthodox Jewish tradition. His search is a poetic one, and his use of the language of the divine is subtle and complex, sometimes even ironic. Often, as in the poem "All is worthy of my roaming eye" (p. 83) the divine 'master' can be interpreted as an expression of his own overwhelming poetic vision of the universe.

In two very important respects, however, the essential Jewishness of his world view emerges in his poetry. The first is the unwavering commitment he felt from the late thirties onward to the Jewish people and the continuity of the "golden chain" of the generations, as has already been discussed. A central component of this continuity was the preservation of the Yiddish language, to which he dedicated himself through his literary journal and his poetic word.

It is indeed in his relationship to the word that his deeply-felt Jewishness is most evident. The poetic word is not only the vehicle, but also the unifying theme of all his work. In Jewish religious and cultural tradition, the written word occupies a place of particular importance. The Torah scroll is handled with great reverence, and may not be destroyed but must be preserved or buried. The mezuzah and *tefillin*, – both being small containers holding sacred texts – are placed respectively on the door posts or on the forehead and arm; both of these objects are a literal interpretation of God's command to Moses: "And thou shalt bind them for a sign upon thine hand, and they shall be as frontlets between thine eyes. And thou shalt write them upon the posts of thy house, and on thy gates."[145] Religious Jews touch the Torah scroll with their prayer shawl then kiss the material which has been in contact with the holy words. These examples are evidence of the central, *corporeal* significance of the word in traditional Jewish life. The word is more than just a sign; the written marks themselves are infused with the holiness of their meaning. Indeed in the mysticism of the Kabbalah the written sign can have a significance far beyond comprehensible 'meaning', as Gershom Scholem has pointed out:

> Letters and names are not only conventional means of communication. They are far more. Each of them represents a concentration of energy and expresses a wealth of meaning which cannot be translated.[146]

---

145 Deut. 6: 8–9. The quasi-religious identity with which Sutzkever invests his own poetic word can be seen in his use of the image of tefillin in the final poem of this volume, p. 205.
146 Scholem 1969: 36.

While it would be wholly inappropriate to ascribe Kabbalistic mysticism to Sutzkever, it seems justifiable to assert that the awe in which the written word is held in the tradition of Jewish mysticism reaches into all Jewish religious and secular life, and it is this tradition which gives the concept of the *word* in Sutzkever's poetry its particular resonance.

In fact it can be argued that the term "mystical" can indeed be used of Sutzkever's poetry, if it is taken in its wider sense of searching for something numinous, beyond normal human understanding. A mystic, according to Gershom Scholem, is "a man who has been favored with an immediate, and to him real, experience of the divine, or ultimate reality, or who at least strives to attain such experience."[147] Sutzkever's imbuing of inanimate matter with quasi-magical or spiritual qualities, his constant and ever-intensifying quest to reach the ineffable, ultimate reality – "the glittering essence" – through his poetic word, which can nourish, protect, and which "expresses a wealth of meaning that cannot be translated," as well as extraordinary moments of illumination in his poetry, where he attains a glimpse of this reality,[148] – all these attributes place the poet and his work in the realm of the mystical.

The ultimate silence

Sutzkever, in common with many Jewish mystical thinkers, seems to regard the silence beyond the realm of words as the ultimate goal of human perception. Religious thinkers see the Torah as the path towards perception of this divine silence: the French philosopher André Neher wrote:

> Psalm 62 teaches all those who vibrate before the divine Infinity that there is no chord more vibrant to express the longing of the soul than silence: "Towards God with silence vibrates my soul" (verse 2),[149]

and the modern mystic Arthur Green asserts that deep intimacy with the Torah "will lead us to the Torah beyond the text, the word that embodies all of divine silence[…]."[150]

In the already mentioned "Notes From My Diary",[151] Sutzkever himself speaks of a silence beyond human words. Describing the בשותפותדיקע ווערטער (*beshutfesdike verter*, words we have in common) that he is seeking in order to communicate with the dead, he says:

---

147 Ibid.: 5.
148 Cf.…געוואָלט (דערצייל, וואָס האָסטו זען געוואָלט (Tell me what you hoped to see…), p. 183.
149 Neher 1981: 11.
150 Green 2010: 84.
151 Cf. above, p. 265, 277.

די אָ ווערטער, אָדער שאָטנס פֿון ווערטער,
געבוירענע פֿון אַ געהיימער סובסטאַנץ,
באַהאַלטן זיך ערגעץ אין די נעסטן פֿון מיד־
בר. זייער אָטעם, זייער מוזיק איז לעבעדיקע
שטילקייט.

Those words, or shadows of words,
are hiding in the nests of the desert.
Their breath, their music, is *living silence* [my emphasis].[152]

The three related concepts of שטומקייט (*shtumkayt*, muteness), שטילקייט (*shtilkayt*, stillness or silence), and שווײַגן (*shvaygn*, silence) are seminal terms in Sutzkever's permanent metapoetic vocabulary from the postwar period on. He speaks of the place ווו שטילקייט ראַנגלט זיך מיט שווײַגן (*vu shtilkayt ranglt zikh mit shvaygn*, where stillness struggles with silence),[153] and of a דריטע שטילקייט (*drite shtilkayt*, third silence, p. 157). In a poem from 1974, the *ikh* longs to descend to the depths of the sea to perceive ווו שטומע שטילקייט לערנט זיך דעם אלף־בית פֿון שווײַגן (*vi shtume shtilkayt lernt zikh dem alef-beys fun shvaygn*, [...]mute stillness learning the alphabet of silence, p. 165). In the final analysis this language of silence beyond human words, which expresses the ultimate reality, is the true and constant goal of his poetic quest. Where religious mystics strive to hear this cosmic silence through ever deeper penetration of the divine mysteries, the great modern Yiddish poet Avrom Sutzkever never ceased to trust in the overwhelming power of the poetic word. It may be that towards the end of his life he felt that he was at one with this ultimate silence, for in one of his very last poems he was able to write:

איך בין די שטילקייט.
בין איר ברויט און זאַלץ.

I am silence.
I am its bread and salt.[154]

152 Sutzkever 1962: 166. "Shadows of words": in Sutzkever's poetry, the word שאָטנס (*shotns*, shadows) often designates the true reality of an object or being.
153 Sutzkever 1963 (II): 37.
154 ברויט און זאַלץ (*Broyt un zalts*, Bread and Salt), p. 197.

Avrom Sutzkever, drawing for Yaron Sachish, 1972, courtesy of the owner

Bibliography

1. Works by Avrom Sutzkever

a. Books (in chronological order)

1937: *Lider* (Poems). Warsaw: Bibliotek fun yidishn Pen-klub.

1940: *Valdiks* (Of the Forest). Vilna: Yidisher literatur-fareyn un Pen-klub.

1945: *Di festung* (The Fortress). New York: Ikuf-farlag.

1946a: *Lider fun geto* (Poems from the Ghetto). New York: Ikuf-farlag.

1946b: *Vilner geto 1941–1944* (The Vilna Ghetto 1941–1944). Paris: Farband fun di Vilner in Frankraykh.

1946c: *Fun Vilner geto* (From the Vilna Ghetto). Moscow: Ogiz melukhe-farlag "Der emes."

1947: *Vilner geto. 1941–1944.* (The Vilna Ghetto 1941–1944). Buenos Aires: Farlag Ikuf.

1948a: *Vilner geto. 'Kapitlen'* (The Vilna Ghetto. "Chapters"). Buenos Aires: Komitet tsu koordinirn dem yidish-veltlekhn shulvezn in Argentine.

1948b: *Yidishe gas* (The Jewish World). New York: Farlag Matones.

1948c: *Geheymshtot* (Secret City). Tel Aviv: n. p.

1952: *In fayer-vogn* (In the Fiery Chariot). Tel Aviv: Di goldene keyt.

1953a: *Sibir* (Siberia). Jerusalem.

1953b: *Fun dray veltn* (From Three Worlds). Buenos Aires: Literatn- un zhurnalistn-fareyn "H. D. Nomberg."

1955: *Ode tsu der toyb* (Ode to the Dove). Tel Aviv: Di goldene keyt.

1957: *In midber Sinay* (In the Sinai Desert). Tel Aviv: Farlag Perets-bibliotek.

1960: *Oazis* (Oasis). Tel Aviv: Farlag Y. L. Perets.

1961: *Gaystike erd* (Spiritual Earth). New York: Der kval.

1963: *Poetishe verk* (Poetic Works), 2 volumes. Tel Aviv: Yoyvl-komitet.

1968a: *Lider fun Yam-hamoves* (Poems from the Dead Sea). Tel Aviv/New York: Farlag Bergen-Belzen, Veltfarband fun di Bergen-Belzener.

1968b: *Firkantike oyses un mofsim* (Square Letters and Miracles). Tel Aviv: Farlag Di goldene keyt.

1970: *Tsaytike penemer* (Ripe Faces). Tel Aviv: Farlag Y. L. Perets.

1974: *Di fidlroyz* (The Fiddle Rose). Tel Aviv: Farlag Di goldene keyt.

1975: *Griner akvarium* (Green Aquarium). Tel Aviv: Hebreisher universitet in Yerusholayim, Yidish-opteylung / Komitet far yidisher kultur in Yisroel.

1977a: *Lider fun togbukh* (Poems from My Diary). Tel Aviv: Farlag Di goldene keyt.

1979a: *Dortn vu es nekhtikn di shtern* (Where the Stars Spend the Night). Tel Aviv: Farlag Yisroel-bukh.

1979b: *Di ershte nakht in get*o (The First Night in the Ghetto). Tel Aviv: Farlag Di goldene keyt.

1982a: *Fun alte un yunge ksav-yad*n (From Old and Young Manuscripts). Tel Aviv: Farlag Yisroel-bukh.

1986: *Tsviling-bruder* (Twin Brother). Tel Aviv: Farlag Di goldene keyt.

1989: *Di nevue fun shvartsaplen. Dertseylungen* / Prophecy of the Inner Eye. Stories. Introduction: Ruth Wisse. Jerusalem: Magnes Press.

1992: Der yoyresh fun regn (The Heir of the Rain). Tel Aviv: Farlag Di goldene keyt.

1993: *Baym leyenen penimer. dertseylungen, dermonungen, eseyen* (Reading Faces. Stories, Memories, Essays). Jerusalem: Magnes Press.

1996: *Tsevaklte vent* (Shaky Walls). Tel Aviv: Farlag Di goldene keyt.

b. Journal articles

Sutzkever, Avrom, 1951: "Mark Shagal in Yisroel." In: *Di goldene keyt* 9, 5–6.

– 1962: "Togbukh-notitsn" (Notes from My Diary). In: *Di goldene keyt* 42, 164–167.

– 1966: "Mayn eydes-zogn farn Nirnberger tribunal" (My Witness Statement before the Nuremberg Tribunal). In: *Di goldene keyt* 54: 5–16.

– 1973: "Frayndshaft mit Mark Shagal." (Friendship with Marc Chagall) In: *Di goldene keyt* 79/80, 5–39.

– 1977b: "Di farb vos loykht vi a shtern (tsum nayntsikstn geboyrn-tog fun Mark Shagal)." (Color that Shines like a Star (on Marc Chagall's Ninetieth Birthday)). In: *Di goldene keyt* 92, 63–80.

– 1982b: "Magye fun yungshaft (Mark Shagal – tsu zayne finf un nayntsik)" (The Magic of Youthfulness (Marc Chagall – on his Ninety Fifth Birthday)). In: *Di goldene keyt* 108, 27–31.

– 1985: "Der goyen fun pashtes" (The Genius of Simplicity), (essay on Marc Chagall). In: *Di goldene keyt* 116/117, 8–10.

– 2001: "Ikh hob shtilerheyt gebentsht aykh! Monolog fun Avrom Sutskever (Silently I Blessed You! Monologue of Avrom Sutzkever)." Recorded by Yankev Beser. In: *Toplpunkt* 2, 6–13.

c. Recordings

– 1959: *Mayn lebn un mayn lid*. Talk held at the at the Jewish Public Library in Montreal on 24 May, 1959. http://www.yiddishbookcenter.org/collections/archival-recordings/fbr-84_4084/farewell-evening-abraham-sutzkever-leo-roskies-melech-ravitch (accessed 21.09.2016).

– 1960: *The Poetry of Abraham Sutzkever, "The Vilno Poet"* recorded and with notes by Ruth Wisse. New York: Smithsonian Folkways Recordings FL 9947 (LP record). Reissued as F-9947 (CD). [Contains 13 poems, read by the poet.]

2. Selected secondary literature

Adamczyk-Garbowska, Monika, 2011: " 'I Know Who You Are, but Who I Am – You Do not Know…': Reading Yiddish Writers in a Polish Literary Context." In: *Shofar: An Interdisciplinary Journal of Jewish Studies*, 29 (3), 83–104.

Amminger, Agnes, 2015: "Sibir. Zu Marc Chagalls Illustrationen von Abraham Sutzkevers Gedichtzyklus." In: *Chilufim. Zeitschrift für Jüdische Kulturgeschichte* 19, 87–124.

Aptroot, Marion and Gruschka, Roland, 2010: *Jiddisch. Geschichte und Kultur einer Weltsprache*. Munich: Verlag C.H. Beck.

Astur, Mikhoel [Michael C. Astour], 1963: "Sutskevers poetisher onheyb." In: Zalman Shazar, Dov Sadan, M. Gros-Tsimerman (eds.), *Yoyvl-bukh tsum fuftsikstn geboyrntog fun Avrom Sutskever*. Tel Aviv: Yoyvl-komitet, 22–42.

Bikl, Shloyme, 1969: *Di brokhe fun sheynkayt. Eseyen vegn Avrom Sutskever*. Tel Aviv: Farlag hamenoyre.

Blum, Jost G., 1992: "Notizen zu Autor und Werk." In: Abraham Sutzkever, *Griner akwarium: kurtse baschrajbungen / Grünes Aquarium: kurze Beschreibungen. Prosastücke*. Jiddisch und Deutsch. Transl. Jost G. Blum, Michael von Killisch-Horn, and Mirjam Pressler. Frankfurt am Main: Jüdischer Verlag, 131–142.

Briedis, Laimonas, 2012: *Vilnius. City of Strangers*. Vilnius: Baltos Lankos (distributed by Central European University Press).

Cammy, Justin D., 2004: "Vision and Redemption: Abraham Sutzkever's Poems of Zion(ism)." In: Joseph Sherman (ed.), *Yiddish after the Holocaust*. Oxford: Boulevard / The Oxford Centre for Hebrew and Jewish Studies, 240–265.

– 2007: "Abraham Sutzkever." In: *Dictionary of Literary Biography*. Vol. 333: Writers in Yiddish. Detroit: Thomson Gale, 303–313.

Cammy, Justin and Figlerowicz, Marta, 2007: "Translating History into Art: The Influences of Cyprian Kamil Norwid in Abraham Sutzkever's Poetry." In: *Prooftexts* 27 (3), 427–473.

Chagall, Marc [Mark Shagal], 1950: "Der kinstler." In: *Di goldene keyt* 5, 29–38.

– 1953: "A. Sutskever der poet un mentsh." In: A Sutskever, Fun dray veltn (antologye). Buenos Aires: Literatn un zhurnalistn-fareyn H. D. Nomberg, 64f.

Dawidowicz, Lucy, 1979: The War against the Jews 1933–1945. Harmondsworth: Penguin Books.

Döblin, Alfred, 1987: *Reise in Polen*. München: dtv Verlagsgesellschaft.

Drucker Bar-Am, Gali, 2016: "Gaystike erd by Avrom Sutzkever: between Personal Mythology and National Ideology." In: *Journal of Jewish Studies* 67 (1), 157–181.

Estraikh, Gennady J., 2004: *In Harness. Yiddish Writers' Romance with Communism*. Syracuse, N. Y.: Syracuse University Press.

Fishman, Dovid-Elyohu [David E. Fishman], 1996. *Shaytlekh aroysgerisn fun fayer: dos oprateven yidishe kultur-oytsres in Vilne / Embers Plucked from the Fire: The Rescue of Jewish Cultural Treasures in Vilna*. New York: YIVO.

Frakes, Jerold C., 2011: *Yerusholayim d'lite. Di yidishe kultur in der Lite / Jerusalem of Lithuania: A Reader in Yiddish Cultural History*. Columbus: Ohio State University Press.

Gilbert, Martin, 1986: *The Holocaust. The Jewish Tragedy*. Glasgow: William Collins.

Gilbert, Shirli, 2005: *Music in the Holocaust. Confronting Life in the Nazi Ghettos and Camps*. Oxford: Clarendon Press.

Gilbert, Shirli a.o., n.d.: "Vilna" In: *Music and the Holocaust*. http://holocaustmusic.ort.org/places/ghettos/vilna/ (accessed 14.05.2015).

Glatshteyn, Yankev, 1947: "A. Sutskever." In: Yankev Glatshteyn, *In tokh genumen. Eseyen 1945–1947*. New York: Farlag Matones, 57–65.

Green, Arthur, 2010: *Radical Judaism. Rethinking God and Tradition*. New Haven a.o.: Yale University Press.

Gries, Zeev, 2008: "Romm Family." In: Gershon D. Hundert (Editor in Chief), *The YIVO Encyclopedia of Jews in Eastern Europe*. New Haven: Yale University Press, II, 1588–1589. http://www.yivoencyclopedia.org/article.aspx/Romm_Family (accessed Sept. 21, 2014).

Gritz, Linda, 2013: "A Shvartse Khupe (Black Wedding Canopy)," National Yiddish Book Centre, https://www.youtube.com/watch?v=Jxs3De-UY2s (accessed Oct. 10, 2016).

Harshav, Benjamin, 1990: *The Meaning of Yiddish*. Berkeley, Calif. a.o.: University of California Press.

– 1991: "Sutzkever: Life and Poetry." In: Benjamin and Barbara Harshav (eds.): *A. Sutzkever. Selected Poetry and Prose.* Translated from the Yiddish by Benjamin and Barbara Harshav. Berkeley, Calif. a.o.: University of California Press, 3–23. Reprinted 2007 in Benjamin Harshav, The Polyphony of Jewish Culture. Stanford, Calif.: Stanford University Press, 253–269.

– 2003: *Marc Chagall and His Times. A Documentary Narrative*. Stanford, Calif.: Stanford University Press.

Katsherginski, Shmerke, 1953: "Mayn khaver Sutskever." In: Avrom Sutskever, *Fun dray veltn*. Buenos Aires: Literatn- un zhurnalistn-fareyn "H. D. Nomberg", 59–63.

Katz, Dovid, 2004: *Words on Fire. The Unfinished Story of Yiddish*. New York: Basic Books.

– 1955: "A. Sutskever." In: *Shmerke Katsherginski ondenkbukh*. Buenos Aires.

Koller, Sabine, 2012: *Marc Chagall: Grenzgänge zwischen Literatur und Malerei (Marc Chagall: Borders between Literature and Painting)*. Köln a.o.:Böhlau.

Kruk, Herman, 2002: *The Last Days of the Jerusalem of Lithuania. Chronicles from the Vilna Ghetto and the Camps 1939–1944.* Edited and introduced by Benjamin Harshav. Translated by Barbara Harshav. New Haven, Conn.: Yale University Press.

Litvine, M., 1968–1986: *Frantseyzishe poezye. Iberzetsungen un komentarn.* 2 Vols. Paris: Undzer kiem.

– 1983: "Der driter period in Avrom Sutskevers poezye." In: Dov Sadan, Yishayahu Avrekh, Chava Turniansky and Chone Shmeruk (eds.), *Yikhes fun lid. Lekoved Avrom Sutskever / Yikhuso shel shir. Likhvod Avraham Sutskever.* Tel Aviv: Yoyvl-komitet, 122–146.

– 2003: *Fun der velt-poezye. Iberzetsungen fun frantseyzish, rusish, daytsh.* Jerusalem: H. Leyvik farlag, 2003.

Lustiger, Arno, 2003: *Stalin and the Jews. The Red Book. The Tragedy of the Jewish Anti-Fascist Committee and the Soviet Jews.* New York: Enigma Books.

Mark, Yudl, 1974: *Avrom Sutskevers poetisher veg.* Tel Aviv: Y. L. Perets farlag.

Miron, Dan, 2003: "A tsvayg mit letste karshn – a shmues vegn Avrom Sutskevers poezye." In: *Toplpunkt* 7, 112–121.

Neher, André, 1981: *The Exile of the Word. From the Silence of the Bible to the Silence of Auschwitz.* Translated from the French by David Maisel. Philadelphia: Jewish Publication Society of America.

Niborski, Yitskhok, 2012: "Avrom Sutskever: der lebediker poet." In: *Yerusholaimer almanakh* 29, 16–27.

– 2013: "Avrom Sutskever: poezye farn lebn / Avrom Sutzkever, un poète pour la vie." In: *Avrom Sutzkever: poète et héros du XXe siècle/Avrom Sutskever. Der poet un der held.* [Catalogue for the exhibition of the same name, at the Maison de la culture yiddish / Bibliothèque Medem, Paris, from 5 December to 25 March 2013], 9–14 (French), 15–19 (Yiddish).

Novershtern, Avrom [Avraham Nowersztern], 1976: *Avrom Sutskever bibliografye.* Tel Aviv: Farlag Yisroel-bukh.

– 1983a: "Der nartsis un der regn." In: Dov Sadan, Yishayahu Avrekh, Chava Turniansky and Chone Shmeruk (eds.), *Yikhes fun lid. Lekoved Avrom Sutskever / Yikhuso shel shir. Likhvod Avraham Sutskever.* Tel Aviv: Yoyvl-komitet, 187–210.

– 1983b: *Avrom Sutskever. Tsum vern a ben-shivim.* [Catalogue of the exhibition in honor of Sutzkever's 70th birthday]. Jerusalem.

Pat, Yankev, 1960: *Shmuesn mit shrayber in Yisroel,* New York: Der kval.

Pollin-Galay, Hannah, 2016: "Avrom Sutzkever's Art of Testimony: Witnessing with the Poet in the Wartime Soviet Union." In: *Jewish Social Studies* 21 (2), 1–34.

Ravitsh, Meylekh, 1959: "Estetik un etik in Avrom Sutskevers lider." In: *Yidisher kemfer,* 22 May 1959, 11–12.

Reznik, Nisl, n.d.: *Geshikhte fun FPO*, Sutzkever-Katsherginski Collection RG223-649, YIVO Archives, New York. http://www.yadvashem.org/yv/en/exhibitions/this_month/resources/partisan_organization.asp (accessed May 17, 2015).

Roskies, Dovid, 1983: "Der tsikl fun oyfkum in Sutskevers a getolid." In: Dov Sadan, Yishayahu Avrekh, Chava Turniansky and Chone Shmeruk (eds.), 1983: *Yikhes fun lid. Lekoved Avrom Sutskever / Yikhuso shel shir. Likhvod Avraham Sutskever.* Tel Aviv: Yoyvl-komitet, 243–256.

– 1984: *Against the Apocalypse. Responses to Catastrophe in Modern Jewish Culture.* Cambridge, Mass.: Harvard University Press.

Roth, Joseph, 1985: *Juden auf Wanderschaft.* Cologne: Kiepenhauer & Witsch.

Rupnow, Dirk, 2005: *Vernichten und Erinnern: Spuren nationalistischer Gedächtnispolitik.* Göttingen: Wallstein Verlag.

Scholem, Gershom, 1969: *On the Kabbalah and Its Symbolism.* Transl. Ralph Manheim. New York: Schocken Books.

Schroeter, Gudrun, 2008: *Worte aus einer zerstörten Welt: Das Ghetto in Wilna.* St Ingbert: Röhrig Universitätsverlag GmbH.

Schwarz, Jan, 2005: "After the Destruction of Vilna. Abraham Sutzkever's Poetry, Testimony and Cultural Rescue Work, 1944–46." In: *East European Jewish Affairs* 35 (2), 209–224.

Sherman, Joseph, 2012: "Introduction." In: Joseph Sherman (ed.), *From Revolution to Repression. Soviet Yiddish Writing 1917–1952.* Nottingham: Five Leaves Publications, 12–34.

Sheyntukh, Yekhiel, 1983: "Di biografye fun lid 'Der tsirk'." In: Dov Sadan, Yishayahu Avrekh, Chava Turniansky and Chone Shmeruk (eds.), 1983: *Yikhes fun lid. Lekoved Avrom Sutskever / Yikhuso shel shir. Likhvod Avraham Sutskever.* Tel Aviv: Yoyvl-komitet, 258–279.

Shpiglblat, Aleksander, 2003: "Zikhroynes fun der 'tsoyber-kuznye'." In: *Toplpunkt* 7, 17–19.

Tory, Avraham, 1990: *Surviving the Holocaust. The Kovno Ghetto Diary.* Edited and with an Introduction by Martin Gilbert. Cambridge, Mass. and London: Harvard University Press.

Valencia, Heather, 1990: "Avrom Sutskevers 'Ode tsu der toyb'." In: Dovid Katz (ed.), *Oksforder Yidish. A Yearbook of Yiddish Studies* I. Chur a.o.: Harwood Academic Publishers, 115–139.

– 1991: *"Bashtendikayt" and "Banayung": Themes and Imagery in the Earlier Poetry of Abraham Sutzkever.* Doctoral Thesis, University of Stirling.

– 1994: "Sibir b'shtey poemot shel Avrom Sutskever." In: Shalom Luria (ed.), *Khulyot. Studies in Yiddish Literature* 2, 181–195.

– 1999: "'Gezang fun a jidischn dichter in 1943': Wort als Schutz und Widerstand in der Lyrik von Abraham Sutzkever." In: Thomas. F. Schneider (ed.), *Kriegserlebnis und Legendenbildung. Das Bild des 'modernen' Krieges in Liter-*

atur, Theater, Photographie und Film, 3 vols. Osnabrück: Universitätsverlag Rasch, II, 603–618.

– 2003: "Abraham Sutzkever." In: Sorrel Kerbel (ed.), *Jewish Writers of the Twentieth Century*. New York, London: Fitzroy Dearborn, 568–570.

– 2004: " 'Farvandlen vil ikh toyt in lebn': Transformations of the Holocaust in the Post-War Poetry of Abraham Sutzkever." In: Joseph Sherman (ed.), *Yiddish after the Holocaust*. Oxford: Boulevard / The Oxford Centre for Hebrew and Jewish Studies, 217–239.

– 2012: "From Der tsirk to Erev mayn farbrenung. The Transformation of Experience in Two Poems by Avrom Sutzkever." In: Marion Aptroot, Efrat Gal-Ed, Roland Gruschka and Simon Neuberg (eds.), *Leket. Yidishe shtudyes haynt. Jiddistik heute. Yiddish Studies Today*. Düsseldorf: Düsseldorf University Press, 109–128.

– 2013: "Nokhvort / Postface" In: Avrom Sutzkever, *Griner akvarium/Aquarium vert*. Bilingual edition Yiddish / French, transl. Batia Baum. Paris: Medem Bibliotek, 109–122 / ‏כח‎–‏ז‎ (Translated from English: French, Fleur Kuhn; Yiddish, Yitskhok Niborski).

Wisse, Ruth R., 1975: "The Prose of Abraham Sutzkever." In: *Abraham Sutzkever, Griner akvarium. Dertseylungen*. Jerusalem: V–XXXIII.

– 1981: "Introduction: The Ghetto Poems of Abraham Sutzkever." In: Seymour Mayne (transl.), *Burnt Pearls. Ghetto Poems of Abraham Sutzkever*, Oakville, Ontario: Mosaic Press / Valley Editions, 9–18.

– 1989: "Abraham Sutzkever the Storyteller." In: Abraham Sutzkever, *Di nevue fun shvartsaplen*. Jerusalem: The Magnes Press, the Hebrew University, Jerusalem, V–XIX (also in Hebrew, ‏יט‎–‏ז‎).

– 1990: "Introduction." In: Abraham Sutzkever, *The Fiddle Rose: Poems 1970–1972*, selected and translated by Ruth Whitman. Detroit: Wayne State University Press, 13–32.

– 2002: "A Prayer of Homecoming by Abraham Sutzkever." In: William Cutter and David Jacobson (eds.), *History and Literature: New Readings of Jewish Texts in Honor of Arnold Band*, Providence, R.I.: Brown Judaic Studies, 339–349.

Volpe, Dovid A. [David E. Wolpe], 1985: *Mit Avrom Sutskever iber zayn lidervelt. Monografye*. Johannesburg: Farlag kayor.

Yanasovitsh, Yitskhok, 1981: *Avrom Sutskever. Zayn lid un zayn proze*. Tel Aviv: Farlag Yisroel-bukh.

Zimmerman, Joshua, 2015: *The Polish Underground and the Jews*. Cambridge: Cambridge University Press.

Illustrations

www.ingramcontent.com/pod-product-compliance
Lightning Source LLC
Chambersburg PA
CBHW080916100426
42812CB00007B/2294